JOURNEY WITHOUT RETURN

ALSO BY TOM LINDLEY

Out of the Dust

Opening Doors

To the Max

Tall Grass, Big Dreams

JOURNEY WITHOUT RETURN

A PALESTINIAN AMERICAN STORY

TOM LINDLEY

IN COLLABORATION WITH

TAWFIK AND SIHAM RAMADAN

FOREWORD BY

YOUSEF KHANFAR

OLIVE BRANCH PRESS

An imprint of Interlink Publishing Group, Inc.
www.interlinkbooks.com

DEDICATION

Dedicated to my ten amazing grandchildren
and the children of the world,
with the hope that they will
build bridges, not walls,
and carry love across every divide.

First published in 2026 by

Olive Branch Press
An imprint of Interlink Publishing Group, Inc.
46 Crosby Street
Northampton, Massachusetts 01060
www.interlinkbooks.com

Cover design by Harrison Williams
Interior design by Carl Brune

Library of Congress Cataloging-in-Publication Data available
ISBN 978-1-62371-527-4

10 9 8 7 6 5 4 3 2 1

Printed and bound in Thailand

CONTENTS

DR. TAWFIK AND SIHAM RAMADAN

ACKNOWLEDGEMENTS

The story of Tawfik and Siham Ramadan has unfolded over more than four years, a journey shaped by their unwavering presence at every step. I am deeply grateful to them for their steadfastness, for the boundless kindness, patience, and hospitality they have shown me as we delved into the profound essence of being Palestinian and the aching yearning for home. Our journey together has been one of its own kind, a privilege I carry with immense honor.

I also owe a special debt of gratitude to Yousef Khanfar. Without his inspiration, wisdom, and intimate knowledge of Palestine and the Middle East, I would have been adrift. A renowned photographer and writer in his own right, Yousef has been the heart and soul behind *Journey Without Return*, a visionary force who believes that the Ramadans embody a crucial, yet often overlooked, facet of the Palestinian-Israeli narrative—one that, until recently, has remained unjustly silenced.

Finally, my sincere thanks go to the meticulous copy editors, Siema Rafiq and Daniel Simon, whose keen eyes and thoughtful guidance have been invaluable. And to every individual who gave me the privilege of their time for an interview, and those who shared their knowledge and insights on this deeply important subject—your contributions mean more than words can express. You know who you are, and I am profoundly grateful.

FOREWORD

The human heart is a musical instrument with harmonious strings that intertwine through its core. When the world's voices echo with sorrow—notes of violence, injustice, and poverty—they strum our heartstrings, crafting a melancholic symphony that envelops us in sadness. Yet when the air fills with cheerful news, laughter of children, and happy tales of love, those same strings vibrate with joy, gifting us a delightful melody that lifts our spirits.

And one fateful day, a vital chime will break away, ignite passionate flames in one's heart, leaving an enduring mark. In that moment, some will choose to embrace it, dedicating their life journey to its profound call. This was the path taken by two souls, one a healer, another a teacher.

Journey Without Return, by Tom Lindley, is the story of two Palestinians, Tawfik and Siham Ramadan. Born in separate villages and maturing in separate time periods, their lives, like diverging rivers, carved distinct paths, only to converge in a love destined for eternity. Little did they know that one fateful day, their tranquil existence would be shattered, and they would be torn from the warmth of their beloved homes and serene villages, cast into the gloom of exile.

They would face the darkest atrocities of humanity, uprooted from their cherished homeland, embarking on an uncharted journey. This book unfolds as a tapestry of hope, forgiveness, and healing, knitting together the threads of homeland, war, and the plight of refugees. It captures the essence of survivorship and the agonizing voices of exile. This book seeks *to enlighten* and not *to convince*. First of all, last of all, and heart of all.

Astonishingly, the Ramadans stand as eyewitnesses to pivotal moments in Middle Eastern history to share with us. Many Palestinian voices vanish into the void, never given the chance to vibrate in the world; yet within these pages, they refuse to evaporate. We are blessed to be gifted with their voices that teach us, inspire us, and, at times, outrage us.

I have been fortunate to fall into the orbit of the Ramadans, who believe life is a precious but fleeting gift, and that each day should be dedicated to good deeds. To them, morality is living with and for others, offering parts of yourself in others' joy and sorrow. It is the only way to heal a fractured society and a wounded planet.

Tawfik is cloaked in high values, bound by unshakable principles, and shrouded in deep wisdom. Doctor Ramadan dedicated over six decades of his life as a pediatrician, healing young souls with compassion and expertise. His generosity to help others extended far beyond the clinic, as he consistently gave of his time and resources to those in need. Siham does not come from tribes that rouge their lips or perfume their wrists, but from the tribes of lionesses, woven from fine silk and resilient steel. She started as a teacher in refugee camps during the most atrocious time. She is feminine, yet powerful; optimistic, yet grounded; cultured, yet simple. Her aura pulses with a vitality that inspires others effortlessly.

The more they shared their story with me, the more I yearned for more. They led me back to my Palestinian roots, enlightening me about the culture, food, poetry, literature, music, and, most of all, the history that shaped them. And so, the seeds of this book were sown.

One might wonder: What purpose does documenting history serve if we fail to learn from it? We seek history recorded with truth, capturing perspectives from both sides. History penned solely by one side, by the victors, becomes drenched in bias, fostering doubt and nurturing propaganda. Colonizers craft their historical tales to justify their invasions, rarely revealing the true essence of their hidden agenda. In times of turmoil—war, violence, and upheaval—we do not need history to whisper in our ears but to scream loudly in our faces. We demand history to hold us up by the collar and shake us, gaze into our eyes, and roar, *Look at me, you are repeating me, you are repeating history.*

History and laws are intertwined like a dense mesh, and I trust, or at least hope, that we all desire virtuous and fair legislation. Laws are living, breathing documents that should embody justice and humanity. Unfortunately, shadows linger in our past where some laws throughout history, which were deemed legal, masked cruelty, injustice, and inhumanity. So come, come all men, women, and truth.

Not long ago, in the history of the United States, Indigenous peoples faced brutal treatment by the European colonial settlers as their lands were seized and their cultures destroyed in the name of expansion. They were uprooted through massacres disguised as progress, with treaties broken and lives shattered. Their existence was criminalized, and their traditions scorned. All this was legal, yet it was profoundly criminal and inhumane.

Not long ago, in the history of the United States, slavery was permitted and legalized. An enslaved African, male or female, could be bought and sold, treated as mere property. Their lives were extinguished through lynchings, hangings, and flames, deemed acceptable under the law. All this was legal, yet it was profoundly criminal and inhumane.

Not long ago, in the history of Germany, a Jewish man or woman could be condemned to death for nothing more than their religion. Neighbors betrayed their Jewish friends, leading them to a deathly doom in Auschwitz. Throngs of Jewish families were torn apart, herded into concentration camps, and thrown into gas chambers—a horrific chapter of cruelty. All this was legal, yet it was profoundly criminal and inhumane.

Not long ago, in the history of South Africa, an apartheid regime established a stark divide where privilege flowed like a river for the whites, while the Blacks were left parched and barren. This was a system that masked oppression in legality, yet it was drenched in injustice and cruelty. Rights were stripped, voices silenced, and freedom denied. All this was legal, yet it was profoundly criminal and inhumane.

And, not long ago, in the history of Palestine, the Nakba (Catastrophe) unfolded. In 1948 the establishment of a settler-colonial state, Israel, through the Zionist national movement, marked the beginning of a tragedy where over 750,000 innocent Palestinians were forcefully uprooted from their homes and shoved into restrictive refugee camps. This exodus was accompanied by the annihilation of villages, brutal massacres, and the confiscation of lands, all while cultures were systematically erased. All this was framed as legal, yet it was profoundly criminal and inhumane.

And that is what tyrants, dictators, and oppressors do when they seek to colonize a land, crush their opponents, or silence their rivals; they manipulate existing laws or craft new ones, so they can carry out their plan behind a legal shield. This gives it the essence of legality, creating an illusion of order and acceptance. One who stays within the realm of the tyrant's laws and obeys has their safety mostly guaranteed, but one who dares to step out of line and resist is often met with the full weight of brutal punishment.

In the end, the more fraudulent the autocrat, political party, or government, the more abundant and heavier the books of law. And herein let us remember, for every colonizer, dictator, and tyrant who sells the blood of others at low price, a day will come when someone buys their blood at the same cheap rate.

Here we must pause and differentiate between Judaism and Zionism. These terms are often conflated, yet they represent separate concepts despite what the propaganda machine wants us to believe. Judaism is a rich, ancient religion with spiritual, cultural, and ethical dimensions, rooted in the beliefs and practices of the Hebrew people. In contrast, Zionism emerged in the late nineteenth century as a nationalist movement advocating for the establishment of a Jewish state in Palestine—which meant replacing one nation with another nation. Which meant an ethnic cleansing of the indigenous Palestinian population. Which meant violence, bloodshed, uprooting, destruction, savagery, and the like. Which meant Palestinians were forced to live in refugee camps, while Zionists live in the stolen Palestinians' homes. Which meant that Palestinians became the victims of victims.

Who would like to have the filthy boots of colonialism on their neck controlling every aspect of their lives? Who would like to live in a refugee camp? No one, surely. The Nakba survivors were forced into refugee camps, enduring unimaginable hardship. The food rations were so controlled that many received very little or nothing. Hunger can dehumanize people, but the Palestinians' generosity and faith ensured no one went hungry. Even basic necessities like water, electricity, medical supplies, daily needs, and freedom of movement were restricted.

The refugee camps are poverty-stricken, where most tents are made from thin fabric or nylon—scorching hot in summer and frigidly icy in winter. After days of heavy rain, mud clings to people's feet, clothes, and tents. The ground of the tents is the ruttiest, and between the tents is the slushiest. Pools of dark water develop where animals grudgingly drink, and children are exposed to diseases. Living becomes miserable, surrounded by the stench of sweat, dirty clothes, polluted drainage, and the suffocating fumes of overcrowded tents. Sadly, some children walk about aimlessly, unaware that their family is dead.

Clouds of sorrow hang over Palestinian refugees, who lose hope with each passing day. Many call on God, wishing for death over life. Men are frustrated and depressed, unable to provide for their families. Fatigued from unemployment, for work is scarce, and when available, it's poorly paid. Women, thin and unkempt, wear the same clothes for months, losing touch with their femininity. They lack basic necessities like sanitary pads and endure painful childbirth without anesthesia. The camp becomes more squalid, unsanitary, and crowded; a place that preaches less hope and more death.

Imagine, for a moment, if this were you. After living peacefully in your own home, on your own land, in your own country, with your beautiful family and successful career, someone brutally forced you out, claiming everything as theirs, justified by their holy book. Of course, for intelligent people, this is not acceptable. I respect all religions, but above that, I respect wisdom and common sense that is not blinded by them.

The heavens and humanity have no greater enemies than those who manipulate religion as a weapon of war and violence. The Holy Scriptures are not miswritten but often misinterpreted and misused to justify murder with carefully selected verses. Intoxicated by power and control, they blur the lines between nationalism and religion, believing themselves entitled to act without regard for others' rights. They declare war, shatter lives in the name of their own ideology and profit, masquerading as instruments of God's will, while trampling on the flesh and bones of innocent people. It is a tragic irony that so few, in the name of God, can cause so such misery for so many.

The political ideology of the Zionist project, although drawing on Jewish historical and religious narratives, uses this as a tool to legitimize and justify the colonization of Palestinian land. By framing the return to Israel as a fulfillment of religious destiny, Zionism sought to galvanize support and consolidate power, often disregarding the rights and existence of the indigenous Palestinian population. This exploitation of religion has complicated the discourse around identity, land, and justice, creating a narrative that intertwines faith with territorial ambition, ultimately leading to lasting conflicts in the region.

Now, some want you to believe that the Palestine case is very complicated, but in contrary, it is very simple. It can be summarized in three words: colonization, colonization, colonization.

Whenever one takes ethnic cleansing, confiscation of land, checkpoints, illegal settlement, an apartheid regime, the kidnapping of children, separation of families, collective punishments, and the like, then tosses them into a frying pan of ideology over a raging fire of politics, the result is a cancerous dish called colonialism. For colonialism not only symbolizes a single, evil vice; it symbolizes all vices.

No nation stands by carelessly while its land is invaded and its people oppressed; this is true for Palestine. No country tolerates ethnic cleansing, nor the destruction of its culture; this, too, is true for Palestine. No republic accepts to pay the price by the blood of their citizens for the crimes and sins of others; this, undeniably, is true for Palestine. No people should endure the weight of colonization, the brutality of apartheid, and daily humiliation; this, without question, is true for Palestine. And since the Nakba of 1948, the spirit of Palestinian resistance has risen—defending sovereignty, embodying the struggle for justice, independence, and liberty. The Palestinian resistance, which is their full right under international law, has become a symbol of resistance and resilience, earning respect and solidarity across the globe.

Today, when one gazes at Palestine and the Palestinians, one not only sees a *Nation of Souls* but also a *Nation of Principles.* Principles of justice, freedom, and independence. Principles of love, passion, and dreams. Principles of honesty, hospitality, and generosity. For between the Palestinians and their principles, there is no chasm; it is their second skin.

In the court of public opinion, we have the responsibility to uphold morality and justice. We have the responsibility to advocate for the truth and nothing but the truth, even though someone who talks truthfully about the tragedy of the Palestinian cause, they might be charged by selfish people or a lobby with being an enemy of Israel or labeled anti-Semitic. One must reject this obloquy and resist the noisy vehemence of those who obscure the truth about Palestine. For the truth is not only essential to you and your community but also essential to the world.

Allow me to touch on a related subject. In today's media landscape, another player in this unfair game, the narratives we consume are often shaped by powerful news corporations and interest groups, which may distort the reality of a subject like the Israeli–Palestinian case. It is crucial for the public to approach this related news with skepticism and discernment, especially when tainted with biased portrayals that favor the Zionist entity while diminishing the legitimate struggles of Palestinians' rights of existence.

To truly understand any situation, one must search beyond the mainstream narrative and seek out trusted, informed voices—scholars, human rights advocates, and credible journalists who approach the issue with balance, integrity, and respect for all human lives involved. Blindly accepting only one side of the story without questioning its facts and sources is a disservice to yourself and the collective understanding. Let us remember, the truth lies not in the loud voices of the powerful but in the quiet voices of the powerless.

The Palestinians, regardless of how hard and long their freedom journey, and regardless of how many generations it will take, and just as they protect Christianity and Islam, they are determined to protect Judaism from Zionism. For the Palestinians, who witnessed so many empires come and vanish—from their numerous colonizers who selfishly sought to build their own Promised Land over the ashes of the natives—history and experience delivered to them wisdom and strength, whereby the Palestinians stopped believing in the colonizer's supremacy, because they stopped believing in Palestinian inferiority.

Before the Nakba of 1948, Palestine was a thriving, vibrant country with its own airport, railroad system, banking system, education system, health care, and more. It was a radiant nation where Jews, Christians, Muslims, and other religious denominations lived together peacefully. The history of Palestine and its culture is vastly documented in poetry, literature, arts, photographs, archaeology, legal documents, holy books, maps, and the like. Its roots are ancient, rich, and spiritual. Despite the painful colonization, her spirit is sweetened by a fidelity that refuses to die. And after every bloodshed, she emerges into the light once more, towering above all else to teach us new lessons about forgiveness, tolerance, and peace.

The Palestinian people carry a pride shaped by centuries of being the guardians of the Holy Land. Their hospitality is their religion, generosity is their shrine, and humanity is their holy book. Their loving spirit embraces all, respects all, and welcomes all who seek refuge or desire to worship. They are friendly people of profound wisdom, shaped by struggle, who know the true cost of peace and the weight of justice. Education is their glowing flame, passed from generation to generation, lighting the way through adversity, something that is embodied in the spirit of Tawfik and Siham Ramadan.

This book's author, Tom Lindley, arrived as rain to a parched and overlooked subject—a rain shaped from knowledge, experience, and common sense. This is the deluge that the thirsty mind craves. He felt that the best way to describe the horrors of what happened to the Palestinians was not by writing fiction but through recording the testimonies of witnesses.

During the crafting of this book, something extraordinary unfolded—an unexpected whisper, a manifestation the writer perhaps wasn't ready for, yet maybe he was. As his pen was marching onward, capturing the voices of the Ramadans, he began to hear voices from the beyond. Familiar voices, resonant and haunting, emerged—testimonies similar to the Ramadans, yet spoken from different lips, across distant space and time.

One of the most profound elements of this book project is the author's transformation and enlightenment. Tom Lindley, born in the United States, educated in American schools, and raised in the embrace of the Christian church, was startled to uncover striking parallels between the plight of Palestinians and the experiences of the First Americans—the injustices faced by Native Americans repeated hauntingly in the actions of Zionists against Palestinian natives. As a writer, Tom was compelled to dismantle all he had learned, to confront the uncomfortable truths, and to rebuild his understanding anew, fortified by the weight of facts, history, and the clarity of justice.

Tom Lindley, a reporter at heart, steeped in journalistic ethics, immersed himself in the stories of the Ramadans, while also plunging into many related books on the subject. He sought trusted, unbiased sources, driven by a quest for truth. To his amazement, some of the most compelling books he encountered about the Israel–Palestine case were penned by Jewish authors and Israeli citizens themselves, standing in opposition to the Zionist entity, because they believe the crimes that happened to them, as Jews in the Holocaust, should never be inflicted on others. For they stand on the side of humanity, and nothing else matters.

Tom realized a troubling truth: how the United States of America is complicit in repeating the very crimes they inflicted upon the First Americans. America, a colonial settler that funds Israel—another force of colonization—perpetuates the same egregious actions against Palestinians: ethnic cleansing, massacres, displacement, confiscation of land, and more. Before our eyes, the past unfurls anew, while countless voices remain shamefully silent. *Yes, I see history repeats itself*, he lamented; *we have not learned from history*.

In this deeply moving narrative, Tom articulates the touching story of Tawfik and Siham, and invites us to journey alongside them. This odyssey unfolds through Palestine, Jordan, Egypt, Lebanon, Iraq, Saudi Arabia, and, finally, the United States of America. Through their voices,

Tom weaves the challenging time of the Middle East—the greatness and madness—while introducing us to renowned figures who changed the course of history. This book will hum in your hands with the enduring power of love, resilience, human spirit, and much more.

The unyielding dream to reclaim their stolen homeland has been the lifeblood of the Palestinian people, a luminous thread that stitches generations together. Shaped by the fires of struggle, nourished by burning tears, clad in faith and principles, this dream transcends time, lighting their way through obstacles and uncertainties. The road to freedom is costly and steep, but it is paved with the strength of shared values, where every act of resistance holds the hopes of those who came before. Parents cradle their children, passing on their ancestry's heroic stories, inspiring in them a fierce love for their homeland. In unity, determination, and sacrifice, they find their power, unwavering in their resolve that this dream will rise, unbroken, toward the horizon of liberation.

And in the spirit of humanity, it is my dream that, one day, we will have human-rich leaders, who build human-rich societies, so we can live in human-rich civilizations. So help us God.

Yousef Khanfar
PHOTOGRAPHER. WRITER. HUMANITARIAN
March 2025

Yousef Khanfar is an international award-winning Palestinian-American author who is listed as one of world's top photographers. He has published three books and is featured globally in many publications. The Fulbright Center for Peace in Washington, D.C., selected his book to celebrate the Global Symposium of Peaceful Nations. He was selected as Artist of the Year by Montblanc and promoted literacy with UNICEF. The Palestine mission to the United Nations honored him for "Appreciation of your extraordinary service to promoting peace and justice in Palestine through art."

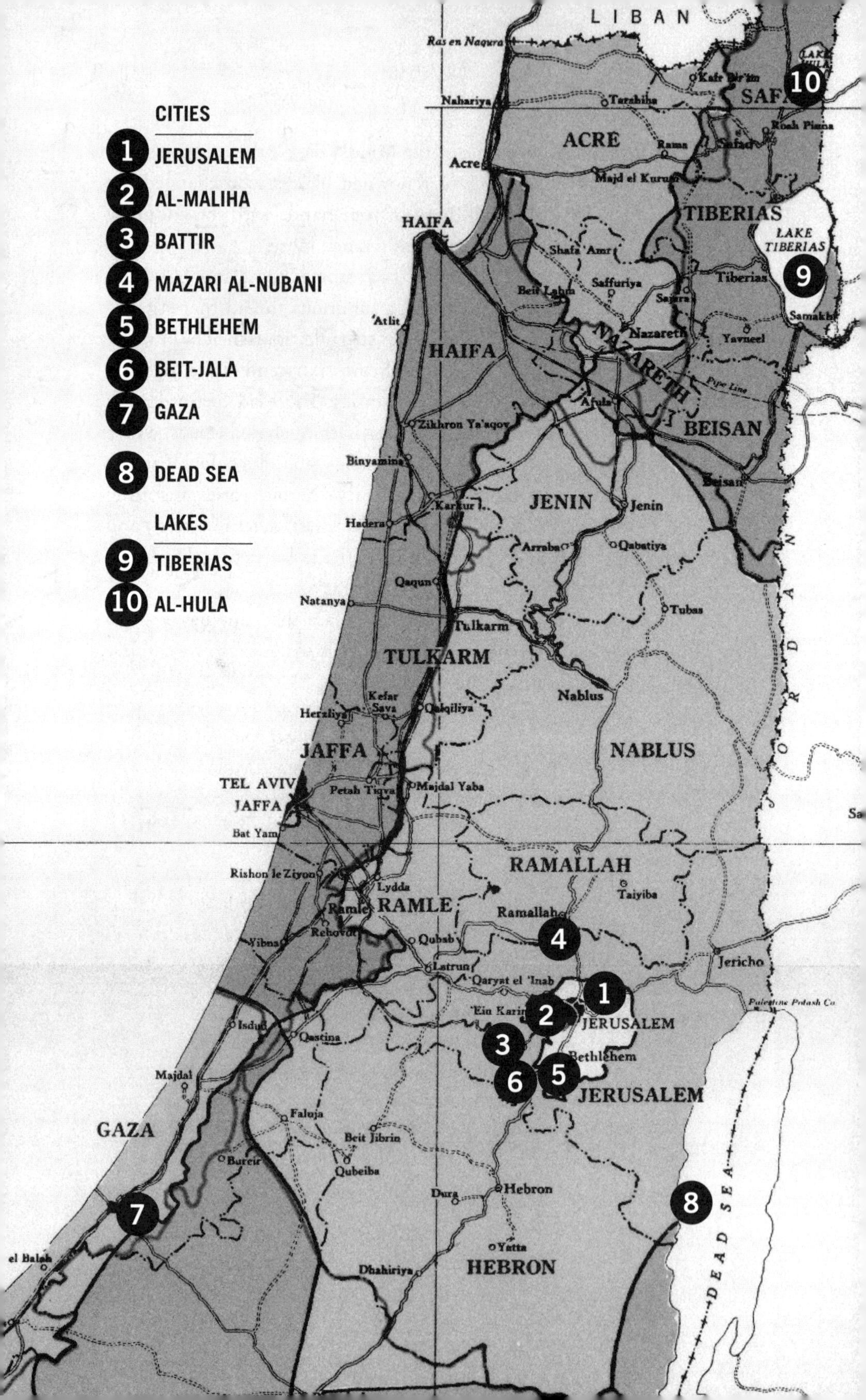
CITIES
1 JERUSALEM
2 AL-MALIHA
3 BATTIR
4 MAZARI AL-NUBANI
5 BETHLEHEM
6 BEIT-JALA
7 GAZA
8 DEAD SEA
LAKES
9 TIBERIAS
10 AL-HULA
LIBAN
Ras en Naqura
Nahariya
Tarshiha
ACRE
Acre
Rama
Majd el Kurum
Rosh Pinna
Safad
TIBERIAS
LAKE TIBERIAS
Tiberias
Samakh
Yavneel
HAIFA
Shafa 'Amr
Saffuriya
Beit Lahm
Nazareth
NAZARETH
'Atlit
HAIFA
Pipe Line
Afula
BEISAN
Beisan
Zikhron Ya'aqov
Binyamina
JENIN
Jenin
Karkur
Hadera
Arraba
Qabatiya
Qaqun
Natanya
Tubas
Tulkarm
TULKARM
Nablus
Kefar Sava
Qalqiliya
Herzliya
NABLUS
JAFFA
TEL AVIV
JAFFA
Petah Tiqva
Majdal Yaba
Bat Yam
RAMALLAH
Rishon le Ziyon
Lydda
Taiyiba
Ramle
RAMLE
Ramallah
Rehovot
Yibna
Qubab
Jericho
Latrun
Qaryat el 'Inab
Palestine Potash Co.
'Ein Karim
JERUSALEM
Isdud
Qastina
Bethlehem
Majdal
JERUSALEM
Faluja
GAZA
Beit Jibrin
Bureir
Qubeiba
Hebron
Dura
DEAD SEA
Yatta
el Balah
Dhahiriya
HEBRON

CHAPTER 1

THE GIFT OF HEALING

There are only two ways to live your life. One is as though nothing is a miracle. The other is as though everything is a miracle.

— ALBERT EINSTEIN

The Christian town of Beit Jala has served mankind as far back as the Stone Age, and, luckily, it was still there on a hill adjacent to Bethlehem waiting for Tawfik Ramadan to come along in the fall of 1948.

Tawfik was twelve years old, and he was on the run.

Only a few months earlier, a new Zionist state had plopped down on top of him and his family with the weight of a mountain, squeezing the very life out of the land his ancestors had inhabited for centuries and leaving about one million Palestinians with neither a country nor a home.

The Arab world called it the *Nakba*, which means "catastrophe," and Tawfik experienced it firsthand. One day, he felt part of a close-knit, extended family in the Palestinian village of Al-Maliha on the outskirts of Jerusalem; the next day, the 1948 Arab–Israeli War knocked on his door, and Tawfik saw his family disperse like quail at the sound of a shotgun.

Some had fled to Bethlehem; others escaped to Amman, Jordan. But one patriarch, Tawfik's grandfather on his mother's side, had traveled with Tawfik's immediate family to Beit Jala, long a welcoming place for Muslims, Jews, and Christians. Tawfik's grandfather was more than one hundred years old but had the face of a much younger man and the stamina of one half his age. Every week after their arrival in Beit Jala, Tawfik's grandfather walked four miles to the mosque in Bethlehem in time for Friday prayers rather than accept a ride.

One day he got sick along the way, and no one in the family knew what was wrong. As he watched his grandfather deteriorate before his eyes, Tawfik suspected he could not afford to wait much longer for a collection of natural herbs to take effect. The day was growing short when Tawfik, accompanied by his uncle Khalil, who was the same age, began their search for a doctor.

"We learned where he lived and went to his house," Tawfik says. "It was after office hours, but we saw his car and knew he must be there."

Tawfik rang the front doorbell, eventually attracting the attention of a woman, who peered out a window. "We need help. My grandfather is sick," Tawfik pleaded. She said the doctor was not there and turned away. So, they waited.

An hour later, Tawfik rang the bell a second time. His attempt was met with a stony silence. Eventually, the woman replied that the doctor would see their grandfather the next day. Not that night or first thing the next day but, basically, when he could find the time.

The look in his grandfather's eyes told Tawfik that tomorrow might be too late. It could be that the doctor had more patients than there were hours in the day. It was also possible that the doctor, knowing the Ramadan family were refugees, realized they had nothing to exchange for his services, not even a hen or a hen's egg.

The circumstances should not have mattered, Tawfik surmised. All that mattered was that someone needed a doctor. Whether it was a stranger or the Grand Mufti made no difference to him.

While standing in the street waiting for the doctor that day, Tawfik made another prognosis: "It struck me that in the future I needed to make something different happen for people who are sick and can't get help. I told myself I would become a doctor. 'I will save humanity,' I said to myself."

The next afternoon, the doctor made his house call. He took a cursory look at Tawfik's grandfather, checked his blood pressure, and rendered a quick verdict. "He is hypertensive and has had a stroke," the doctor said. "Nothing can be done for him. Just pray for him."

So, that is what the family did. They prayed until Mohammad Ahmad Ramadan died about a week later. But Tawfik's dream did not die with him. His desire to help others grew and grew until one day it crossed a great ocean.

CHAPTER 2

HOPE EMERGES OUT OF A STORM

Children are the living messages we send to a time we will not see.

—JOHN F. KENNEDY

For centuries in Palestine, respect has been as widespread as the taste for *maqluba* (the country's revered main dish). At the top of the list is respect for one's elders, as personified by Tawfik Ramadan's concern for his grandfather.

The reality is that Palestinians have turned the practice of respecting others into a ceremonial display of generosity and hospitality that can overpower the whole room. The Palestinian welcome mat is like no other, in part because the countryside has always been defined by clusters of small villages whose inhabitants clung to one another and the land for survival. When guests showed up at a Palestinian's doorstep, tradition called for them to be greeted by sweets, Arabic coffee, and a benevolent host.

It did not matter whether the visitor was expected or not. It did not matter whether they were part of the same tribe or a stranger passing through a village, whether rich or poor, whether they called themselves a Jew, a Muslim, or a Christian. Everyone was embraced for who they were, not who they represented.

But the accommodating ways of the Palestinian countryside were not meant to last. A pot was boiling on the stove, and there was no one to tend it. Fear and distrust filled the air, for which a simple act of kindness was no match.

By the summer of 1936, it had become apparent to the midwife of the peaceful Palestinian village of Al-Maliha (*maliha* means salty in Arabic) that the time-honored healing agent of a spoonful of olive oil with one's morning coffee would no longer be enough to preserve the serenity of her village.

For one thing, Hajah Safiyah, Al-Maliha's dutiful midwife, was worried about a growing conflict between two families that was not getting resolved in the typical amicable fashion, what might be called a form of "ancient Palestinian mediation." Something else was on her mind, too.

A growing unease had been seeping into Palestine ever since Britain's announcement of the Balfour Declaration in 1917, a sweeping public statement that essentially promised a national home for the Jewish people in a land overwhelmingly inhabited by Muslims and Christians.

How mere words could undo so much was not apparent to Hajah Safiyah at the time, but it was clear to her that the next baby she delivered would have a rude awakening.

Za'al Rashid Ramadan and Khadrah Mohammad Ramadan were husband and wife as well as first cousins from the same tribe. Fortunately, both sides of the family had been blessed with good health. Khadrah even had a twin sister, which was rare in Palestine at the time as healthcare was limited and survival rates for one baby, much less two, were low. The first child of Za'al and Khadrah, a son they named Ibrahim, died in infancy, as did their sixth child, Sabri. But their other children, three girls (Izziah, Fatimah, and Hamdah) and two boys (Tawfik and Daoud), survived. Za'al always kept the health of his children in mind, often telling them to "keep space in your stomach, one third for water, a third for food and one third to breathe." Za'al practiced what he preached as he had a passion for life, was eager to lend a hand, and was always on time for morning prayers. Khadrah, in contrast, was calm and quiet. Mostly, she was known for her devotion to her family and her *maqluba*. A Palestinian staple dish, *maqluba* means "upside down" in Arabic and is the name for a pot of stewed meat, rice, and fried vegetables that, after being cooked, is flipped onto a serving dish to form an impressive tower.

Large families through intermarriage were customary in Al-Maliha as they were throughout the country. Khadrah's father sired five girls and two boys in his first marriage and three boys and two girls when he remarried after the death of his first wife. Za'al's father had two boys and one daughter by his first wife, and three boys and one girl from a subsequent marriage.

Partly due to a lack of medical care, death often arrived ahead of schedule on the dirt tracks of Palestine. But when you dig deep, what remains is the simple fact that Palestine for thousands of years has been left in the care of peasants – peaceful, simple, caring, hard-working people who depended on agricultural and pastoral pursuits for survival. Each year, they struggled and persisted in the face of the elements, the politics of the day, and the fragile state of the economy.

Most of the men of Al-Maliha either worked in the fields or cut stone from nearby mountains, while the women worked even longer hours managing the household and the children. None of it was easy, but it was apparent from the state of their mental and physical health that the pace of life suited them.

The tranquility in this part of Palestine also was owed in large part to the emphasis people placed on their rich culture – the love poems they wrote, the distinctively Palestinian music they played, the delicacies they prepared and shared, the vibrancy and intricacy of the embroidery (*tatreez*) Palestinian women had been perfecting for centuries, and the premium Palestinians placed on family, generosity, and hospitality. Much as America became a melting pot for immigration, Palestine has served as the cultural capital of the Middle East, having blended its own diverse and vibrant culture with those of surrounding countries, such as Jordan, Lebanon, and Syria.

A tribal people whose history dates to the Bronze Age, the villagers of Al-Maliha had functioned without turmoil for generations in multifamily compounds made of Mediterranean white stone on two mountains overlooking the Bani Hassan region of the District of Jerusalem. The Ramadan compound contained four homes, all in a row. There was room behind the homes for an orchard that produced plentiful fruits. Besides Tawfik's family, there was his uncle Ahmad (Za'al's brother) who had two children; Uncle Ahmad (Khadrah's brother) who had six children; and Uncle Esa (Khadrah's other brother) who had six children. Located on the road connecting Jerusalem and Jaffa, Al-Maliha fell under the shadow of the expansion of Jerusalem over time, although its fertile hillsides helped preserve its pastoral past.

The son of Za'al and Khadrah Ramadan was just coming into the world when life as it had existed for eons was being undercut daily with the arrival of more and more Jewish immigrants from Germany, Poland, Russia, and elsewhere, who defined themselves as the Jewish Diaspora.

Between 1932 and 1936, more than 130,000 Jews immigrated to Palestine, tens of thousands of them illegally as the Zionist movement easily outmaneuvered the British Mandate's lax attempts to enforce immigration laws. On top of that, Jewish immigrants were seizing more land and increasing their economic gains, further marginalizing the Palestinian population. In retaliation, Palestinians launched a spontaneous strike and boycott of the British and Jewish economy that became known as the Great Revolt, or Great Palestinian Revolt, a three-year movement that sought the end of British rule and its support for Zionism.

Against this ominous backdrop, Tawfik Ramadan was born on August 22, 1936, in the large upstairs room of a stone house with concrete walls and no electricity. In desperation, Hajah Safiyah, the midwife who had her finger on the pulse of Al-Maliha and Palestine as a whole, offered a solution: "Name your baby 'Tawfik,'" she said to Za'al and Khadrah.

In Arabic, the name Tawfik signifies a person who is successful and can bring people together. Something or someone had to save the day, and she prayed Tawfik could answer Palestine's cry for peace.

Alas, Tawfik Za'al Rashid Ramadan could not bring peace. Peace was not to come. Not then. Not now. Maybe never.

CHAPTER 3

ESSENCE OF A HOMELAND

We see our homeland more clearly when we are away from it than when we are in it.

— NAWAL EL SAADAWI

Palestine is perhaps the most coveted piece of real estate in the world. Jerusalem alone has been captured and recaptured more than forty times, and the land known as Palestine has been controlled by Ancient Egypt, Persia (modern-day Iran), Alexander the Great and his successors, the Roman Empire, and the Crusaders. In 1516 Palestine was invaded by the Ottoman Turks, who ruled for four hundred years. It's not necessarily safe to have been born in a place where, for as long as anyone can remember, someone has been willing to die over every speck of land.

Exemplifying the confusion over whose land this was, Tawfik Ramadan's Palestinian birth certificate was written in three languages: Arabic, English, and Hebrew. Looking on the bright side, the document reflected the rich diversity of the region and bore the stature of a passport, implying that the bearer would be welcome anywhere.

But reality is another story.

The document could not have been more worthless had it been written in invisible ink. Once, when Tawfik attempted to cross into the West Bank from Jordan, a young Israeli security guard eyed his passport, which listed his place of birth as Palestine, and told him, "There is no Palestine, so why do you carry it?"

Tawfik answered, "When I was born in 1936, there was no Israel."

Touché.

Unfortunately, Tawfik's factual point does not carry weight with six members of the esteemed G20 (twenty of the world's largest economies) who do not recognize Palestine as a state. Notably, the United States and the United Kingdom are among the naysayers. It is confirmation that the Arab population of Palestine essentially stopped being viewed as people and became permanent refugees almost seventy-five years ago when they were driven from their homeland by the Zionists, whom Tawfik believes migrated to Palestine primarily for the purpose of forming their own state.

"The tale of Palestine from the beginning until today is a simple story of colonialism and dispossession, yet the world treats it as a multifaceted and complex story – hard to understand and even harder to solve," says Jewish historian and writer Ilan Pappé in the 2015 book *On Palestine*, co-written with Jewish American scholar Noam Chomsky.

To clarify what Palestinian people have lost, Tawfik explains that as a child he could point to the spot on a globe where Palestine is located and see the name "Palestine" in print. Likewise, the carefully folded piece of paper that serves as his birth certificate bears the same name. While many mapmakers have since changed the name of "Palestine" to "Israel," Tawfik refuses to go with the flow. "Now we call it occupied Palestine," he says.

It is no wonder Tawfik is determined to keep Palestine from becoming another Atlantis. At the age of ninety, he is among a select few – the last surviving children of a free Palestine. When his generation speaks wistfully of the past, they are doubling as guardians of a proud culture.

So, what was it like, this land called Palestine that the Zionist movement has been so intent on destroying?

In the 1950s Aziz Shihab, a Palestinian then living in the United States, enthralled American audiences with stories about his childhood in this simple but incredible place, where toys were unnecessary, of the echoing streets of Jerusalem, the friendliness of people, the openness of his own Muslim family to different backgrounds and faiths, as shown when he wanted to march, as a boy, with candle-carrying Christian pilgrims to Bethlehem on the second day of Advent to mark the hope for peace that Jesus brings to the world. "Palestinians. Bagpipes. Kids traded desserts (or *helwyat* in Arabic for sweets). The world was full of mixing and mingling," Naomi Shihab Nye wrote in memory of her father in the "Palestine Voices" issue of *World Literature Today* magazine (Summer 2021).

Tawfik had the same experience not far away in Al-Maliha. It also came as a shock to no one that one of Za'al's best friends was a Jew. The other was a Christian.

By and large, Tawfik's childhood memories were formed amid the commotion of a large family in a peaceful, neighborly village. Growing up, his father's strength gave him comfort, his mother's loving nature warmed his heart, and the school he attended filled his head with knowledge. The truth is Tawfik was more eager to learn than he was to play.

"I think I was always thinking about the future," he says, when asked to describe himself as a boy.

Early on, it became apparent to his father and everyone else that Tawfik's appetite for learning, coupled with his powers of comprehension, set him apart from other children. His father was proud of his son's study habits and smiled with delight at Tawfik's ability to recite Palestinian poetry on cue from the time he was a small boy.

Tawfik is too modest to acknowledge he was the obvious favorite of his parents, but that was the case. Perhaps it was because he was always trying to do the right thing.

Throughout school, Tawfik had a penchant for being the first student to arrive in the morning. "My father used to wake up very early every morning, and pray. After the Morning Prayer, he would say to all of us, 'If you sleep late in the morning, you will inherit poverty.' He also would always say, and instilled in all of us to 'wake up early.'"

His example is apropos of an old Arab proverb: "Someone would ask the farmer, 'Why are you so hard on your kids in the field?' The farmer would answer, 'I am not raising a crop, I am raising men.'"

Above all, Tawfik's father taught him the value of education. "When we would sit there doing our homework, he would come in and say, 'Show me what you did today and what you are supposed to do tomorrow.' Every day he did that, although I don't think he knew what the words or numbers on the page meant. But he taught me the importance of education. 'Education is your life,' he said." It seems Za'al, the champion of education, had never been taught to read or write.

Today, Palestine is well respected in the Arab world, Europe, and the United States for producing more than its fair share of physicians, engineers, scientists, and teachers. "Because we have lost our homeland, it is important that we succeed in other countries. And to get a good job, you have to be educated and go the extra step to prove yourself," Tawfik says.

A basic education was not easy to obtain in rural Palestine, where money for schools was scarce and teachers were in short supply. To attract an educator, a village often had to offer lodging to convince a teacher to move there, and because schools were drastically underfunded, students often brought their own stools and supplies with them to class.

Under British Mandate governance, Palestinian students had limited opportunities to extend their basic education beyond the tenth grade (around the age of sixteen). Tawfik recalls that there were only five secondary state-run schools in the entirety of Palestine serving eleventh and twelfth grades while he was in school, not counting private schools.

Fortunately, Tawfik was a self-starter whose curiosity stretched far beyond the fields he helped tend. As a child, Tawfik had a big part in one of the village's most celebrated events – a play in honor of Caliph Omar ibn al-Khattab, the second of four caliphs (*Al-Khulafa' Ar-Rashidoon,* or wise men) who succeeded the Prophet Muhammad, and was known for his pious and just nature.

"I was in the fourth grade and acted out a scene where Caliph Omar ibn al-Khattab passed a poor woman on the street who was sitting outside her house stirring a pot filled with boiling water and some small rocks," Tawfik says. "When he asked her why she was engaged in such a futile task, she answered that she did not have any food to give her children, so in order to give them some hope she decided to put rocks in the pot as a last resort.

"Omar was struck by her explanation and later returned with some food for her and her family without ever telling her who he was. I very much liked doing that play about him."

While news of World War II filtered in on the radio, not much separated Al-Maliha from the distant past. The mosque still towered over the village, and its inhabitants and the patriarch of each tribe controlled everything else. Government of any form played a very small role in anyone's life in rural Palestine.

Al-Maliha had been settled by three main tribes. The largest tribe was the Jawareesh, to which Tawfik's immediate family (Dar Hmoud) belonged. The other two prominent tribes were the Fawagsah and the Abo Kamel. Al-Maliha and surrounding villages fell under the leadership of a small family called the Darweesh, whose principal leader, Abdel Fattah Darweesh, owned the only private car in the district. Each tribe in Al-Maliha had its own public house (*saha*) that was used for special occasions and where village guests were housed.

Even after Palestine became subject to the British Mandate in 1922, to say that Palestine was loosely governed would be an understatement. British civil officials attempted to set up a government that maintained order, minimally interfered in economic life, and provided basic services that met European standards. Rural Palestine, however, continued to be largely left to its own devices. The British did not seem interested in improving roads and infrastructure; and the locals, who were overwhelmingly champions of education, especially for males, did not want foreigners to tell them how to run their schools.

In Al-Maliha, for example, there was no form of municipal government. One wasn't necessary because the elders in the village were considered the wise men – the leaders – and when problems arose, they got together to solve them. For example, the people of the village raised enough money in 1947 to add a second floor to their school in order to establish a secondary education program.

They obviously still had hope for the future, albeit misplaced.

And why shouldn't they keep the faith? After all, the land had provided them a living for a long time. Life was good for other reasons, too. For one thing, the climate and the soil were well suited for growing wheat and barley, and the olive and fruit trees seldom produced a disappointing harvest. And while no one from Tawfik's village had ever attended college, they all took pride in their work, particularly the men who cut stone for a living.

Ranging in color from white to pink, yellow and tawny, limestone from the nearby mountains came to be known as Jerusalem stone and eventually grew popular around the world, which meant there was a steady source of income for the men from Al-Maliha when they were not working in the fields. One reason was because of the color and quality of the stone. The other reason, which ultimately comes into play in all things related to Palestine, was the fact that the stone, in essence, came from the sacred ground near Jerusalem, the holiest city in the holiest of lands and home to sacred places for three of the world's greatest religions: Islam, Christianity, and Judaism.

Za'al was molded in that tradition, long before tunnel-boring equipment and laser-cutting machines were put into service. The history of stonecutting dates back centuries to when peasants began working with mud and stone. Eventually, they grew skilled enough to test the mountain, and soft Senonian limestone began to be used as an inexpensive building material. The more durable layers were more expensive to quarry while the Turonian layers, which were soft and easy to chisel, became the most prized building stones because of the speed by which the stone hardened when exposed to the atmosphere.

Still, it was hard work. At the same time, it was considered artwork.

"There are many famous families of stonecutters," Tawfik explains. "The stonecutting involves three specialties. The first one (*hajjar*) is to blow the stone out of the mountain and cut it into smaller pieces. This was a specialty of my father. The second phase (*kasheeb*) was to cut it into rectangular pieces, which is called reshaping the rock. The third specialty (*daqqiq*) involves people who work the stone using a chisel and hammer and another tool with teeth to make the face of the stone for the construction site. Not everyone can do it."

It took an artist with muscles to know where and how to cut the stone from a huge rock that has to be a certain color, such as white to yellow to red, and have certain specifications, and then to go into that pile of stone and start cutting and shaping it to the approximate size.

Because they were cut by hand, the stones were never exactly the same size. But when you looked at a house constructed of stone that had been shaped by Al-Malihan hands, you would never notice that one piece was bigger than the other. The highest honor for Tawfik's father was being one of the stonecutters who produced Palestinian stone that was shipped to Baghdad for the construction of the palace for King Faisal II, heir to the Hashemite Iraqi monarchy.

His grandfather, King Faisal I, was held in high esteem across the Arab world and in Za'al Ramadan's household for his attempts to promote Pan-Arab nationalism and pro-Palestinian positions. But he endeared himself to Palestinians most of all with his support of the Arab position during the 1929 al-Buraq Uprising, the bloody week of riots between the Arab and Jewish communities over access to the Western Wall. Faisal pressured the British to find a pro-Arab solution to the Palestine crisis and said that he would support a "Jewish national home" to which Jews fleeing persecution around the world might go, although he stopped short of offering them a "Jewish state."

Anticipating the fall of the Ottoman Empire, which had controlled Palestine from 1515 to 1918, the fate of Palestinians was sealed when the British, French, and Italians entered into a secret arrangement (the Sykes-Picot Agreement) in 1916 to divide the Ottoman provinces outside the Arabian Peninsula (the territory of Palestine among them) into areas of British and French influence.

The Sykes-Picot Agreement gave control of Palestine, Jordan, and southern Iraq to the British; southeastern Turkey, northern Iraq, Syria, and Lebanon to the French; and Libya to the Italians. The agreement marked the first official step along Palestine's painful road to colonization.

The other shoe dropped in 1917 when the British government issued the Balfour Declaration announcing support for the establishment of a "national home for Jewish people" in Palestine. The document greatly enhanced the popularity of Zionism – a national and political ideology that called for the creation of a Jewish state – within Jewish communities worldwide and became a core component of the British Mandate for Palestine.

The first Zionist colony in Palestine was founded in 1878 with the initial wave of Zionist immigrants arriving four years later. Baron Edmond de Rothschild, a French Jewish millionaire, began supporting the colonization of Palestine around the same time, and Theodor Herzl, a Hungarian Jew, provided substance for the movement with the 1898 publication of *Der Judenstaat*, a treatise that integrated prevailing Zionist ideas and outlined a program of implementation, according to author Walid Khalidi. And in 1901 a Jewish National Fund was established in London to acquire land in Palestine on which only Jewish labor would be employed.

"The Ottoman authorities repeatedly tried to legislate controls on Zionist mass immigration and land acquisition only to be frustrated by the pressure of European powers, the corruption of their own local officials, the greed of individual landowners, and Zionist ingenuity in exploiting the 'Capitulations system,'" Khalidi wrote.

Although the Balfour Declaration did not spell out what would happen to Palestinian Arabs who called Palestine home, the Zionists were never cryptic about their intent: they foresaw a Jewish state that would exclude their Arab neighbors.

The breaking point for the Palestinian Arab community centered on what it perceived to be a threat to the al-Aqsa Mosque on the part of the Jewish community, which sought to make improvements at al-Buraq Wall, or the Western Wall, a place where Jews gathered for prayer. The wall is in close proximity to al-Aqsa and has long been a source of friction because Islamic law holds that no non-Muslims may pray near a mosque while prayers are held in the mosque, lest it disturb prayers of the faithful.

In 1928, while long-neglected mosques in Jerusalem were under repair, bricks fell on Jewish worshipers at the Western Wall. Arabs were accused of driving mules through the Jewish prayer area and of turning up the volume on the public address systems that called worshipers to prayer, which interrupted Jewish prayers.

Perceiving the actions as a warning, the Zionist community, especially its radical element, demanded Jewish control of the wall. They went a step further by pushing to rebuild the Temple, further alarming Muslims. On August 14, 1929, about 6,000 Jews paraded in Tel Aviv, and that evening, about 3,000 gathered in a cramped space at the wall in Jerusalem for prayer. Rumors circulated that the Jews were about to march on the *Haram al Sharif* – the al-Aqsa Mosque compound. Arabs circulated leaflets accusing their enemy of raping women and murdering widows and babies. The riots that followed killed 133 Jews and 116 Arabs.

There were immediate repercussions: on June 17, 1930, three Arab Palestinians, Fuad Hijazi, 'Ata Al-Zeer, and Mohammad Khaleel Jamjoum, were executed at Acre Prison for their roles in the revolution of 1929. Their executions were intended to silence the Palestinian-Arab protest movement, but they had the opposite effect as the three men became Palestine's first recognized martyrs, particularly after Hijazi's final words circulated across the Arab world: "I am not just your brother or son, I am the brother and son of our *umma* (nation). Do not cry or wail after me ... you must sing and be happy ... my death should be celebrated ... [because the] *umma* that stands in the face of this misery and fights, it is an *umma* that we will forever survive."

During his school days, Tawfik was selected to play the role of Fuad Hijazi in a play based on the poem *Red Tuesday*, penned by Palestinian poet Ibrahim Toucan. "At the school, a stage was built from wood, and in the center of the floor there was an opening used by actors playing the roles of the martyrs," Tawfik says. "I played the soul of the first martyr, Fuad Hijazi, and it was a special moment."

The First Hour: Translation of the Arabic Text

I am the hour of the supercilious soul
I have the honor to be first
I am the first hour of the three
famous hours
All are symbols of fervor
O daughter of Palestine's homeland cause
I have great influence on the causes
The influence of the mashrafiyah famous swords
The influence of the famous Zaghibiah spears
I have instilled in the hearts of the youth the fragrance of the faithful souls
There has to be a day for them (the enemies) when they will be terminated
I swear by the soul of Fuad coming sweetly out of his chest
It comes smoothly to the heavens respected and resides there
No one received the eternal flame without acceptable sacrifice
Long live the souls of those who sacrificed themselves

The tragedy of 1929 had thus launched two recurring themes: the first was the growing Jewish anger with Muslims related to the al-Aqsa Mosque and their desire for separation from the Arabs of Palestine, for self-protection, followed by an unrelenting advancement of a Jewish state. Palestinian Arabs held a totally opposite view.

Family. Palestinian stone. King Faisal I. Conflict over Jerusalem between Muslims and Jews. All things seemed to be connected in the Middle East. Tawfik was old enough to begin to get the picture, for he was present at the beginning of the end of the cherished Palestinian way of life.

CHAPTER 4

THE MASSACRE OF DEIR YASSIN

Only the misfortune of exile can provide the in-depth understanding and the overview into the realities of the world.

— STEFAN ZWEIG

It was about six o'clock in the morning, Friday, April 9, 1948, still too early to get ready for school, when a piercing scream caused Tawfik Ramadan to jump out of bed. A man's voice echoed from atop a nearby hill and penetrated the thick morning air like the clap of thunder: *"People of Maliha, Deir Yassin has been massacred. Please come help. Please come help."*

And, just like that, the Jewish people were about to have a new country of their own while the Palestinians would soon have nothing.

Like dead leaves being raked in the fall, other Palestinian villages would soon be devoured by well-armed and well-trained Jewish paramilitary forces. It really didn't matter whether you called them Zionists, Haganah, Stern, guerrilla fighters, Jewish immigrants, or simply terrorists, as Arab Palestinians considered them to be. The fact was, one horrific morning in Deir Yassin marked the tipping point in a tug-of-war for God's most hallowed ground.

Really, it was no contest as the mournful cry from one of Deir Yassin's survivors made clear. "It was a voice and a day I cannot get out of my mind," says Tawfik, who was twelve years old when he ran through the fog to the main road to make sense of what was happening.

"The weather felt gloomy and the road was already filling up with mourners who were going to Jerusalem for the funeral of Abdul Qadir al-Husayni, a war hero and great leader. He had driven past me and a crowd of people in his Land Rover on the same road only two days earlier. He briefly stopped the vehicle and I waved at him and encouraged him to save Palestine. He was dressed in military fatigues and had a gun in a holster at his side. He was telling us we would win and that he would recapture the village of al-Qastal."

The very next day he was killed.

First, Abdul Qadir al-Husayni, then Deir Yassin.

It was a one-two punch from which the Palestinian belief system never recovered, demonstrating that neither the man on the hill nor Tawfik was exaggerating the gravity of the moment.

Today, the Deir Yassin massacre remains an open wound for Palestinians, serving as confirmation to them that the ethnic cleansing of their homeland is what the Zionist High Command always had in mind. It also produces anxiety in the hearts of many Jews who feel as if remembering the massacre will diminish the magnitude of their own tragedy and somehow displace commemoration of the Holocaust.

Likewise, al-Husayni's death, coupled with the Arab coalition's refusal to lend its full support to Palestine's Army of the Holy War, sucked much of the will out of Palestine's resistance efforts.

Before daybreak that morning, about 130 Jewish fighters from the Irgun and Stern paramilitary groups burst into Deir Yassin, a Palestinian village about three miles west of Jerusalem, and began to spray homes with machine-gun fire. By the time the firing stopped, almost 200 villagers (some accounts list a higher death count), including women and children, had been murdered. Deir Yassin put up stiffer resistance than the Haganah-backed Jewish guerrillas had expected, but the village fell within several hours of house-to-house fighting. Some inhabitants were killed during the battle, others while trying to flee or surrender. Some of those who were still alive were rounded up and executed in cold blood in the village square in front of their wives and children.

The attack on Deir Yassin was neither random nor retaliatory in nature. Deir Yassin was described as a pastoral and cordial village of about 600 mostly Arab inhabitants that lay on a hill west of Jerusalem not far from the Jewish neighborhood of Givat Shaul. Deir Yassin was not considered necessarily helpful to the Palestinian resistance movement, having only a few months earlier signed a non-aggression pact with the Haganah. Deir Yassin also did not hold much military significance related to the Palestinian Arabs' blockade of Jerusalem that was then underway. In fact, the villagers of Deir Yassin and those of the nearby Jewish village of Givat Shaul had signed a peace pact, later approved by the Haganah, in order to maintain good relations, exchange information on the movement of outsiders through the area, and ensure safety of vehicles from the village.

Deir Yassin's residents lived up to the bargain and then died for it.

In a dispatch from Fletcher-Cooke of the United Kingdom Delegation to the United Nations Palestine Commission ten days later, the following information was transmitted regarding the attack:

(1) The operation is believed to have been a joint National Military Organization – Stern Group enterprise undertaken with the knowledge of the Haganah (Zionist Defense Force).

(2) The deaths of some 250 Arabs, men, women and children, which occurred during this attack, took place in circumstances of great savagery.

(3) Women and children were stripped, lined up, photographed, and then slaughtered by automatic firing. Survivors have told of even more incredible bestialities.

(4) Those who were taken prisoner were treated with degrading brutality.

(5) Although the Haganah is unable to deny that it gave covering fire to the terrorists responsible for this outrage, the action as a whole has been condemned by the Jewish press and denounced by the Chief Rabbinate.

(6) Owing to other preoccupations, the Security Forces were not in a position to act before the 14th of April, for which day an airstrike at Deir Yassin was arranged.

(7) On the 13th of April, it became apparent that the Haganah had taken over the village from the terrorists, and the operation was, therefore, suspended.

(8) The Government of Palestine reported on the 14th of April that it had not yet been possible to enter Deir Yassin and that a Jewish Police Officer sent to investigate was not allowed by the Haganah to proceed beyond Givat Shaul.

(9) A representative of the International Red Cross who visited Deir Yassin on the 11th of April is said to have stated that in one cave he saw heaped bodies of some 150 Arab men, women and children, whilst in a stronghold a further 50 bodies were found.

Few bureaucratic responses will ever be as chilling in their straightforwardness.

In a letter revealed in the recent documentary film *Born in Deir Yassin* by director Neta Shoshani, a Zionist participant in the massacre wrote: "This was the first time in my life that at my hands and before my eyes Arabs fell. In the village I killed an armed Arab man and two Arab girls of sixteen or seventeen who were helping the Arab who was shooting. I stood them against a wall and blasted them with two rounds from the Tommy gun."

A young girl in hiding said she saw guerrillas force a number of men to line up and face a wall before they shot them dead in front of her. She said she held back her tears until everyone was gone.

Tawfik was also told that when some parents heard the screaming and killing, they feared they would be shot if they opened their doors so they broke the window glass in their homes and threw their children out of the windows. "Run, run," they told them.

Two days later, fifty-five children from Deir Yassin were found huddled next to the wall of a church in the Old City by Miss Hind Husseini, a cousin of Abd al-Qader al-Husayni, who took them to her home upon learning about the massacre. To shelter them from the chaos, she rented three rooms in the American Colony Hotel, which later became the Dar El-Tifl El-Arabi Orphanage and then a girls' school.

Deir Yassin was a pivotal piece to fall in the Zionist leadership's implementation of Plan Dalet, the fourth in a series of steps, collectively known as Plans A, B, C, and D, whose ultimate goal was to take control of the country and remove the Palestinian population. As Deir Yassin demonstrated, the Zionists would stop at nothing to reach their goal.

In *The Ethnic Cleansing of Palestine*, Ilan Pappe wrote: "On a cold Wednesday afternoon, 10 March 1948, a group of eleven men, veteran Zionist leaders together with young military Jewish officers, put the final touches on a plan for the ethnic cleansing of Palestine. That same evening, military orders were dispatched to units on the ground to prepare for the systemic expulsion of Palestinians from vast areas of the country."

Plan D came with a detailed description of the methods to be used to forcibly evict Arab residents by whatever means necessary, including "large-scale intimidation, laying siege and bombarding villages and population centers, and setting fire to homes, properties, and goods. Clashes with local Palestinian militias, especially after the UN partition resolution of November 1947, provided the perfect context and pretext for implementing the ideological vision of an ethnically cleansed Palestine."

Once Plan D was finalized, it took six months to complete the mission. When it was over, 531 villages had been destroyed and 11 urban neighborhoods had been emptied of their inhabitants.

Pappe's research concluded Plan D clearly laid out what was in store for the Palestinian population in contrast to three precious plans that "had articulated only obscurely how the Zionist leadership intended to deal with the presence of so many Palestinians."

Ten years after the massacre of Deir Yassin and the forced exodus of almost a million Palestinians, Israeli premier David Ben-Gurion admitted that Palestine "was virtually emptied of its former owners." Although he went on to claim that "pre-state Zionism could not have conceived of such a thing," the Palestinian perspective is far different. As noted in *The Transformation of Palestine by Ibrahim Abu-Lughod,* Zionists had been conceiving such a thing for fifty years or more.

It had been attempted between 1917 and 1947, but a politically expedient time or method had never been found. By the beginning of 1948, the Zionist Movement had decided that the international calendar would not synchronize itself with its desire to create a Jewish state.

Architects of the plans maintained the goal was to take control of Mandatory Palestine, declare a Jewish state, and defend its borders and people, including the Jewish populations outside of the borders, before and in anticipation of the invasion by regular Arab armies.

Those who lived through the Nakba reached a different conclusion. They believe Deir Yassin was meant to serve as an example to all Arabs in Palestinian territory that they had two choices: get out or get killed.

Militarily and logistically, Plan D was an overwhelming success. After the attack on Deir Yassin, four nearby villages – Qalunya, Sarris, Beit Sourik, and Biddu – quickly fell. The Haganah units became more proficient in the practice of blowing up houses and expelling people. By May 14, 1948, the day the Jewish state was declared, fifty-eight villages had been wiped out. And when the details of the Deir Yassin massacre began to circulate throughout Palestine, people fled their homes, sparing Haganah and newly trained and militarily equipped Jewish settlers the need to use force to remove the remaining Arab population.

Prior to the Deir Yassin massacre, residents of a small nearby Arab village called Lifta, which had already been engulfed by encroaching Jewish settlements, had taken shelter in Al-Maliha, fearing that something would happen to them if they did not get out.

"Everybody was in the same boat," Tawfik says. "If I see you are having to leave your home, and if I can protect you, then you are coming in. Deir Yassin created tremendous fear for us and all of the surrounding villages because we all felt that if we stayed, we would be killed, like those at Deir Yassin. And this was the Zionists' strategy. They had some groups go into more villages and kill more people so that the news would spread that we would all be killed."

It was not by coincidence that the attack on Deir Yassin came only one day after Palestine's most popular warrior met his death. Desperate for help, many Palestinians had pinned their hopes on al-Husayni, the nephew of Mohammed Amin al-Husayni, the leader of the resistance movement and the Grand Mufti of Jerusalem.

Tawfik says al-Husayni was returning from Damascus, where Arab leaders had turned down his plea to provide him with more troops and weapons to counter the Haganah's strategy of forcing Palestinian Arabs from their villages and allowing Jewish immigrants to move in.

Abd al-Qadir Husayni was killed in battle on the morning of April 8, while leading a counterattack to recover the village of al-Qastal, an Arab village that was importantly militarily to both sides.

"I am told he left a letter to his wife, asking her to take care of the children," Tawfik says. "He probably knew he was going to die after realizing he would not get the men and arms he needed. I saw him on a Wednesday, he died on Thursday, then Deir Yassin was massacred on Friday. This tells you how unorganized and unprepared we were for anything. And when our leader was killed, we gave up."

What many Palestinians perceive to have been a long-term strategy on the part of the Western powers to create a Jewish state was entering its final phase.

"I realized as a child that the Jewish people suffered under the Nazis," Tawfik says. "They were persecuted, but to solve the problem, why should they bring Jews from Germany and around the world only to create a new problem by uprooting Palestinians from their land? This is what happened, you know."

CHAPTER 5

THE SEEDS OF ZIONISM

Education is the passport to the future, for tomorrow belongs to those who prepare for it today.

— MALCOLM X

It was only a matter of time before the drip, drip, drip of colonization reached flood stage at Tawfik Ramadan's very front door.

"Looking back, what we began to have a problem with when I was young was colonization, the fact that somebody would want to put their boots on your neck every day," he says.

Based on what he experienced from the time he was old enough to form a sentence all the way to today's destruction in Gaza, Tawfik's disapproval remains focused on the role the British played in helping the Zionists accomplish what he called their "colonizing project" in Palestine and the creation of the State of Israel.

Pappé captures the plight of the Palestinians by saying: "In January 1948, the level of war rhetoric in the Arab world had reached new heights, but the Arab governments by and large never moved beyond talking about the need to salvage Palestine, at the same time that both local media and dailies, such as *Filastin*, and the foreign press, especially the *New York Times*, were methodically reporting Jewish attacks on Palestinian villages and neighborhoods."

By 1947, Palestine was a major trouble spot in the British Empire, requiring some 100,000 troops and a huge maintenance budget. To ease the burden, the United Kingdom requested that the question of Palestine be handled by the United Nations General Assembly, which commissioned the United Nations Special Committee on Palestine (UNSCOP) to find a solution.

Ultimately, UNSCOP proposed the creation of an "independent Arab State, an independent Jewish State, and the City of Jerusalem," the last to be under "an International Trusteeship System." A slightly amended version of the plan, known as Resolution 181, was adopted by the General Assembly on November 27, 1947, after what was termed "intense lobbying" by pro-Jewish groups and over the objections of Palestinians and the Arab states that had fought for self-determination for decades. Furthermore, they said 181 unfairly assigned about 55 percent of the land, including the most fertile areas in Palestine and the only major ports, to the country's Jewish minority. At the time, Arabs comprised about 65 percent of the population to 30 percent Jewish representation.

In the end, Resolution 181 called for the creation of independent Arab and Jewish states with Jerusalem to fall under international control, marking the end of British military occupation. Finally, in a desperate nod to unity, Resolution 181 proposed an economic union between the two states and sought the protection of minority religious rights.

Adopted by the UN General Assembly on November, 29, 1947, Resolution 181 did not give the Zionists all they wanted. But their success in constructing an ideological, cultural, economic, and political network over four decades gained them a huge advantage over the fragmented agrarian Arab population when it came to nation building. The months-long lead-up to 181's passage also gave Ben-Gurion time to prepare for war and the removal of the Palestinian people. He did so by mandating that every Jewish man and woman receive military training, including combat training for females. Thanks to Golda Meir's fund-raising ability, Ben-Gurion also raised enough money to buy and smuggle $12 million in heavy arms from Czechoslovakia into Palestine in January of 1948.

By the end of British rule, approximately 10,700 rifles, 1,200 machine guns, 25 field guns, and 11 million rounds of ammunition had arrived in Palestine. The rest was on site by the end of May, allowing the Haganah to accelerate its offensive. In a series of operations carried out from early April until mid-May, the Haganah used force and intimidation to change the face of Palestine. In the meantime, President Truman was convinced to reverse himself and pledge his support for the proposed Jewish state.

Palestinians rejected Resolution 181, saying it violated the principles of national self-determination in the UN charter and was unfair to the population that would remain in Jewish territory under the partition.

It was not long before violence broke out, escalating into the overthrow of Palestine. With the Zionist movement's declaration of independence imminent, parts of Jerusalem became war zones, commencing with the Haganah's bombing of the Semiramis Hotel in the Katamon neighborhood on the night of January 5, 1948. The blast killed a reported twenty-five civilians, including a child. The Haganah claimed the hotel, which was owned by a Christian, was an important meeting place for Arab fighters, but British authorities strongly denounced the attack as the "wholesale murder of innocent people."

In the aftermath of the hotel bombing, Tawfik's father, who had taken a job at a power plant less than a mile away, was among those trapped inside the building as armed Zionist forces controlled the streets. "For almost a month, my father could not get back home," Tawfik says. "The plant was still operating, and people would bring him and others food and water to survive, but there was no way out of the crossfire that had started.

"One day, to his surprise, a Jewish co-worker who had been missing most of that time showed up suddenly in military gear. My father had not previously realized it, but this man was a high-ranking officer for the Haganah. My father called him Cohen (a name Palestinian Arabs commonly used to identify Jews), and Cohen said he was there to help my father escape."

Cohen had a vehicle and drove Za'al safely through the adjacent Jewish-controlled neighborhood (Mekor Chaim). "When they reached the border to Beit Safafa, a Palestinian village east of Al-Maliha, Cohen told my father he would have to walk the rest of the way."

But along that route, Za'al was hit by a sniper's bullet from Mekor Chaim. Some Palestinians took him to a small hospital in Beit Safafa, and for more than a week, his family did not know what had happened to him or if he was even alive.

"Finally, my father's brother gave us the news that he had been shot in the thigh but would recover," Tawfik says. "So, we came to take him home."

After thinking his father was dead, seeing his father alive marked one of the happiest days of Tawfik's entire childhood. "The other part of the story is that this man Cohen was a friend of my father," Tawfik says. "He had been to our house several times in the past. That is why he came to help my father. They were friends."

There are several lessons to be learned from Za'al's rescue. On a personal level, it is a poignant reminder of how friendships can survive in the most toxic of environments. The man known only to Za'al as Cohen had been his friend, and in this case a Jew came to the rescue of a Muslim. On a tactical level, their story demonstrates how the Zionists were far better trained, equipped, and prepared for the all-out war that would soon engulf Palestine. In contrast, the rest of the Palestinian people, both

Muslims and Christians, were still living in the past, or what was left of it.

While anti-Semitism was increasing worldwide at the dawn of the twentieth century, the Jewish people were not considered threats by the majority of the Palestinian Arab population. After all, Jews, Muslims, and Christians had been sharing the land out of respect for one another for centuries. Jewish immigration totals remained small as the Jewish population in Palestine constituted less than 10 percent of the population by 1935.

"The increase in the number of Jews mostly came from Russia and Europe, while the increase in the Palestinian Arab population was a natural increase," Tawfik says. "We (Palestinians) welcomed them as guests until the Balfour Declaration when Palestinian Arabs, the real people who had been living in Palestine for generations, began to get mistreated as a result of actions taken by the British Mandate, particularly the confiscation of their land by means of large tax increases."

In Tawfik's mind, the Jewish people, per se, were never his enemy. That designation is reserved for the British and Zionist leadership, which he believes orchestrated the removal of Palestinian families much the same way U.S. president Andrew Jackson led the effort to confiscate land owned by the Five Civilized Tribes and offer it to white settlers.

Tawfik breaks down the colonization into five well-coordinated steps:

The Balfour Declaration: The declaration turned the Zionist aim of establishing a Jewish state in Palestine into a reality when Britain publicly pledged to establish "a national home for the Jewish people" in a letter on November 2, 1917. The declaration was contained in a letter from the United Kingdom's foreign secretary, Arthur Balfour, to Lord Rothschild, a leader of the British Jewish Community, for transmission to the Zionist Federation of Great Britain and Ireland. The letter included a statement that contended Britain would do nothing to prejudice the civil and religious rights of existing non-Jewish communities in Palestine. But that phrase was reportedly included to falsely appease the Arabs.

Herbert Samuel, as the first Jewish and Zionist ruler of Palestine during the British Mandate: During Samuel's administration, the Churchill White paper was published on June 3, 1922 on Palestine. Among other things, it supported Jewish immigration within the absorptive economic capacity of the country. As an example of how it empowered Jewish people at the expense of native Palestinians, Samuel granted Pinhas Rutenberg, a Russian political activist and Zionist who participated in establishing the Haganah, exclusive rights to produce and distribute electricity in Palestine and Trans-Jordan. Samuel promoted Zionism within the British Cabinet, beginning with his 1915 memorandum entitled "The Future of Palestine." He recognized Hebrew as one of the three languages of the territory and recommended the admission of 50,000 Jews annually to Palestine.

Formation of the Jewish Brigade and the Special Night Squad: Recruited among Yeshiva Jews from Mandatory Palestine and commanded by Anglo-Jewish officers, the Jewish Brigade was a branch of the British Army. Members of the brigade returned to Palestine with their weapons. In 1948 they were part of the organized Zionist group that participated in terrorizing and ethnically cleansing Palestinian Arab villages. Thirty-five of them became generals in the Israeli army.

The Settlement Guards: The Jewish Settlement Police were trained and equipped by the British Mandate Authority. It was reported in 1938 that there were about 40,000 Settlement Guards. During the British Mandate, several paramilitary groups were formed, including the Haganah. The Palmach, the elite fighting force of Haganah, formed on May 15, 1941, was trained and equipped by the British Army and played a big role in 1948. The other Zionist paramilitary organizations operating from 1931 to 1948 were the Irgun, Stern, and Lehi (an underground branch of Stern). It was reported that the number of paramilitaries ready to fight was more than 70,000 well-trained and well-equipped men. This number exceeds the total number of all Arab armies, who were poorly trained, disorganized, and ill-equipped.

The 1948 withdrawal of British Troops from Palestine and the end of the Mandate: There were 100,000 British troops by 1948, and when they withdrew they left a large number of weapons and armored vehicles for the Zionist groups to confiscate. It is not unlike what happened before World War I when the British relied on the help of Arabs to defeat the Ottoman Empire at the same time they were working secretly with the Zionists to devise a plan to colonize

Palestine at the expense of the Arab people.

It is Tawfik's contention that while a Palestinian could be sent to prison for possessing a knife, the Zionist leadership could plan and execute atrocities against both Palestinians and Mandate personnel without retribution.

One example of the extremes to which the militant Zionist paramilitary unit Lehi (also known as the Stern gang) would go was the 1944 assassination of Dublin-born Walter Edward Guinness, the 1st Baron Moyne, who served as British secretary of state for the colonies and minister resident in the Middle East. In November 1944 Moyne was assassinated near his home in Cairo by two young members of Lehi, who were later hanged. Lord Moyne's death was one of the steps on the road to British withdrawal from Mandate Palestine.

Knowing it could cost him his life, Lord Moyne had remained resolute in his belief in compromise between Jews and Arabs. While he dismissed his Egyptian police escort and a police guard that was stationed at his house day and night, he did recognize the mounting pressure on the British in Palestine, writing that the previous attempted murder of a high-ranking high commissioner incited violence by Zionist circles in Palestine.

If there was any question about whether the Zionist paramilitary units would bite the hand of their British trainers, it was answered on July 22, 1946, when Irgun, the militant right-wing Zionist underground organization, bombed the King David Hotel in Jerusalem, the headquarters for the British administration in Palestine, a tragedy that Tawfik remembers well.

Menachem Begin, who went on to become the first Likud Party prime minister of Israel, was commander in chief of Irgun at the time of the bombing. Disguised as Arab workers and hotel waiters, Irgun members planted a bomb in the basement of the main building of the hotel. Tawfik, who was about ten years old at the time, said the story he heard then was that members of Irgun carried bottles of milk to the hotel from a local dairy and put the explosives inside the milk containers. The blast, which went off at 12:37 p.m., blew off the western half of the southern wing of the seven-story hotel, killing ninety-one people of various nationalities and injuring forty-six others.

"I first became informed that the King David Hotel was blown up by one of the Jewish guerilla groups while listening to a neighbor's radio that he had placed on a table outside his house," Tawfik recalls. "The announcer on the newscast from Jerusalem said they blew it up because the hotel was part of the headquarters for the British people working in Palestine. But there were other people there, too. I mention this because after the newscast one of our other neighbors said she knew people there, a Palestinian lady who worked as a secretary. She was among those killed."

Zionist sympathizers claimed the attack was in response to Operation Agatha, during which British troops had searched the Jewish Agency on June 29, 1946, and confiscated large quantities of documents directly implicating the Haganah in the Jewish insurgency against Britain. The intelligence information was taken to the King David Hotel where it was initially kept in the offices of the Secretariat in the southern wing. The claim was that the bombing was an attempt by Irgun to destroy incriminating evidence.

British Mandate authorities responded by restricting the civil liberties of Jews in Palestine and denounced Zionist terrorist tactics. The measures also ultimately shifted British public opinion against the Mandate system and alienated the British Jewish population from their government, which had been the objective of Begin, the leader of Irgun, from the beginning.

CHAPTER 6

THE PALESTINIAN *NAKBA*

It is during our darkest moments that we must focus to see the light.

— ARISTOTLE

Tawfik's father carried his house key with him until he died, long after he ever got the chance to use it again. The point is if you want something badly enough, you don't want to let go, and Za'al was not one to give up easily.

After the death of Abdul Qadir al-Husayni and the massacre at Deir Yassin, Za'al knew his courage was about to be put to the test. "The thought was we would be next, and we were not prepared," Tawfik says.

Some villagers did flee Al-Maliha in the aftermath of the massacre, but Za'al and Tawfik's uncle, Ahmad, had already decided to fight for their homes, if necessary.

"The British Mandate might hang you if they found a weapon on you, but I remember my father and my uncle, both of them, sold their wives' jewelry to buy a black-market rifle," Tawfik says. "I remember hearing my father talk about going into the desert of Libya to procure a gun. At that time, rifles were very expensive. They paid 110 Palestinian pounds (100 Palestinian pounds was equivalent at the time to more than three years of wages for a skilled worker in Palestine) for the rifle and shared it so they would have a weapon to fight with. But they only had ten bullets."

Prior to Deir Yassin, Al-Maliha villagers had already fended off one Jewish incursion on March 6, 1948, according to a report in the Jaffa-based Palestinian daily *Filastin*. With probably no more than fifty guns in a village largely populated by farmers and stonecutters, Al-Maliha was easy prey.

Tawfik agrees that the situation quickly grew unsustainable around the end of May after the family again awakened to gunfire. This time the sound was coming from not far down the road.

It did not take long before Za'al said it was time for them to go. First, he hid the gun – yes, his only means of resistance – and some jewelry in a secret compartment under the tile floor in their living area. If he had not been under immense stress, Za'al might have held on to the weapon, but panic, not logic, ruled the day. They had lived with the constant fear of being slaughtered the way the residents of Deir Yassin were, and now that moment was at hand.

In their mad rush to escape, the family took little more than the clothes on their backs. Once outside, Za'al took out a key and locked the front door. He expected to be returning soon. At least, that was the impression he wanted to leave. "I thought we would be coming back the next week, or sooner," Tawfik says.

The key was never used again.

The village was not completely emptied until mid-July during Zionist operations conducted around Jerusalem in conjunction with Operation Dani.

On the night of July 13–14, an Irgun Zvai Leumi (IZL) company and two platoons from the Yonathan Company of the Gadna (Palmach Youth Battalions) entered Al-Maliha, taking up positions in the village. Arab forces launched a counterattack on July 15, forcing the IZL unit to withdraw from the farthest position in the village. That same day, Egyptian irregulars operating south of Jerusalem alongside Palestinian guerrillas announced taking Al-Maliha in a communiqué quoted by the *New York Times*, but it was soon reoccupied after the arrival of IZL reinforcements. The *Times* reported Zionists were using medium artillery and mortar fire to mount diversionary attacks on the Jerusalem front on July 14. The objective was to take the "important supply base and assembly center of Al-Maliha," according to the paper's correspondent.

Tawfik's paternal grandfather was among the villagers and volunteers who launched an unsuccessful counterattack. It cost him his life as he was shot in the groin and died in a French hospital in Bethlehem. "I vividly remember visiting him in the hospital and seeing how pale he looked," he says.

By July 16, the village was in Israeli hands, although fifteen Irgun invaders died in the process, and another twenty were wounded. The IZL said it had been "let down" by the Haganah, which withdrew from a flanking height and failed to give covering fire during the Arab assault, but the Haganah denied the charges. A few days later, on July 22, the Zionist commander of the Jerusalem area, David Shaltiel, told the *Times* correspondent that the "strategic" villages of Al-Maliha and 'Ayn Karim had been occupied between the truces, thus ending a "threatened Egyptian invasion of Jerusalem."

Tawfik questions that claim, saying the Egyptian fighters were volunteers, not regular military.

What goes without question is that on that day late in May 1948 when the Ramadans fled Al-Maliha, no one thought it would be the start of a journey with no return.

The day also marked the end of their lives together as the Ramadan family was split like a watermelon – Za'al and his cousin Ahmad headed south toward Battir, four miles west of Bethlehem, while Ahmed and Esa, their other cousins, took their families to Bethlehem. The crisis unfolded so quickly it was as if they came to a fork in the road, and two went one way and two went the other with their families in tow.

Within less than an hour of leaving home, Tawfik's caravan was caught in the middle of gunfire while venturing down a dirt road. "It was chilling because the shots were all around us. And we had my sister, who was four years old, with us. Somebody had to carry her as we ran. We had nothing except the clothes we were wearing. I didn't think about it then because I was still a boy, but now I realize our journey represents the suffering of all Palestinians."

The family stopped briefly at Al-Hania spring at Walajah to drink water and wash their faces. It was late in the day when they arrived in Battir. "We were glad to be alive," Tawfik says. "By chance, my father met a man, Ahmad Hammad, who rented us his house. When I say it was a house, I mean it was really one big room. He charged one Palestinian pound a month, which was expensive at the time. But he came to be a good friend."

The story goes that most of the people in Battir had already left as well. The few who stayed behind would light candles at night and take out the cattle in the morning to convince Israeli attackers that Battir was still inhabited, in the hope it would discourage them from attacking.

The two families took shelter there from May until July, when the Israelis decided Battir was a valuable link on the railroad line that ran from Java to Jerusalem. The Israelis met resistance from the villagers, giving Tawfik's family time to escape. "We moved about two or three miles into the country, to an orchard that the man we rented the house from owned and that the Israelis didn't know about," Tawfik explains. "We built temporary shelters from tree branches and lived under the trees for about three months. The same man befriended us as well because we lived off the tomatoes and other vegetables from the gardens he owned."

From there, the Ramadans found lodging in Beit Jala. In Arabic, "Beit" means house, meaning Tawfik was now in the "House of Jala." It was a town of about 4,000 people, the majority of whom were Christians (mostly Greek Orthodox), and in the wake of the 1948 War fell under Jordanian rule.

In addition to protection from his newfound enemy in the Haganah, Beit Jala afforded Tawfik Ramadan a chance to resume his education. His father would have it no other way.

CHAPTER 7

A TRIBE OF LIONESSES

Everyone has oceans to fly,
If they have the heart to do it.
Is it reckless? Maybe.
But what do dreams
Know of boundaries?

— AMELIA EARHART

In some ways, it was as if Siham Saleh Taha Alzaben had been born on the opposite side of the world from her future husband. While the villages they came from were only about thirty miles apart, every mile seemed like one spin of the globe because a few steps either way in 1948 Palestine marked the difference between breathing free air and living like a refugee.

War would eventually bring Siham and Tawfik together, but in those dark early days of the Nakba, one's fate was decided by whether Jewish immigrants were waiting to occupy your home the minute you went running for your life.

Fewer than four miles from Jerusalem, Al-Maliha was ripe for resettlement. Located on strategic high ground, it was an important military location for the Israelis. By contrast, the farming village of Mazari al-Nubani, where Siham was born on February 10, 1948, lay about fifteen miles to the northwest of Ramallah and went largely unnoticed as part of the Bani Zaid area in Ramallah Province.

Her village also was not within the United Nations' boundary of a proposed Jewish state. Plus, by the time Siham was old enough to know that a large part of Palestine was occupied by the Israelis, her village had become part of the West Bank of Jordan that was united with the East Bank in the Hashemite Kingdom of Jordan. Mazari al-Nubani remained under Jordanian control until the Israelis gained that territory as a result of the 1967 Arab–Israeli War.

"I knew there was fear in the people's hearts because they would talk about the Zionists, about their enemy, and that part of their land was taken. But I was so young, and for me there was no information about this, nobody to sit down and say that all these Palestinian cities, like Jaffa on the Mediterranean Sea, had been fully occupied or taken over by the Jews."

One might say that she simply had geography on her side and Tawfik didn't. The other difference between the two is that Siham still has a home to go to, if not a country. The luck of the draw – the way the boundary lines fell when control of Palestine was divvied up after every war – had a lot to do with how Siham's childhood evolved.

The true guiding light in her life was her mother, whose determination to nurture and protect her children and her land was nothing short of extraordinary. Siham, for example, remains a part owner of her mother's land to this day, even if she is only allowed to visit on a ninety-day visa.

Aysha Mustafa would be deemed phenomenal anywhere and at any time in history, and Siham has done her best to walk in her footsteps. You can start with the fact that Siham's mother was thirteen years old when she married Saleh, who was forty-seven years older, in an arranged marriage between tribes in the same village. Two years later she had a son, and then another son, and soon she was sixteen years old and responsible for a whole household.

"After they were married, they say that in the nighttime she used to wake up, unlock the door and run across the street to go to her mom's house," Siham says. "You would call it brutal now, not an easy thing. I cannot imagine someone who's not even fourteen years old marrying a man who's over sixty years old. But, somehow, she made it."

Her father, a prosperous landowner and farmer, had two daughters, Saliha and Ezyah, by his first marriage. Both girls were already married with grown children by the time Aysha married their father.

"I remember I was about ten or twelve years old when someone who was in their thirties came to our house and called me '*Khalto,*' which means aunt," Siham says. "That was done out of respect for the family, which is important in our culture."

Saleh and Aysha produced two sons and three daughters. Siham's eldest brother, Taha Saleh, was already twenty years old when Siham was born in 1948 (Taher, the younger brother, was eighteen). Her two older sisters, Samiha and Nazeeha, were twelve and six years older, respectively.

Siham's father died when she was less than a year old, putting into question whether Aysha was strong enough to carry on without him because the expectation was that farming would not be profitable if left in the hands of a female. Boys were stronger and ordained to work the fields. Aysha certainly debunked that stereotype and many others that fit into the proverbial concept of a "man's world." Not only did Aysha demonstrate her resolve in taking control of her late husband's estate, she went on to tend the land as successfully as any man.

"The old mentality still existed then. My father had been the eldest son in his family, and some of my uncles tried to take over the responsibility of working the land from my mother," Siham says. "But she told them, 'I have kids; I have to make a living to survive and keep them, the same as everybody else.' To me, she was trying to protect her chicks, like the hen spreading her wings, while trying to keep her land from being taken away. We owe everything to her. For me, I have always wanted to be like her and learn to survive the way she survived."

As the youngest child, Siham had a unique upbringing. She has only seen grainy photos of her father, as she was still a baby when he died. All she had heard was that while he may have been an old man when he married her mother, he remained a formidable figure in the community.

Not only was there no father figure in her life, but Siham's older brothers had already joined the Jordanian army by the time she was born. Aysha could have appealed to their sense of duty to the family, but she encouraged them to leave home. Their departure left Siham's mother totally responsible for her daughters, their home, the land, and the crops.

Aysha had never been to school, but she had a PhD in survival training. Instead of cratering under the strain of having no husband, no sons at home, and in-laws who wanted what was hers, Aysha worked and saved until she could afford to buy more land. She bought more sheep and cattle to raise, and she sewed dresses for twenty-five cents apiece.

"I never woke up and found my mother still asleep," Siham says. "I never even saw her go to sleep. She was always working unbelievably long hours."

Those were the lessons Siham learned under the protection of a resilient woman whose work ethic was only matched by the love she gave her children. As a result, Palestine never strays far from Siham's head or heart. Sometimes she gets the sensation that she is back home, eating green almonds from the three big almond trees near her house in the spring and then cutting the almonds off the trees after they dried in the summer.

Sometimes she is walking up a big hill with her sisters – more like a mountain in her recollections – until she reaches a terrace that is full of grapes and figs, pomegranates, plums, and peaches.

When the summer sun started to bake them, they would cool off in the shade and eat lunch, maybe some bread with olive oil and some *zaatar* (a wild herb similar to oregano) and fruit. Meanwhile, their mother kept working.

There are four defined seasons in that region of Palestine. Winter is usually dominated by cold weather and heavy rain. Spring is comfortable; summer is hot, sometimes as hot as 100 degrees; and traditionally, mild fall weather follows summer and is marked by the turning of the leaves on the fruit trees, other than the olive trees, which remain green all year long. When it was time to pick the fruits and vegetables, Siham's mother would bring them into the house and share them with neighbors.

As followers of Islam, residents of Mazari al-Nubani strictly observed the two most celebrated religious holidays: Eid al-Fitr, which marks the end of Ramadan, the holy month of fasting from dawn to sunset, which includes introspection and prayer; and Eid al-Adha, which marks the end of Hajj, the Islamic pilgrimage to Mecca, Saudi Arabia, the holiest city for Muslims. Ramadan is celebrated as the month during which the Prophet Muhammad received the initial revelations of the Qur'an, the holy book for Muslims. It falls on the ninth month of the Islamic calendar, a lunar calendar in which months begin when the first crescent of a new moon is sighted. Consequently, the Islamic year is ten to eleven days shorter than the solar year, which means Ramadan will be observed at a different time every year.

As a child, Siham always marveled at the way her village came together to celebrate Eid, marking the end of the holy month. In preparation, usually half a dozen women representing the various families in the village would gather to create delicious sweets and pastries, each accented with dried fruit. The bakers would pool the ingredients; maybe one woman brought two pounds of almonds, and another brought walnuts. The ingredients did not matter as much as the fact that they were all being shared.

"The preparation for the end of the month and the big feast went on for about a week and involved the whole village," Siham says. "Everyone also had to have new outfits for Eid, so you either traveled to the city on a bus where you could buy new clothes, or, in our case, our mom always used to sew my and my sister's clothes. Everything had to be special for that day."

Although they were away much of the time, Siham's two brothers, Taha and Taher, also played important roles in Siham's upbringing, particularly Taha, the oldest. "When I was young, I thought that my oldest brother was my father," she says. "So, all the time I was looking forward to the day when he would come home from the Jordanian Army. I remember it vividly, the times when he would come in and sit in the chair. I would run over and hug him tight. It has been that way for us all our lives. I have looked at him as my father. And I think his love for me is more like a father's than a brother's."

When on leave from the military, Taha and Taher often traveled to Ramallah where they would catch a bus to Mazari al-Nubani. The bus made five stops, starting in the morning with Siham's village (Mazari al-Noubani), followed by Arora, Abwein, Jiljilyha, and Sinjil and then on to Ramallah, a distance of about twenty miles. After five or six hours, the bus would make the return trip.

Although Siham always grew antsy waiting for her brothers to arrive in the afternoon, she was never disappointed. "Taha and Taher always came with all kinds of goodies with them," Siham says. "The kids from the neighborhood would come, calling my mom's name. They would say, '*'im Taha.*' My brother's name was Taha. T-A-H-A. They would say, *'im, 'im, 'im Taha, 'im Taha.*" *Im* means mother, mother of Taha.

"Then some boys playing near the bus parking area start saying, 'Taha has come. Taha has come.' And my mother would say to the boys, 'Go back, go back, and go help him bring the stuff.' They did the same for Taher."

The most anticipated item was a bag, a jute bag full of oranges. They call them Jaffa oranges, which were really from Jericho, she says. Before 1948, Jaffa was known for its citrus fruit, but many of those farmers fled after Jaffa became occupied, one of the many casualties of Israeli occupation, according to her.

Growing crops and cutting stone had been the primary means of survival in rural Palestine for centuries. There was nothing easy about either endeavor, which may be one reason that Tawfik's father and Siham's mother insisted they receive the best education possible.

Siham's opportunities were limited by the fact that she was a girl. Her village didn't offer girls an education until 1953, when a room in the local mosque was set aside for girls and a teacher was recruited from out of town.

"I was about five years old when there was talk over town that there was going to be a school for girls," she says. "And the following year, as soon as girls were allowed, my mom took me and my sister, who was six years older than me, to school to enroll. Both of us started school at the same time."

When she showed up at school carrying paper, pencil, and an eraser, Siham discovered that the "school" consisted of a big square room with a single teacher.

Whether there was one or a hundred teachers, Siham felt honored because teachers, like physicians, were held in high esteem. As Ahmad Shawqi, an Egyptian poet, wrote: "Stand up for the teacher and honor his rank . . . for a teacher is almost as a prophet. . . . Do you know of someone nobler than . . . he who nurtures minds and hearts?"

Siham's teacher was named Nawal. She was a young woman from Beit Jala who came to live and teach in Mazari al-Nubani with the encouragement and support of Siham's mother, who regularly supplied her with fruit, vegetables, and fresh meat. Siham, who was in the second grade, remembers carrying a half-gallon jug of clean drinking water on her head to share with the teacher.

It happened that Siham's aunt, who also lived in Beit Jala, knew the parents of that teacher. One day Nawal asked Aysha if she could take Siham with her when she went to see her family so that Siham could see her aunt. On Thursday mornings the bus would take her to Ramallah, and from there she would take a taxi to Beit Jala where she would spend Thursday and Friday, before returning in the afternoon in time for class on Saturday morning.

"Somehow, my mom accepted the offer, and she permitted me to go with *Sitt Nawal* (*sitt* means miss in Arabic) knowing that I'm going to be safe and going to come back. For me, it was lots of excitement. I had barely seen a car at that point in my life, so riding the bus was a big, big thing, plus there was the excitement to be in a city for two or three days and see what it was all about.

"My aunt had a very nice second-story apartment with a balcony that faced a church in Beit Jala. It was a beautiful church with a big cross on a hill. We were standing on the balcony of my aunt's house and looking around, and I saw this handsome-looking man walk by my aunt's house. I could not see his face, but I could tell he was dignified. He had a robe on and wore a big cross on his chest. At that point, he was heading up the hill toward the church. My aunt knew him, and she knew his name. She said, 'Good morning, Father . . .' in a loud voice. I can't remember what his name was, but the man turned around and returned the greeting. Then they spoke for a minute. As for me, I got confused because that was the first time I heard anyone call someone else a 'father' who was not their father."

Siham looked at her and said, "What are you saying? Why are you calling him father?"

"He is a Christian and is the priest of his church," her aunt answered.

"What are Christians?"

Her aunt's response has stuck with Siham ever since. "He is a follower of the Christian religion, and we respect them, and they respect us." There could not have been a more valuable lesson for Siham to learn at that point in her life.

"It resonated in my mind that the world is a lot bigger than my village . . . and, like my aunt told me, we are all God's children."

CHAPTER 8

A YOUNG DREAMER WITH CONVICTION

Those who fear climbing the mountains will spend their lives in the ditches.

— ABO ALQASIM AL-SHABBI

Boys and girls all over the world are encouraged to strive for the kind of no-mountain-too-high goals both Tawfik and Siham set for themselves. He decided he would grow up to save lives rather than have them brushed off, as did Siham once she was old enough to grasp how much suffering was going on beyond the protection of her mother's arms.

Young dreamers with conviction, oh, how big they dream. Of course, the bigger the dream, the higher the climb. The thought of a poor Palestinian refugee kid trapped in a hopeless state defying incredible odds to become somebody, well, that was almost unthinkable in occupied Palestine. Better set your sights lower, kid.

Or so the world thought.

What the law of averages fails to calculate correctly in the Palestinian equation is exemplified by Tawfik's and Siham's own journeys. By virtue of the fact that he was twelve years older than Siham, Tawfik got a head start. They also took separate routes to reach the same place in life. His was rockier; hers more spiritual. They did so only because they shared a common thread: devoted parents who stressed the importance of an education and their own undeniable determination to make a difference.

Tawfik knew his father slid the key to their home into his pocket the day he left Al-Maliha and motioned his family to follow him down a treacherous road. What he did not know at the time was that the other pocket contained the actual key to Tawfik's future.

"This will tell you how much my father emphasized education," Tawfik says. "When we were forced to leave our village, I didn't think we were able to take anything except the key to the door. But I discovered later that he carried all the certificates my school handed out evaluating my performance. That's the only other thing he carried with him."

Throughout the summer and early fall of 1948, Za'al held on to the batch of papers while the Ramadan family joined the ranks of refugees seeking shelter in Palestinian villages not yet occupied by Israeli forces.

It was already October by the time the Ramadans reached a small rural neighborhood on the outskirts of Beit Jala, a city only a mile from the Church of the Nativity in Bethlehem City in the West Bank. The area contained quarries where Za'al continued to cut stone. It is not known whether he deliberately went to Beit Jala in 1948 searching for a school for his son or whether it was by pure luck. Either way, Za'al went to the right place, if not at the right time, as Tawfik and his family arrived two months after the start of the school year at a nearby Christian school.

"When we got to the school, my father took me with him to the principal, George Khoury, and told him that I had finished the fifth year of elementary school and that he wanted me to advance to the sixth grade.

"The principal said, 'No, I cannot do that,' citing the fact that the school year was already well underway."

To which Za'al stood up, leaned over the desk, and said, "You will take my son." Then he reached into his pocket and pulled out Tawfik's school certificates from elementary school. The papers confirmed that Tawfik had scored first in his class in the first, second, third, fourth, and fifth grades.

"Just put him in the sixth grade. He can do the work," Za'al said in summation. The principal capitulated, and Tawfik did not disappoint.

"We were still living in the rural area outside of town at that point, and I had to walk a few miles a day to school until we eventually moved to a house in Beit Jala," Tawfik says. "My brother decided he didn't want to attend school any longer, so I walked alone on the road."

Tawfik attended the Beit Jala Christian Orthodox Elementary School for the sixth and seventh grades, where he was the only Muslim student. From there, boys either advanced to secondary school or found a vocation and learned to make a living. The school of about five hundred students was a welcoming place where boys from several religious backgrounds learned and laughed together. Tawfik even joined the Boy Scout troop organized by the new principal, Qustandi Nicola, when Tawfik was a seventh grader.

"That was my first time taking an overnight camping trip. I liked the motto 'Be prepared' and have kept it all my life."

For high school, Tawfik attended a small public school in Bethlehem where he thrived by having more than one teacher. His English teacher was a Palestinian and a graduate of Oxford University in England. As impressive as this might sound, Tawfik was not overwhelmed as he had been learning English since the fourth grade.

"But all of us students had difficulty understanding the teacher when he used the word 'turnstile' because we had never seen one. As a frequent visitor of London, he took it for granted that everyone had," Tawfik says.

His education extended beyond the classroom as a master's level course in how to survive as a Palestinian refugee was being taught on the streets of Jerusalem, only a few miles from where Tawfik was now attending high school.

The lesson was driven home by the crack of a revolver on July 20, 1951, amid tight security at the Al-Aqsa Mosque in the heart of Jerusalem. The target was Abdullah Ibin Al-Hussein, the founder and ruler of the Jordanian realm and a direct descendant of the Prophet Muhammad. His assassin, Mustafa Shukri Esho, was a twenty-one-year-old tailor's apprentice who was reportedly associated with the ex-mufti of Jerusalem, Amin Al-Husseini, whose nephew's death deflated the Palestinian resistance. Abdullah Ibin Al-Hussein's assassination came only three days after the assassination of Lebanese prime minster Riad Al-Sulh in Amman.

"This was an important event because King Abdullah I was brought into power by the British and was meeting with the Zionists secretly," Tawfik says. "He was not elected by the Palestinians, and it is my view that the assassin represented the young generation of Palestinians at the time who believed in democracy and freedom of speech."

Not long afterward, something else transpired to convince Tawfik to fully take up the banner of Palestinian justice and equality. The boy was becoming a man who, like so many other Palestinian boys of his day, had adulthood thrust upon him, ready or not.

The event, known as the Qibya massacre, took place on October 14, 1953, and it was to be the next turning point in Tawfik's life.

Qibya was yet another small village targeted for destruction by the Israelis. The motives varied: sometimes the Israelis attacked in retaliation; sometimes for military and logistical purposes; and sometimes it was to set an example and stoke more Palestinian fear. Choosing to call it an act of retaliation, Ariel Sharon led Israeli troops into the West Bank village at night, killing sixty villagers, two-thirds of whom were women and children. Forty-five houses, a school, and a mosque were destroyed in the process.

Officially, the attack was launched as part of "Operation Shoshana" in response to a grenade being thrown into a home in Yehud that killed an Israeli woman and her two children. Palestinians suspect the Israeli military fabricated the incident as a pretense to clear out more Palestinian villages in the area. A part of the Israeli neighborhood was in al-Abbasiyya, a Palestinian Arab village before the 1948 war not far from the dividing line between the West Bank and the new state of Israel.

The Israelis were adamant that Operation Shoshana was justified because of what happened at Yehud, and Jordan drew a sharp rebuke from the Mixed Armistice Commission because it reportedly had been perpetrated by Palestinian infiltrators from Jordan. Although they remained skeptical, the Jordanians offered to collaborate with Israel to apprehend the guilty parties.

It was a school day when word of the Qibya massacre reached Bethlehem. And it was there that Tawfik Ramadan realized he, along with other students in his school, had finally had enough. To express their outrage, they took to the streets to demonstrate, a time-honored means of protest for those seeking a voice.

"We marched, we chanted, we held signs," Tawfik says. "The whole school that I attended went out to demonstrate." For the first time, Tawfik felt the need to stand up and fight, not with a weapon, but as one of many voices.

CHAPTER 9

ABOVE ALL ELSE

Education is the key to unlock the golden door of freedom.

— GEORGE WASHINGTON CARVER

Aysha had been married at the age of thirteen. Now her youngest daughter was approaching the same age, and she wanted Siham to have more than one choice in life.

Above all, she wanted Siham to continue her education. But her Mazari school only went as far as the sixth grade for girls, partly because Palestinian culture placed more emphasis on males and partly because under the British Mandate, educating rural Palestinians of either sex had not been a priority.

So, Aysha and Siham's oldest brother, Taha, cooked up a plan. Still in the army, Taha lived in the East Bank of Jordan in the city of Zarka. The plan called for Siham to move in with him and his wife in order for her to attend a public secondary school and become proficient in English and prepare her for college.

It sounded like a wonderful opportunity and ended up being one. But it came at a high price because it removed Siham from her birthplace and the protection of her mother. Aysha accepted the consequences of her plan because she would do anything to better her daughter's future. Two decades earlier, Tawfik's father did virtually the same thing so his son could get his degree. The difference was he was able to keep Tawfik close to him through high school, and he knew Tawfik wanted an education as much as Za'al wanted one for him.

Tawfik was now figuratively running toward something as opposed to running from the Haganah. And his performance in secondary school reflected his determination as he churned out exemplary reports from the Bethlehem Secondary School for his father to file for future reference.

The true test came at the end of his senior year in secondary school in 1954 when Tawfik sat down to take the standardized aptitude test administered by the Jordanian government. "It is designed like the ACT (American College Test) that children take here in America," he says.

Despite scoring near the top of the Jordanian Secondary School exam,

Tawfik was again at the mercy of events beyond his control. He wanted to be a physician, but only a few of those scholarships were allotted to Palestinian refugees. His father had faith in his son, to be sure. If only he had enough money to pay for the next round of Tawfik's education...

What came next was straight out of a prophecy.

In the fifth grade, of the fifty-four students in Tawfik's classroom in Al-Maliha only a handful would go on to complete their primary education. Because of the hardships forced upon Palestine's young people at the time, Tawfik became the only member of his fifth-grade class to eventually obtain a college degree.

"What were the odds, I have to tell you, that the principal in my elementary school in Al-Maliha became the principal of a school in Hebron and somehow saw my name on the list of secondary school graduates," Tawfik says. "When he saw my name, he said, 'I want this man to be a teacher.' So they called me and said, 'You need to see what opportunity has been presented to you.'"

With some hesitation, Tawfik, who still wanted to be a doctor, signed up to be a teacher. Teaching was a revered profession in Palestine. It did not take an advanced degree to obtain a teaching position, but beginners needed some luck, some prayers, someone to vouch for them, and someone to get them in the door. Teaching fulfilled his desire to help others and earned him a little money, but teaching was not the same as being a doctor, and that was what Tawfik was determined to be.

Tawfik worked briefly as a teacher while his application for a scholarship through the United Nations Relief and Work Agency (UNRWA) was under consideration.

"When I went to interview for the scholarship, the man (Ahmad Toqan) who interviewed me, he later became a member of the Jordanian cabinet. Well, he oversaw higher education for UNRWA and came from a big city, and I came from a small town, a village, actually."

Examining Tawfik's scholarship application, Toqan paused when he got to a line on the page where Tawfik had stated he wanted to use the scholarship to study medicine.

"Do you really want to be a doctor?" the educator inquired. It was as if he had never heard of anyone from a small village becoming a doctor and didn't consider it possible. "Why don't you choose something else?"

Thinking to himself, Tawfik thought, "Impossible? Really? Who was the man kidding?"

The word "impossible" did not register with Tawfik then, and, most likely, the word has not entered his mind since. There is overwhelming evidence to support how Dr. Tawfik Ramadan has brushed aside the impossible his entire life. But given that the word "impossible" was staring him in the face that day in the form of one of the foremost educators in Palestine, Tawfik rose to the challenge. The next words out of his mouth would determine the course of his life.

Without hesitation, Tawfik answered, "Yes, I want to become a doctor."

Tawfik will never know whether his interviewer was testing his resolve or if he truly thought a young man from a small village had neither the ability nor the background to succeed in medical school. Really, only two things mattered at the time: first, he had no intention of giving up on his goal to become a doctor; and second, UNRWA and Tawfik needed each other. The relief agency was the single stabilizing force in a region where the Israelis, Arab states, and Western governments lacked the political will to solve the refugee crisis. However, the refugee crisis had overwhelmed the relief agency from the beginning, and having a medical officer such as Tawfik, who was as dedicated to UNRWA's mission as he was to his own family, would be a godsend.

Since its inception in 1949, UNRWA has been supporting the relief and human development of Palestinian refugees, including those displaced by the 1948 Palestine War and subsequent conflicts, as well as their patrilineal descendants and legally adopted children. As of 2019, more than 5.6 million Palestinians were registered with UNRWA as refugees. The total number of Palestinians worldwide is about 15 million.

Sometimes depicted as "the original sin" of the Israeli state, the displacement of Palestinian civilians during the 1948 War contradicts the Zionist myth of the right to "a land without people for a people without a land," writes Riccardo Bocco in the 2009 *Refugee Survey Quarterly*. "Denying, ignoring, or sweeping the refugee issue under the rug, therefore, has been the main approach of most Israeli governments since 1948."

Bocco goes on to say that the impact of UNRWA's operations and the objectives of its donors (about one-third of its annual budget comes from the U.S.) have been used to justify the unwillingness of the international community to implement United Nations General Assembly Resolution

194, which was considered by the Palestinian refugees as a guarantee of their right of return and/or compensation.

"In the mid-1950s, UNRWA turned to the provision of 'essential services' (primary health care, relief, and social services) and focused on education," Bocco writes. "This concentration of activities on human development also contributed indirectly to the protection of Palestinian refugees and their legitimate cause, without jeopardizing the right to return."

If education was to be UNRWA's focus, no one would serve the cause better than Tawfik Ramadan, whose grades and passion for being a physician earned him a scholarship from the agency. His next stop would be Cairo, Egypt.

CHAPTER 10

RISING WITH CAIRO

The best way to predict your future is to create it.

— ABRAHAM LINCOLN.

The fixed-wing airplane flight from the Jerusalem airport to Cairo took about two hours and carried Tawfik Ramadan across Palestine, over the Dead Sea, to a world far beyond the scope of his imagination. While the thought of the unknown did not unsettle him, the air pockets the plane encountered along the way did.

The curious child from the Jerusalem suburb of Al-Maliha was now a focused eighteen-year-old on his way to the University of Cairo to study medicine. He was joined on the plane that day, October 27, 1954, by twenty-nine other UNRWA scholarship recipients, all with dreams as big as the sky must have seemed to them, particularly the first-time flyers, of which Tawfik was one. The only reason the thirty Palestinians were making the trip that day was because Egyptian president Gamal Abdel al-Nasser had allowed them to join the pool of about 80,000 Egyptian students who were taking a general education test for admission into higher education.

Given the lack of emphasis the British Mandate had placed on educating Palestinians, Tawfik making it this far was remarkable in itself. Tawfik and a fellow classmate in high school were the only two Palestinian students who planned to study medicine, making him even more of an oddity and creating a high bar for him to scale. On top of that, the only money Tawfik had was the twelve Egyptian pounds his scholarship provided him with every month. How would he find food and lodging on so little? To compound matters, Tawfik had landed in Cairo not knowing where he would even eat his next meal or sleep for the night.

It was the fall of 1954, and the calendar was serving up yet another series of earth-shattering events across the Arab world, similar to what had unfolded in Palestine in 1936, 1948, and 1953 (the Qibya massacre). Again, Tawfik Ramadan found himself living history the hard way in the fog of real time in the most turbulent corner of the world, rather than comfortably reading about it later under the precise light of history.

But the significance of the moment slapped him hard across the face from the moment his plane landed. "It was the second day after the assassination attempt on Nasser, and Cairo was in turmoil," he says.

To this day, Nasser remains an iconic figure in Egypt and all of the Arab world as a champion of the Arab Nationalist Movement and a worthy adversary for Israel for his victories on the battlefield and for his social and economic reforms. To implement his ideology of positive neutrality and bolster regional solidarity, Nasser developed a Pan-Arabism movement to counter pressure from the West and the Soviets. He diverged from Marxist socialism in that he did not abolish private property or attack systems that protected the rich. He also did not implement anti religious or family reforms, knowing how closely held family and religious views were in Egypt.

Besides benefiting from Nasser's deference to the Palestinian cause, Tawfik arrived in time to see all of it unfold while he trained to be a physician for the next seven and a half years. Egypt was the springboard for Nasser's secular movement and the unification of the Arab world, and Tawfik got to see it firsthand, sitting in the catbird seat in the middle of Cairo. For a young man who had been stripped of his home and country almost overnight, Nasser offered strength, comfort, and hope.

How could Tawfik not want to be a part of such a grand and glorious cause? It would not take him long to cast his lot with Nasser's vision for the Arab world, but at that moment he was more concerned about how he would get from the airport to where he was staying, given that the buses were not running. Besides, with his family and the Palestinian people counting on him, Tawfik went to Cairo to succeed in school, not start a revolution.

"Initially, all of it was a big, big shock for me and very difficult," he says. "You see, I was someone who lived in a small town, and now here I was in a big city with no relatives, no friends, only the other students whom I arrived with on the plane from Jerusalem. And they were going into different fields of study from me. Plus, Cairo was very advanced at the time regarding technology, music, arts, everything."

His bumpy arrival in Cairo was soon cushioned by the pillowy grace of hospitality shown to him by the Egyptian people. For example, Tawfik managed to find a room to rent in a boarding house, or pension, owned by a retired woman originally from Syria. "She was cooking for us, and she was helping us, so it wasn't a big change from home," he says, except of course the word "home" no longer meant his true home, and he would only see his family occasionally in the summers from 1954 to 1961.

Otherwise, it could be said that he went on to literally "see it all," from the emergence of Nasser as president of Egypt, to the rise of a movement, to a firsthand look at the rise to power of future Palestinian Liberation Organization leader Yasser Arafat, to Nasser's bold takeover of the Suez Canal from the French and the British, and to the futility and desperation of Palestine's spiraling refugee community.

For example, Tawfik was twenty years old, in his second year of pre-med courses, and living in what was called "New Egypt," a suburb of Cairo near the military airport, when the Israelis invaded Gaza and Egypt's Sinai Peninsula to regain control of the Suez Canal.

"We could see the British Canberra airplanes bombing the airport," Tawfik says. "We had to take shelter downstairs in the basement."

Nasser may have been a thorn in the side of the West who drew the wrath of religious Egyptians by pushing the social margins in his secularization of the state, but his vision defined the new Arab modernity, which led the decade of the 1950s to be called the New Golden Age of Egypt.

In 1952 the Mojamma El Tahrir, the towering new seat of Egypt's bureaucracy and Egypt's "other temple," opened. Two years later, *Al Jomhuria,* the influential state-owned Egyptian Arabic-language daily newspaper, began publication. In 1956 Cairo Stadium opened and a city master plan was adopted, while in 1959 the Cairo Conservatoire opened, and the Academy of Arts and Cairo Symphony Orchestra were founded.

Although not all of the population was educated, people demonstrated a touch of class in their thoughts, looks, and conversations. "Just watch an Umm Kulthum concert; it's evident in the audience," one historian said. Without television to distract them in the 1950s, Cairo residents depended on radio, newspapers, and books as sources of information and knowledge, which made them better informed. Furthermore, the streets were clean thanks to the legacy of King Farouk, who was said to have ordered the washing of Cairo's streets every day in the 1940s, and because the number of cars and means of transportation were much less predominant than today. Finally, a healthy economy made life affordable because of the higher value of the Egyptian pound.

"Cairo was a big city, and it was a beautiful place with great hotels and the Nile River running through it. My favorite thing was to eat out at the restaurants along the Nile, a scenic spot with good food. The food wasn't too different from what I was used to, as food across the Arab world is very similar."

Tawfik completed two years of pre-med courses and five and a half years in the Cairo University School of Medicine. But he also got an advanced degree in overcoming tyranny, thanks to Nasser's fiery speeches and bold moves, and the daring attempts of African freedom fighters to defeat colonialism.

His exposure to the world stage also extended far beyond the Suez Canal crisis. For example, he supported a revolution in 1958 against the monarchy in Iraq, and that same year he was among thousands of people in the streets when the formation of a political alliance between Egypt and Syria was announced in Cairo. Known as the United Arab Republic, the UAR was the first step toward a larger Pan-Arab state and was thought to have prevented a Communist takeover of Syria. In addition, Tawfik actively supported Nasser's prominent role to resist the domination of the superpowers. Called the Non-Alignment, the worldwide movement served as an impediment to both the United States' containment policy and the Soviet Union's systems of influence, as noted by Ohio State University's *PressBooks* report.

During the decade between 1951 and 1961, demonstrations, strikes, and artistic and intellectual pursuits were an Egyptian national pastime. Tawfik was exposed to a variety of people and countries across the Middle East and Africa, from Lebanon, Syria, Yemen, Iraq, Saudi Arabia, and Algeria. In those days, Cairo was the epicenter of the Arab world, and Tawfik witnessed many of the major political events of the times: the nationalization of the Suez Canal; the Tripartite invasion and 1956 war on Egypt and Gaza; the announcement on February 11, 1958, when the United Arab Republic took steps to forming a larger Pan-Arab State; the July 1958 revolution in Iraq that resulted in the overthrow of the Hashemite monarchy in Iraq; and the formation of the Baghdad Pact on February 24, 1955, by the Central Treaty Organization (CENTRO), a military alliance between Iran, Iraq, Pakistan, Turkey, Jordan, and the United Kingdom.

Indeed, Cairo offered the young Palestinian a rare glimpse into the world whereby Tawfik became more convinced that Nasser's desire for a united Arab polity would afford Palestinians their best hope for the future.

More importantly, Cairo is where Tawfik went to fulfill a promise he made to become a physician. He spent his first year preparing to take the national exam (*Tawjihiyah*) at the Ibrahimiyah Secondary School. Then came six and a half years of medical school. During the first two years, he studied anatomy, physiology, biochemistry, and histology. "During my one-month vacation between my first and second year, I had to dissect the human brain. I brought it home with me to Beit Jala, dissected it, and drew the section as requested," he says.

Tawfik's third year included courses in parasitology, forensic medicine and toxicology, pharmacology, and an introduction to hospital rotation. During his fourth year of medical school, Tawfik studied pathology and completed his hospital rotation in medicine and surgery, ophthalmology, pediatrics, dermatology and viewed doses, urology, obstetrics and gynecology, infectious diseases, orthopedics, and psychiatry.

"As part of that, I studied textbooks, attended lectures, took classes at the College of Medicine, and completed rotations at the hospital, Qasr El-Eyni (which has expanded into a 4,000-bed hospital today)," he says. "The professors at the College of Medicine were all highly educated and PhD trained in Egypt and England.

"I remember my professors: Dr. Batrawi, professor of anatomy; Dr. Talaat, professor of physiology, who later became the dean of the school of medicine; Dr. Mohammad Sulaiman, professor of forensic medicine; Dr. Alkhyyal, professor of pharmacology; and Dr. Mehrez, professor of surgery. I also bought many textbooks, plus a complete real human skeleton. Besides some money my father sent, I had only the scholarship from UNRWA that paid twelve Egyptian pounds a month. I still remember going to the UNRWA office to get the money, and the representative who gave it to me, Ibrahin Abu Khadrah.

"The hardest exam came at the end of my second year of medical school, a test that covered the four basic medical sciences: anatomy, physiology, biochemistry, and histology," Tawfik says. "I remember sitting at my desk for forty-eight hours studying for the anatomy portion. When I got tired and sleepy, I would stop, take a shower, and resume studying. One of the textbooks was called *Gray's Anatomy* and contained more than 2,000 pages."

During his first two years in Cairo, Tawfik lived in "New Egypt" or Masr Aljadeedah (Heliopolis) in the northern part of Cairo, not far from both airports. He would take the metro from his apartment to Bab Al

Hadid Central Station, called Ramses Square. From there, he took a bus to the School of Science at Cairo University's main campus. At the start of his third year in medical school, Tawfik moved with two other students to Dukki, which was closer to campus.

One of Tawfik's friends was in engineering school and had a brother in medical school. During his last four years in school, he shared an apartment in Manial with three other students. "There was Khalil Awad, his brother Ibrahim Awad, his cousin Ahmed Awad, and me in the same apartment," Tawfik says. "We hired a cook whose name was Abdu. I remember we used to pay him five Egyptian pounds a month. The building even had an elevator, which was unusual in those days."

Given the seductive nature of Cairo, medicine and Arab national interests did not consume all of Tawfik's attention. Some of his spare time was spent doing what young men like to do – have fun – whether playing soccer, frequenting the gym, learning to ride a motorbike, roller-skating, or checking out Cairo's celebrated belly dancers at various clubs. "But we did not drink alcohol there," he stresses.

The highlight for him was the celebration of Egypt's most popular holiday, Sham Al-Naseem, a national festival marking the beginning of spring. In an age-old celebration tied to Egypt's agrarian roots, Muslims, Christians, and Jews would spend the day picnicking at the parks and public gardens along the Nile River and at the zoo. Tawfik fondly recalls taking a Nile boat to El Qanater El Khayreya, where he could admire the greenery and smell the clean air. "We would spend the whole day there playing, eating, and singing," he says. "I very much enjoyed the traditional food during the festival, mainly *fesikh* (a fermented, salted, dried gray mullet fish with lettuce, scallions, green onions and colored boiled eggs)."

During the month of Ramadan and the two Muslim feasts – Eid al-Fitr and Eid al-Adha – Tawfik again celebrated with the residents of Cairo. "We spent the whole night mainly at a famous place called Assayida Zainab Mosque and the square carrying the same name," he says. "Crowds of people spent the night there reciting the Qur'an, singing and dancing while vendors were selling all kinds of food. I enjoyed those gatherings."

To Tawfik, the food in Cairo was unsurpassed. He and his companions ate at a variety of restaurants in Cairo, many of which were located along the banks of the Nile. One of them specialized in hummus-foul (fava beans) falafel.

With Cairo's abundance of gathering places and talented artists, there also was plenty of cuisine to soothe both the mind and the body at a next-to-nothing cost. Once a month Tawfik would join all of Egypt in tuning the radio to listen to Umm Kulthum, the legendary "Voice of Egypt," perform her monthly radio concert. Known for songs that dealt with love, longing, and loss, she also was closely aligned with Nasser. One of her songs, "It's Been a Long Time, O' Weapon of Mine," was adopted as the Egyptian national anthem from 1960 to 1979.

Umm Kulthum's husband, Dr. Hasan Al-Hafanawi, happened to be one of Tawfik's professors during his medical school rotation in dermatology and venereal disease. "He was thirty-nine years old and she was fifty-six," Tawfik says. "It was her first marriage and the second for him. No one knew how they got together, but he was always on the front row watching her perform her monthly concerts. It is said that one of Umm Kulthum's conditions in marrying him was that he continued to pay support for his ex-wife.

"He was not particularly tall, but he was a good-looking man who would come to class dressed in a shirt with cuffs and always wore a necktie. When he entered the room, we would always ask him, 'Sir, how is the lady?' He would laugh and say that she was okay."

Poetry evening at the Kuwaiti Student Center, or Kuwaiti House, was another popular venue for Tawfik, which was frequented by politicians, asylum seekers, and freedom fighters. He recalls vividly the night Abdel Muti Hijazi, a pioneer in the resurgence of contemporary poetry, read to the audience. On one of the many occasions he spent sitting, chatting, and reading the newspaper at the popular Groppi Café, Tawfik found himself at the table next to famous Egyptian actor Yousef Wehbe.

A student of history, Tawfik visited the Aswan Low Dam and got to see the Abu Simbel temple and monuments carved in the cliffs overlooking the Nile from 1298 to 1235 BCE, which were painstakingly removed in three- to twenty-ton sections and precisely repositioned on higher ground prior to the Aswan High Dam's opening in 1970. "It was like moving a mountain," Tawfik says. "Our group was among the last to see the temple before it was moved."

He took a train from Cairo to the construction site at Aswan with other students, with the Egyptian government paying the way. The architect who planned the dam also planned a city to relocate thousands of Nubian people who were living in primitive conditions, but many of them would not go to the city he built for them. Nasser's desire to harness the Nile with a project equal to the Pyramids forced about 60,000 Nubians, whose ancestors conquered and ruled Egypt 2,800 years ago, to relocate to the less fertile, arid lands north of Aswan. The Nubians of Ballana still talk of going home, much like the Palestinians. But Nasser's dream of increasing Egypt's farmlands by one-third and bringing electrical service to a vast contingency won out.

CHAPTER 11

A FORK IN THE ROAD

You must be the change you wish to see in the world.

— MAHATMA GANDHI

Tawfik Ramadan had a clue early on that Yasser Arafat was going to be something special. Of course, the same could have been said for Tawfik on that day in March 1955 when a small contingent of Palestinian students arrived for a private audience with Gamal Abdel Nasser, the president of Egypt, whose sudden rise to power captivated the Arab world and sent shivers across the seats of power in Europe and the United States.

Tawfik was only a second-year pre-med student at the University of Cairo, yet his eloquent defense of the Palestinian cause had won him a place in the room as one of a small number of student representatives there to complain about the Egyptian army's harsh treatment of Gaza citizens who had protested Israeli attacks on refugee camps and other facilities inside Gaza.

An insignificant moment in an otherwise memorable day for Tawfik demonstrated what a mistake it would be to underestimate Arafat under any circumstances.

"I will tell you a joke about Yasser Arafat that tells you a lot about him," Tawfik says. "When we went to the governmental headquarters for our meeting with President Nasser, a guard stopped us. Yasser looked directly down at the soldier and said, 'Stand up, soldier. I am Yasser Arafat, a high-ranking officer in the Egyptian army, and we are here to see President Nasser.' The soldier looked shocked and overwhelmed. He stood up and let us go through."

Another guard led the students into a big room, where they waited for the Egyptian leader. After Nasser arrived, Arafat, who was president of the Palestinian Students Union, did most of the talking.

"We wanted the president to know that we were angry and frustrated with the British government over their support of Israel, and we asked him whether we should protest the arrival of the British envoy who was scheduled to arrive in Cairo in the next few days."

Nasser offered a response: "As head of state, I cannot encourage you to protest, but you can make your own decision."

It was said in jest, but Tawfik can only surmise what Nasser might have been thinking.

While he was impressed by Arafat's passionate and convincing manner, Tawfik believed Nasser's modern take on Arab unification would best serve the Palestinian cause, while Arafat wanted a laser focused on the Palestinian–Israeli conflict. Tawfik's take is that Arafat wanted to be in Israel's face at every turn because he thought the liberation of Palestine was a Palestinian–Israeli matter. Tawfik and Arafat did share the overarching goal of granting Palestinians the right of return and something as finite as improving scholarship opportunities for Palestinian students.

The Palestinian student protest that earned them a meeting with Nasser is an early example of how Arafat, as president of the Union of Palestinian Students, learned to apply pressure to the main players in the Middle East: the Egyptians, Israelis, British, and Americans.

According to an article in *Vanity Fair*, Arafat seemed to have won and held that office as president of the Palestinian group "for exactly the same reason he later won and held the chairmanship of the PLO. This student organizer simply out-organized – and outworked, out-talked, and out-maneuvered – everyone else."

Nonetheless, Tawfik's vote went to the other guy.

Leading up to the meeting with Nasser, Palestinian students had launched a series of off-campus sit-ins at the Palestinian Student Union to draw attention to Israel's raid on Egyptian military outposts in February 1955, including a hospital in Gaza and an Egyptian army base where thirty-nine Egyptian soldiers were killed.

The Israeli position was that the raid, named Operation Black Arrow, was designed to curb both the growing number of fedayeen (Arab freedom fighters) attacks as well as send a message to the Egyptian army to stop turning a blind eye to the fedayeen.

Tawfik can only speculate as to what impact their Palestinian student protests in the heart of Cairo may have had on Nasser. However, it is clear the Gaza raids changed Nasser's mind about the threat Israel posed to Egypt, leading him to turn to the U.S., Britain, and France for military aid. When that attempt failed, Nasser set up commando training camps to better prepare the fedayeen for more retaliatory attacks, and he obtained military assistance from the Soviet Union. A year later, Nasser announced the nationalization of the Suez Canal.

When Nasser showed enough courage to unilaterally take control of the Egyptian landmark, the Arab world was as stunned as it was proud. "There was like an explosion among the crowd," Tawfik remembers. "People jumped for joy because the Suez Canal was a big, resourceful project that should bring money to the country. Instead of going to France, the money would come to Egypt. Because of colonization, people in the Middle East had been living with this experience for many, many years. The French colonized a part of the Arab world, the British colonized the rest of it, and Palestine was now being colonized by the Israelis.

"With every colonization, people would come in and take some of the resources, some of the artifacts, some of the art, and some of the treasures, and then take it back to England, to France, and do whatever they want with it. And they benefited from that. The Suez Canal was on Egyptian land and is an Egyptian canal, and Nasser thought that is where it should stay. And the people did, too."

Not everyone agreed because Nasser's bold proclamation brought a quick response from the Israelis, who struck back on October 29, 1956. Two days later, British and French military forces, who were supposed to attack in concert with the Israelis but were delayed, landed at Port Said and Port Fuad and took control of the area around the Suez Canal.

The Suez Crisis, or the Second Arab–Israeli War, put the world's superpowers in the precarious position of being at odds with one another and heightened tensions between the U.S. and the Soviet Union. President Dwight Eisenhower warned the Soviets that reckless talk of nuclear conflict would only make matters worse and cautioned Soviet leader Nikita Khrushchev to refrain from direct intervention. However, Eisenhower also issued stern warnings to the French, British, and Israelis to give up their campaign and withdraw from Egyptian soil.

The threats did their work. The British and French forces withdrew by December, and Israel finally bowed to U.S. pressure in March 1957, relinquishing control over the canal to Egypt. Nasser was the big winner as it raised his stature while diminishing Britain and France in the eyes of the world. But the Cold War between the U.S. and the Soviet Union was merely beginning.

"The sense was the people were supportive of Nasser's willingness to fight and hold on to the Suez Canal and take back Port Said and the area the British had occupied," Tawfik says. "There was a big British presence in Cairo, but the people differentiated between the British people and the British government, much like we differentiated between the Jewish people and the Zionist government in Palestine. You do not take out your anger on ordinary people."

No one else has ever impressed Tawfik quite like Nasser, and the movement that evolved out of a reaction to the onslaught of European domination drew its strength from the core premise that Arabs are unified by language, culture, and a shared sense of Arab and Islamic history.

"This was eye-opening for me," says Tawfik. "Cairo, during the time I was in Egypt, was a center of freedom for freedom fighters from the Arab world and Africa, like the Kenyan freedom fighters in the Mau Mau uprising and Ahmad Sékou Touré of Guinea. During those leaders' visits to Cairo, I had the opportunity to learn about them, their countries, and their efforts to end British and French colonization.

"I still recall the five leaders of the Algerian revolution against France when they came secretly to Cairo to meet with Nasser and how, on their way back, their airplane was intercepted by the French and forced to land in Algeria. This was the first act of piracy in the history of aviation. The five leaders were arrested and put in jail. The next day there were demonstrations in Cairo against the French in support of the Algerian freedom fighters, and I attended a meeting held in a big hall in Cairo with many speakers and poets. I particularly remember one poet, Abdel Muti Hijazi, and his poem called 'Auras' and the birth of freedom in the mountains."

It was not long before Nasser's influence and charisma turned Cairo into a showcase for the Pan-Arab movement, giving Tawfik a front-row seat to an extraordinary period in time. A steady parade of anti colonial activists, political leaders, intellectuals, and poets came to counsel with Nasser, and the spillover filled the Cairo University campus and Tawfik with hope for what a unified Arab world might accomplish. "Some students went to the movies, but for me there was little social life because my thoughts were on our political activity and my academics," he says.

He was there to become a doctor, but the time Tawfik spent in Cairo also gave him hope that his fellow Palestinians could find their way home. While rejecting Marxism, Tawfik tolerated the socialistic overtones in

Nasser's Arab nationalist movement because it reflected his own pro-Arab and anti-colonialist viewpoints.

Throughout the 1950s, all the Arab world was in what Tawfik calls "rapid movement and change." He did not say "turmoil," "chaos," or "upheaval." One, he never thinks in those terms because it would demonstrate a lack of self-control; and two, Nasser's message of a unified Arab world made sense to him as it was being vigorously but thoughtfully debated among the Arab student body at Cairo University (formerly known as Egyptian University from 1908 to 1940 and King Fuad I University from 1940 to 1952).

"I was not an angry person lashing out," Tawfik says. "I was more involved in studying and in doing my activities with my student union peers, although I did become involved in supporting Palestinian causes.

"The goal was to organize people together, to educate them. We used to meet and read books and discuss creating a movement to unite the entire Arab world. The Arab world was divided by the Sykes-Picot agreement. The British took Sudan, Egypt, and Palestine; the French took Lebanon, Algeria, Morocco, Tunisia, and Syria; the Italians took Libya. It was like a game."

Nasser taught Tawfik three things: one, that unity was the Arab world's best hope; two, that his commitment to helping others would be best served by helping those most in need – his fellow Palestinians; and three, that both his father and Nasser were teaching him to not give up, to hold on tightly to his family and to rely on his instincts for survival.

CHAPTER 12

EYES ON GAZA

SILENCE FOR THE SAKE OF GAZA

Gaza is not the most beautiful of cities.
Her coast is not bluer than those of other Arab cities.
Her oranges are not the best in the Mediterranean.
Gaza is not the richest of cities.
And Gaza is not the most polished of cities, or the largest. But she is the equivalent to the history of a nation, because she is the most repulsive among us in the eyes of the enemy – the poorest, the most desperate, and the most ferocious. Because she is a nightmare. Because she is oranges that explode, children without a childhood, aged men without old age, and women without desire. Because she is all that, she is the most beautiful among us, the purest, the richest and the most worthy of love.

— MAHMOUD DARWISH

Those passionate and stimulating philosophical debates over Pan-Arab nationalism, colonialism, Marxism, and revolution that took place inside the Palestinian Student Union were eventually put into practice.

Arafat was particularly eager to do so. As a teenager, he had smuggled arms into Palestine to be used against the Zionists. After the establishment of the new Jewish state, he became so despondent that he applied for a visa to study at the University of Texas. But the dream of the restoration of a Palestinian state would not die, and two years later he withdrew from the University of Fuad I, reportedly to join Palestine insurgents fighting the Israelis in Gaza.

After obtaining his degree in civil engineering from Cairo University in 1956 and working in Kuwait as a contractor, Arafat decided to go big and construct a movement. Two years later, he and several like-minded members of the Palestinian diaspora working in Arabian Gulf states devised the concept of a political and military organization to rally the

Palestinian people to retake their homeland. The symbols on Fatah's original flag – two crossed rifles and a grenade – indicated Arafat was ready for battle from the outset.

While Arafat went to Kuwait to hone his passion, Tawfik chose a different route. And if he ever had any doubts about the unified Arab world theme Nasser was promoting, they were answered the minute Tawfik landed at the airport in Damascus in September 1958. His impromptu flight from Cairo to celebrate the recent political union of Egypt and Syria showed him what it felt like to have complete freedom of movement, something Americans take for granted.

"I wanted to know how it felt to be free, to not have to answer a hundred questions to obtain a visa in order to cross the border of one country into another. Because of Nasser, I got to go somewhere without encountering checkpoints, barriers, and blockades, and it felt liberating."

The open border between Egypt (including Gaza) and Syria was formalized in February of the same year as part of the creation of the United Arab Republic (UAR) and became the first test case of Nasser's vision of how a unified Arab world might function.

Unfortunately, the UAR was rushed into existence, largely to keep Syria from falling into the hands of the Communist Party, which had gained a foothold in the ranks of the military. Fearing a takeover could jeopardize his plans, Nasser offered the Syrians a way out. At a meeting with a pro-Nasser wing of the military, Nasser opted for a quick merger under a harsh set of terms calling for a vote by members of the electorate, the dissolution of political parties, and the withdrawal of the army from politics.

At the time, Syria's ruling class felt its only choice was to accept Nasser's terms. But Syria's attitude changed after Nasser established a new provisional constitution that gave all the power to Egyptians, and a 1961 Syrian coup ended the Egyptian–Syrian union.

Nonetheless, Tawfik's "freedom flight" in 1958 emboldened his pursuit of the liberation of Palestine under the banner of a unified Arab world and gave him an inkling of what the world had to offer.

He had already pleaded directly with President Nasser in 1955 to do something about Israel's attacks on Gaza, so in the summer of 1959 Tawfik, in the company of fellow classmates, decided to go there for himself. Inspired by Nasser, they were on a recruiting mission on behalf of the National Arab Movement.

It seems like people have been debating over what's best for Gaza for more than 4,000 years, often destroying the city in the process. None of those incursions matched the scale of destruction caused by Israel in the aftermath of Hamas's attack inside Israeli-occupied territory that killed about 1,200 IDF (Israeli Defense Forces) personnel and Jewish settlers inside Israeli-occupied territory adjacent to Gaza on October 7, 2023.

The thin strip of land along the shore of the Mediterranean Sea has always been too attractive to pass up, particularly for those seeking to build an empire. A popular trading post for centuries, Gaza has fallen under the control of the Canaanites, Egyptians, Philistines, Alexander the Great, the Romans, the Crusaders, Muslims, the Ottoman Empire, the British Mandate, Egypt, and now the Israelis, who captured the Gaza Strip in the 1967 Middle East War, at which point Gaza's population had mushroomed from 70,000 to almost 400,000.

The will of the people of Gaza has also been tested over time by floods, earthquakes, the bubonic plague, and other acts of devastation. In spite of it all, Gaza – which loosely means "Strong City" – always seems to rise from the ashes or ruins. It takes proud people to make a strong city, and Gazans are nothing if not proud.

They are especially proud of their history, their culture, and the bountiful surroundings. Gaza has been described as a painting colored by the refreshing orange and yellow and demure green of its citruses and olives; and scented by their fresh sour and sweetened bitter essences. It is the basket of fresh natural fruits, tended by farmers, fishers and the simplest workers who make the small land a home for large industrial exports and supply food to the Middle East and Europe.

After Egypt relinquished control in 1967, many Gaza laborers took jobs inside Israel, but their harsh treatment at the hands of Israeli troops and the rapid expansion of Jewish settlements cast a foreboding shadow over the Gaza Strip, heightening Palestinian resentment. The mounting tension led to the first Palestinian uprising in 1987 and the formation of Hamas by the Muslim Brotherhood, which escalated the cycle of revenge and retaliation that goes on today.

As the world looks on today in disbelief, it is noteworthy that to Tawfik Ramadan, Gaza unfolds not only on the pages of history, social media, and television. With Israel barking at the door, he walked along Gaza's popular beaches sixty-five years ago, dined in popular restaurants by the sea, visited Palestinian refugee camps outside the old city, and met with numerous public officials, merchants, and students to better understand what made Gaza unique – and to hopefully convince them his message of Arab unity was the best way to help save it.

Gaza was much different then; not a paradise, but not the world's largest open-air prison, as it came to be known in 2007 when Israel shut off Gaza from the world, and certainly not the new ground zero of the Palestinian holocaust. In that regard, Israel has gone where even none of Gaza's previous conquerors dared to go.

Tawfik takes issue with the acceptance of Gaza as a "prison," because it implies its residents must be guilty of some crime. "Captives in their own home" is the way he would put it. Likewise, Nezar Azimi painted a vastly different picture of life in prebombardment Gaza in a *Washington Post* opinion piece:

> "Home. Park. Zoo. School. Bakery. Church. Mosque. These are just some of the fundamentals of Gazan life that have been blasted, bombarded and bulldozed since the Israeli siege began this past October (in 2023). As of this writing, more than two-thirds of the buildings in the Gaza Strip have been damaged or destroyed by Israeli strikes. More than 4 out of every 5 Gazans – some 1.9 million people – have been displaced. All historians have come to refer to infrastructural devastation at this scale as 'urbicide,' or 'violence against the city.' Sometimes, it can be hard to imagine what this place was like before the war."

In the same article, Deena Kishawi, a physician, conjured up thoughts of the aroma that wafted through Gaza before it was leveled:

> "My father's parents lived around the corner from Al-Ailat, the largest bakery in Gaza. Al-Ailat, which means 'the family' in Arabic, is run by the Shehada clan, Christians who have been in Gaza for centuries. While the bakery started as a storefront in the Al-Rimal neighborhood, it has expanded over the years to occupy half of an entire block. Al-Ailat is more than a bakery; there's a café with cute bistro chairs where you can eat sweets and drink coffee.

"The place is famous for its *ka'ak*, a kind of sesame-covered biscuit, as well as the *mouajanat*, a bread pie filled with spinach or cheese. When I was younger, we'd buy steaming hot pita bread there and then run across the street to Abu Talal, the popular hummus shop. The combination was heaven."

The bakery was bombed on November 4 and November 9, 2023, and is now inoperable.

Tawfik remembers similar sights and sounds. His journey to Damascus started on an airplane; his trip to Gaza in 1959 began on a train. He and two roommates rode a train from Cairo to Rafah at the Egyptian–Israeli border and then to Gaza City.

Three years had lapsed since the end of the Suez Crisis, and about 139 square miles of what became known as the Gaza Strip was now under the control of the United Arab Republic and administered by the Egyptian military. Israel, meanwhile, controlled all of Beer al-Sabi (now called Beersheba) and most of the Gaza subdistrict, which led to the destruction of forty-nine villages and the displacement of about 200,000 villagers, according to *The Interactive Encyclopedia of the Palestine Question.*

Refugees were originally housed in mosques, schools, homes, military barracks, and open spaces, but by the time Tawfik arrived, UNRWA had supervised the construction of eight refugee camps. Those long lines of white tents and the people crammed into them became as symbolic of the Palestinian resistance movement as the PLO flag.

In his memoir *Mapping My Return,* Salman Abu Sitta, who hails from the village of Almain in the Beersheba District of Mandatory Palestine, reminds us that the oppressed will always find a way to foil their oppressors. "Those wretched lines of tents were crowded, but certainly were considered a step up, as people had previously found themselves living under trees...

"Of course, there was a price to pay for the crowding. The tents were so close that their pegs and ropes intertwined. There was no privacy to speak of; even a whisper could be heard at the next tent. So it was inevitable that scandal would erupt in this conservative society. I remember once, a young man and woman were caught in an indecent act. The judge (a societal structure existed among extended families inside the camps) scolded them for their unforgivable behavior.

"'Have you no shame? In these trying times, you make improper advances toward your neighbor?' the judge asked the young man. 'Judge, sir, our tent was crowded. There was no room to sleep. My leg stretched out of the tent at night. Apparently she also had the same problem. Our legs got mixed up. What could I do?' the guilty man pleaded."

Almost one million Palestinians had been displaced in 1948, more than half of the inhabitants of Palestine, and about 60 percent of them lost their livelihoods. By the end of the Arab-Israeli War, refugees outnumbered inhabitants three to one in the Gaza Strip. Almost 70 percent of Gaza's residents have been living in refugee camps ever since.

Nonetheless, Gaza was a mixture of old world charm, resilience, and a reflection of the determination of the Palestinian people to keep their land when Tawfik saw it for the only time in his life.

The contrast between then and now makes him weep.

He says he and his traveling companions from the University of Cairo medical school were warmly welcomed, to the extent that they occasionally found lodging in the old city because of a connection they had made in Cairo with the mayor's cousin. But it also was not unusual for them to throw down a towel and sleep on the beach.

Tawfik was not on a vacation – he had come to empower hearts and minds. "We met a lot of people in Gaza that summer. Our mission was to recruit a new generation of people who would work for Palestine and rebuild Palestine. Many of them went on to become leaders in that effort."

The effort involved talking to secondary school students and teachers about continuing their education in Egypt. He knows several of them went to obtain their master's and PhDs. He recalls one student who researched Palestinian fertility rates after the 1948 Nakba; another researched the psychological impact moving to Kuwait had on a group of Palestinian refugees.

Tawfik's summer in Gaza eventually came to what he called a successful conclusion, and his life moved on – first back to Cairo to complete his degree, and eventually to Jordan to answer his calling.

CHAPTER 13

THE CALL OF DUTY

The tragedy of the people of Palestine is that their country was "given" by a foreign power to another people for the creation of a new state. The result was that many hundreds of thousands of innocent people were made permanently homeless. . . . It is abundantly clear that the refugees have every right to the homeland from which they were driven, and the denial of this right is at the heart of the continuing conflict. No people anywhere in the world would accept being expelled en masse from their country.

— BERTRAND RUSSELL
statement to the International Conference
of Parliamentarians, February 3, 1970

Today, the six million Palestinians housed in fifty-eight recognized refugee camps in three countries, the West Bank, and the Gaza Strip are among the most unique in the world. And right behind them are another eight million Palestinians whose new lives will never fill the hole in their heart.

Tawfik Ramadan knows the story better than most because he has lived it from all sides throughout his entire life.

It is not a stretch to suggest that the term "refugee" refers to someone who has taken flight and will eventually settle somewhere else. However, Palestinians simply don't fit anyone's definition, which is why much of the world appears aghast that one can maintain refugee status for seventy-five years. The typical response is, "Why haven't they moved on?"

The simple answer is that Palestinians have largely been forgotten. It gets more complicated when you factor in the fact that Palestinians, unlike other refugees around the world, fall under the authority of the UNRWA, whose sole responsibility is to assist and protect them "pending a just and lasting solution to their plight." In other words, they are in limbo. Not to mention that Palestinians are as hell-bent on going back to their homeland today as they were in 1948.

Tawfik is no different than the rest. With his graduation from Cairo's medical school approaching in December 1961, his future appeared limitless, including the possibility of going to the United States to work. Instead, Tawfik chose to return to the West Bank, where he had three choices: join the Jordanian army, work for the government, or sign up with UNRWA to treat exiled Palestinians at a refugee camp. Tawfik was now a full-fledged physician, although he would seek more specialized training. He had also become the first person from his small village to graduate from medical school.

He had a road map, at least. Besides nation-building, reading had been Tawfik's other main interest as a student in Cairo. Not only did he revel in huge medical and academic volumes, but he read about philosophy, history, and the politics of the region at that time. From there, he toured the world in print. He read *The Dialectics Theory of Hegel* and the work of Friedrich Engels, Karl Marx's *Das Kapital*, Mao Zedong's ideological books, and many other novels and books of poetry, in addition to preparing a weekly summary for his Palestinian student sessions. He followed current events in the newspapers: *Aljumhoriyah, Almasa, Al-Ahram, Roza Eliousef,* and *Sabah El Khair.*

One other form of the written word intrigued him: the Palestinians' path on paper that would take them home. As far as their enemies were concerned, it was not worth the paper on which it was written. But that did not stop Tawfik Ramadan from doing what he had to do.

Adopted near the end of the 1947–49 Palestinian war, United Nations General Assembly Resolution 194 (III) resolved that "refugees wishing to return to their homes and live at peace with their neighbors should be permitted to do so at the earliest practicable date, and that compensation should be paid for the property of those choosing not to return and for loss of or damage to property which, under principles of international law or equity, should be made good by the Governments or authorities responsible."

Adopted in 1967, United Nations Resolution 242 also declared that Israel's occupation of the West Bank was illegal under international law and that Israel should withdraw. Of course, that did not happen.

By any measure, Resolution 194 reflected the honorable and humane thing to do when it was approved in the wake of the Nakba. Out of the approximately 1.2 million Arabs living in former British Mandate of

Palestine, about 85 percent of the population (about 750,000) fled or were driven from their homes in 1948, and more than four hundred Arab villages were depopulated. Thousands of other displaced Arabs remained inside Israeli-controlled territory. After the Arab villages were cleared, newly enacted Israeli laws made it virtually impossible for Palestinian refugees to return home or reclaim their property.

History tells us that in the process of seizing the land, the winner almost always plows under the loser. There is no better example than the colonization of America by Europeans at the expense of the Native American population. Despite an invader's best efforts to purge the land, it is unavoidable for seeds of injustice to be sown along the way, seeds that eventually grow into a thorny thicket bristling with retaliation. Such is the case of land now claimed and occupied by Israelis. Bocco, in *UNRWA and the Palestinian Refugees: A History Within History*, explains it as follows:

> "It is difficult to conceive a sustainable, long-lasting solution to the Palestinian–Israeli conflict without examining the refugee issue and identifying a just solution to it for both sides. Over time, and besides its emotional dimensions, the refugee issue has been increasingly regarded as a 'problem' for the Israeli and the Palestine Liberation Organization (PLO) / Palestinian Authority (PA) leaderships, who have generally taken uncompromising positions. The international stakeholders have been unable to suggest compromises acceptable to the parties concerned."

Nonetheless, the light of hope still burned bright by the time newly minted medical officer Tawfik Ramadan arrived at the Ein el-Sultan camp. The camp was on the road to Jericho, considered the oldest city in the world and best known from the biblical story of a great victory over its Canaanite citizens by the Jewish leader Joshua. It was a hard road, but follow it he must.

Tawfik Ramadan showed up for work in February 1962, fourteen years after the fall of Palestine.

The year 1962 marked the first time an American (John Glenn) orbited the Earth, and it was the year Imam Muhammad al-Badr of Yemen was overthrown by a military coup less than a week after assuming power following his father's death, triggering a civil war that ensnared Egypt on one side and Saudi Arabia, Iran, and Jordan on the other. In 1962 Algeria won independence from France after 132 years of colonial rule and a seven-and-a-half-year war that left 1.5 million Algerians dead and the country devastated. In South Africa, anti-Apartheid activist Nelson Mandela was jailed. In the United States, the Cuban Missile Crisis was coming to a head, and St. Jude's Children's Research Hospital was founded in Memphis, Tennessee.

The year 1962 seems like a long time ago and too long for Palestinians to remain housed in some of the refugee camps where Tawfik first set foot.

The first baby Tawfik Ramadan helped deliver after he arrived at the main gate of the Ein el-Sultan refugee camp near Jericho in the Jordan Valley in February 1962 would now be old enough to be a grandfather or grandmother or even a great-grandfather or grandmother. Yes, the Palestinians' status as refugees dates that far back in time.

Over time, the Palestinian refugee camps where Tawfik spent ten years have become defined as questions without answers that can be put off for another day. Put in harsher terms, the camps are seen by Palestinians as proof of Israel's desire to cleanse the Jewish state of Arabs.

Many Jews argue that when the UN voted to partition Palestine into two states in 1947, one Jewish and one Arab, Palestinian Jews joyfully accepted the compromise while Palestinian Arabs and surrounding Arab states all rejected the partition and vowed to destroy the Jewish state. But there is no denying that Palestine as it was known was dismantled without regard to what that would mean for almost one million Arab citizens.

Tawfik, given the predicament his countrymen faced as refugees, had a lot on his mind: two things, really. "I chose the path I did because I believe in the cause," he explains. "I believed the Palestinians had a right to be allowed to return to their land. I also was an Arab nationalist who believed in Arab unity, and I wanted to work to achieve it. So that was another important cause that kept me from going to the United States when I had the chance."

He quickly learned there would be nothing routine about the practice of medicine in any of the UNRWA camps where he served. Making life better for the camp's occupants would not leave time for much else, whether it was politics, marriage, or advancing his formal education. Sleep only interfered with the amount of work required to get the job done, and he was expected to espouse wisdom about any and everything that moved in the camp.

At that point, Ein el-Sultan was teeming with people, many of whom had fled in haste to the camp after the 1948 War, much like Palestinians for centuries had flocked into any village that offered spring-fed drinking water during the arid summer months. Clean spring water in these parts of the Middle East was a gift meant to be shared.

Tawfik's arrival doubled the number of medical officers serving what Tawfik estimated to be about 30,000 refugees. Try imagining one physician treating that many patients.

"Well, it was a first experience for me to go and work in an outpatient clinic. What struck me was the realization that UNRWA worked under a very limited budget in which to provide health, education, food, and shelter. The senior doctor, Nadeem Nahawi, was Palestinian and, like me, had studied in Egypt. But he was older than me and had been at the camp for five or six years.

"When he welcomed me, he made sure to tell me that we have to work hard. He said in addition to seeing patients and taking care of them, that I would have to supervise the sanitation system in the camp, supervise the kitchen and the staff, and inspect the foodstuffs and every other aspect. And he said there were only two of us for the whole camp."

Surgeries were the only procedures in which Tawfik did not get involved since the camp's medical facility was not equipped for that level of care. If anyone needed hospitalization, there was an ambulance driver and a trained nurse available to transfer patients to the nearest hospital.

Tawfik was stationed at Ein el-Sultan for about a year until a senior physician position opened not far away at Nuway'imah camp, where he became responsible for the health center, school health, camp sanitation, and the camp kitchen, which provided hot meals and milk for needy mothers and their children. He also established a rehydration nutrition center for sick children.

The rows of hastily erected canvas tents had been replaced by mud huts, or small structures, mostly made of cinderblock. It was hardly anyone's first choice for a home. "There was peace, at least there were no hostilities at the time, but life in the camp was not easy, and a camp was not a neighborhood by the traditional definition," he says. "There were small alleys, no drainage, no sewage disposal, and there were only a few places in the camp where there was running water."

One of Tawfik's toughest assignments was overseeing the camp sanitation and sewage disposal systems. "We tried our best," he says. "I had a good crew who took good care of the camp and kept it clean. Even after all that, when you walk in between the alleys, and you see the water running and you see the children walking in mud... It's not an easy life for a human being to live there."

On top of it all, the heat was stifling. "In the summer, imagine the heat in Jericho when the temperature gets to 104 or even 107 degrees, and people are living in those small huts with no running water. No refrigerators, no electricity. And they lived where they could not take showers.

"Can you imagine the life of these people during that time?" Tawfik says. "A small fan was considered a luxury. In 1966 a physician in private practice in Jericho bought a small air-conditioning window unit for his home and invited everyone over for a viewing party."

Despite the poverty, the unemployment, the wretched living conditions, and other impediments, an overwhelming number of refugees remained optimistic that the United Nations would make good on its promise to them. It is why Tawfik wanted to work so hard on their behalf. "They never thought they would be there as long as they were, and that was in 1962," Tawfik says. "It is why they carried the keys to their homes with them, thinking that one day they were going to go back home."

By 1965, UNRWA was aiding more than 1.3 million Palestinian refugees registered with the agency in the West and East Banks of Jordan, Lebanon, the Syrian Arab Republic, and the Gaza Strip. The actual number of refugees, Tawfik believes, was more than 5.5 million. All the while, a back-and-forth blame game was playing out at the United Nations as prospects for negotiating a settlement between Israel and the surrounding Arab states hung by a thread.

To make matters worse, no aspects of the Palestine question were brought before the UN Security Council for consideration in 1965. It was another year that succumbed to violence and the mounting vitriol.

The deaths, denials, and disappointments pertaining to the peace process went on year after year, and Tawfik Ramadan was there to pick up the pieces. He spent five years in three refugee camps around Jericho from 1962 to 1967, starting with Aqabat Jaber, Ein el-Sultan, and Nuway'imah. After the 1967 War, he moved to old Karameh and had responsibility for the emergency camps of Karameh I and II. From there, he went to three camps established in the East Bank, Souf north of Jarash in Jordan, Baqa'a, and al-Wehdat.

As both a physician and a Palestinian, it was an extraordinary period in his life. There were so many people who depended on him, from his own family to the thousands of refugees, all in survival mode, all wanting to go home, all wondering. Nameless faces to the rest of the world, they brought purpose and meaning to Tawfik's life, especially the children.

CHAPTER 14

AGONY IN THE REFUGEE CAMP

Only a life lived for others is a life worthwhile.

— ALBERT EINSTEIN

Clean water. Life is worth nothing without it.

But the paltry amount of clean water that was available in Palestinian refugee camps was reserved for drinking, leaving little for cooking and bathing. Often, those who lived in the camps had to walk several blocks to the source of water, fill their jugs, and return to camp along dusty roads.

Of course, cleanliness doesn't come with so little water. That's how children get infections and gastroenteritis. When they get diarrhea and vomiting, they lose a lot of water, so they get dehydrated. When they are dehydrated, the brain and the kidneys don't get enough water, so they die.

It is one reason that living in the early Palestinian refugee camps was described as not being fit for a dog. There were others: poverty, overcrowding, high unemployment, unsafe sanitary conditions, and a sense of abandonment and helplessness that provoked anger and resentment.

Keeping children healthy is what drives Dr. Tawfik Ramadan, and no place has been in greater need of his services than the children of Palestine and Israel. Children and children's rights have long suffered disproportionately throughout the Israeli–Palestinian conflict, starting with the 1929 Hebron massacre and the 1948 Deir Yassin massacre, which claimed the lives of many children.

The trend escalated after the 1967 Arab–Israeli War and then again during the first and second Intifadas (Palestinian protests that turned violent), to where it is today – more children died in 2023 than any other year.

"Unlike children in refugee camps elsewhere, children born in refugee camps under occupation drink their mothers' milk while their camp is under curfew; they wake up in the middle of the night to the sound of rubber bullets and rumors of a possible settler attack," Daoud Kuttab wrote for the *Journal of Palestine Studies* in 2021. "As they grow up, they quickly learn the political lesson of the occupation. Soldiers, batons, tear gas, rubber bullets, arrests, torture, curfews, the closure of camp entrances, administrative detention, and town arrests are all prominent entries in the refugee camps' daily dictionary."

International organizations have called for both sides to adhere to international conventions on the rights of children. According to B'Tselem's calculations, as of 2021, some 2,171 Palestinian children had been killed in the last two decades by Israeli forces, and 139 Israeli children had been killed by Palestinian forces. Since the October 7, 2023, Hamas attack and Israeli retaliation, more than 13,800 Palestinian children have been killed in Gaza while 33 children were killed in Israel. As of May 2024, another 12,000 children have been injured in Gaza and at least 725 children have been injured in the West Bank, according to the UN Office for the Coordination of Humanitarian Affairs.

Today, all one has to do is turn to social media or turn on the television to see the suffering of Gaza's children. Tawfik cannot stop watching, and he cannot stop thinking about how conditions are more deplorable for the children of Palestine now than they were forty-five years ago when he rolled up his sleeves to help at Ein el-Sultan camp.

"When I was watching Al Jazeera television recently and saw starving children who were only skin on a skeleton, a picture came to my mind of a long line of parents standing in line outside our clinic holding their sick and severely dehydrated children," Tawfik says. "They were very distressed and didn't know what to do."

There was not much Dr. Ramadan could do either, other than get creative because a fast remedy, such as the use of intravenous therapy (IVs), was not available to him at the time. Instead, UNRWA physicians set up a rehydration nutrition center to treat children with nutrition and protein deficiencies using oral hydration and a nasogastric tube line (NG) inserted into the nose and threaded into the stomach.

"We didn't have IVs or Zofran (a drug that prevents nausea and vomiting) so we had to use the NG tube because the children were vomiting up everything they swallowed, and the fluid we ran through the line was a mixture of sodium, potassium, chloride, and glucose. It was an early form of Pedialyte that I think was invented by a pediatrician from Lebanon."

In those days, the primitive conditions were offset by the dedication of UNRWA medical personnel, Dr. Ramadan chief among them. From

1962 until 1967, he was among the first physicians to volunteer for the Al-Makassed physicians' organization, which was established in 1955 and provided free medical care to all citizens of Jerusalem at six outpatient clinics.

Primarily with the help of Palestinian and Kuwaiti donors, the Makassed Islamic Charitable Society was founded in 1956 with the goal of assisting people "in all aspects of life and to offer them the educational and health services for the needy by establishing hospitals, polyclinics and educational institutions."

Among them was the Makassed Hospital, a 250-bed facility on Olive Mountain in the West Bank that today still provides medical services regardless of gender, color, race, or religious, political, or social affiliations.

Dr. Ramadan was also proud to administer the first oral polio vaccine at the Nuway'imah refugee camp and share it with nearby schools. And he was proud of the rehydration nutrition measures he helped establish. "We were doing this in the 1960s, long before many countries," he says.

But it was not enough. This is how Dr. Mohayya Khilfeh entered the picture.

Her story is like Tawfik's: her parents married young and worked hard to operate a small grocery store in Jaffa. Mohayya was five years old when they were driven from their home during the 1948 War and returned to Nablus, where her parents were raised. Like most Palestinians, her father took the key to their house with him, sure that they would return home within six months. He held on to that key for twenty years before he accepted the fact that he would never get to unlock their front door again.

After attending medical school in Iraq, Dr. Khilfeh returned to Palestine to undertake her residency in pediatrics at the Augusta Victoria Hospital in Jerusalem, which is where Dr. Ramadan transferred children from his camps who needed special care.

Although they were no more than twenty miles apart when they were consulting with each other before 1967, the two physicians did not actually meet until 1990 when both were living in the United States. They were connected by a telephone and a sense of urgency as the spread of gastroenteritis and dehydration among Palestinian children living both in and out of the refugee camps was sweeping the country like a plague. They were two young physicians overwhelmed with sick children and without a road map to follow.

"The hospital was crowded with refugee patients, and there were things we could not even treat," she says. "In the beginning we did not have a method by which to hydrate children because all the needles were made for adults, and trying to do it by mouth was ineffective. I was very devastated because every day we would lose two or three kids to dehydration."

In desperation, Dr. Khilfeh read up on bone marrow infusion and used the procedure to save lives. Eventually an American physician who visited the hospital gave her a small supply of butterfly needles he had with him. "He showed me how to use it, but, of course, if I have only twenty-five of them, I have probably fifteen patients a day admitted with gastroenteritis, so, how am I going to use this needle after I take it out of another patient?" So, just as Dr. Ramadan got creative in the field with his rehydration efforts, so did Dr. Khilfeh, who, instead of discarding a used needle, boiled it in water every time she used it until the plastic melted away.

The strain under which they practiced medicine prior to the 1967 War was something neither Tawfik nor Mohayya will ever forget: twelve to sixteen hours a day, six days a week, sometimes seven; aching for the children they lost, thankful for the ones who survived. "In our time, a doctor was a community servant," she says. "You go and see a patient anytime they need you in the hospital. If they do not have money, you do not ask them to pay. I know Tawfik was a dedicated, hardworking guy who cared about his patients. When he sent me a patient, he would call me and tell me this and that about the patient. Then, sometimes if the patient was still sick, he would call me again to discuss what happened. And I would call him, too. We were very young at the time. Dr. Ramadan went on to become a most generous man, a family man. He is like a big tree that grew up and flourished but stayed close to his roots."

Dr. Khilfeh was right. Tawfik was not one to rest. Besides treating patients all day at the camp, Tawfik opened his own clinic not far away, where he treated the general population, often well into the night. Although he was approaching thirty years of age, his plan was to remain in the medical field with UNRWA to be close to his family. His father had stopped cutting stone at Tawfik's insistence, and he was sending home money to ensure his father complied with his wishes. His brother had gotten married and joined the army. It was Tawfik's turn to step up. There was plenty of evidence to show that he had spent his life preparing to serve others.

Other than maybe the long-term duration of a Palestinian refugee camp, nothing is forever in the Arab world, especially normalcy. After all, Palestine is a country that has been occupied many times over throughout history, a list that includes the Assyrians, Babylonians, Persians, Greeks, Romans, Arabs, Fatimids, Seljuk Turks, Crusaders, Egyptians, and Mamluks, the British, and the Israelis.

When the end comes for most untenable situations, it usually comes with a whimper. But given that relations between Israel and its neighbor states were never normalized after the 1948 War, it was only a matter of time before politicians would defer to generals to settle the score with firepower.

CHAPTER 15

THE PALESTINIAN *NAKSA*

Success is not final; failure is not fatal: It is the courage to continue that count.

— WINSTON S. CHURCHILL

Many titles have been ascribed to the period between June 5 and June 10 in 1967: the 1967 War, the Six-Day War, the June War, the 1967 Arab–Israeli War, and the Third Arab–Israeli War. The Arab world had another name for it: "The Setback," or *Naksa*, which provided Egypt, Jordan, and Syria some cover in defeat and did not force them to acknowledge the sweeping magnitude of Israel's victory. Tawfik Ramadan was born in 1936 in the middle of the Great Palestinian Revolt, a nationalist uprising designed to pressure the British administration of Mandatory Palestine to bring about Arab independence and the end of the policy of open-ended Jewish immigration, land grants, and purchases intended to create a "Jewish National Home."

The Six-Day/1967 War seemingly walked in off the street out of nowhere when in actuality it was always inevitable once the Israelis determined there was no place for Palestinians in their new world. The war was also forecast from afar by the U.S. and the Soviets, who had made the threat of nuclear war a game of chess using the Egyptians, Syrians, and Israelis.

"It started on a Monday morning," Tawfik says. "I remember it vividly because I had spent the weekend in Beit Jala with my parents and my brother, who was a colonel in the Jordanian army. His battalion was staying in a camp north of Jerusalem, and I drove him there early that Monday morning, probably before five a.m. Then I continued on to the Nuway'imah camp. I was there the morning the war broke out, and we stayed there in the camp trying to convince people not to move on. But the people got scared when the air raids hit. We could not hold them."

Of course, Tawfik was on the scene that day, scrambling to save lives on both sides of the Jordan River. Where else would he be when a war was going on? "Most of the population of the refugee camps around Jericho fled because the air-raid sirens were becoming so intense and because of the rumors that the Israeli army was coming," he says. "Most of them were forced to flee in 1948, and they were in the camps trying to make their homes all over again. They were settled and getting jobs, and their kids were going to school. But they had experienced the first occupation and how they were taken out of their lands, so again they were frightened."

On the second day, Tawfik was having little luck convincing parents in camp to not run headlong into a combat zone with their children when he was drawn into a medical emergency the likes of which he had never seen before. "I treated a man with napalm burns," he says. "He was an army officer who was brought to me because I was still at the camp's clinic. He was screaming because of the very painful burns all over his body. I had to give him a shot of morphine, and that's all that I had. And then they took him back. We saw a lot that day."

In a flashback to 1948 when Palestinian farmers and their families ran for their lives, people in cars, people on tractors, people on bicycles, and people on foot were now swarming out of Jericho and the West Bank into Jordan. One man in camp who had a disease called myasthenia gravis was afraid to stay, but he also could not walk. Dr. Ramadan gave him a shot of physostigmine. "I knew it would not last him. I'm afraid he probably died on the way to the East Bank."

Tawfik was twelve years old in 1948 when Zionist guerrillas drove him out. When Israel invaded the Sinai Peninsula in Egypt in 1956 to force the reopening of the Suez Canal, he was close enough to Cairo to hear the bombs falling. And now, here he was again – twenty-nine years old and caught in the throes of war, clinging to a tiny piece of land at the Nuway'imah camp as if it contained castles filled with gold rather than huts.

By the fourth day, war was descending upon Tawfik, who was still trying to prevent thousands of refugees from running blindly into gunfire. "I held a meeting with some of the police officials in camp, along with what you would call the wise people of the camp," he says. "And then we had another meeting with the imam of the mosque, at which point I said that we were not going to move. But when the air raids became more intense, we could not stop the people who moved to the East Bank where there were some other refugee camps. So, I had to move with them." Because he owned a vehicle, Tawfik volunteered to transport the family of his friend, the UNRWA school superintendent, Emran Al-Tarsha, whose sister was visiting him at the time. "He had a car, and he took her, so he asked me if I would drive his family to Amman. At that moment, there was no easy way to get there."

Tawfik successfully crossed the King Hussein Bridge from Jericho to Amman behind a Jordanian army convoy. Israeli planes hit the front and back of that convoy after it crossed the bridge to Amman, trapping him in the middle.

"I couldn't go anywhere all day, and when I got out of my car I saw my brother, who was an officer in the Jordanian army, walking toward me. Both of us were surprised. When he saw the children in the car were thirsty, he went to get water for them (there were five children and the school superintendent's wife in the car), and we talked for a while until finally the Jordanians got the tanks moved. Later on, I tried to get back to Jericho again, but by this time the bridge had been blown up, meaning I ended up on the East Bank."

Egypt and Jordan agreed to a ceasefire on June 8, and Syria capitulated on June 9. A United Nations–brokered ceasefire went into effect on June 11, 1967, ending the war. In less than a week, Israel had managed to capture the Sinai Peninsula and the Gaza Strip from Egypt, the West Bank and East Jerusalem from Jordan, and the Golan Heights from Syria.

It was six days of war that still resonate as loudly as they did the morning Israel launched its surprise attack. Almost overnight, the Six-Day/1967 War redrew the region's landscape in a way that rocks the world to this day. In those six days, Israel defeated three Arab armies, gained territory four times its original size, and became the preeminent military power in the region.

The Arab coalition suffered the consequences, and the blame fell on Nasser. His defeat brought with it the demise of Pan-Arabism, and although he survived the war, Nasser's influence was never the same.

Embarrassed by the magnitude of the defeat and the ineptitude of his once-proud military forces, Nasser resigned but soon changed his mind after millions of people went out into the streets to mourn and protest his decision. Answering their pleas, he remained in power until his death in 1970. Yet nothing got settled. Field Marshal Abdel Hakim Amer committed suicide. King Hussein of Jordan lost East Jerusalem but kept his throne; he continued his secret dialogue with Israel and made peace in 1994. In Syria, the air force commander who had been in the ruling junta seized sole power in 1970. His name was Hafez al-Assad. His son, Bashar, succeeded him as president upon his death in 2000.

Between 280,000 and 325,000 people were a part of the 1967 Palestinian exodus, which included the "emptying" of the refugee camps of Aqabat Jaber, Ein el-Sultan, and Nuway'imah. Approximately 145,000 of the 1967 Palestinian refugees also had been refugees from the 1948 Palestine War. Until 1967, roughly half of all Palestinians still lived within the boundaries of former Mandatory Palestine.

Undeterred, Tawfik Ramadan resumed treating refugees at the old Karameh camp on the opposite side of the Jordan River. The only thing certain at the time was that refugees would always need medical care. Regrettably, the river was no barrier to despair, and neither Tawfik nor Karameh proved to be out of harm's way.

CHAPTER 16

THE PIVOTAL POINT OF KARAMEH

I, for one, know of no sweeter sight for a man's eyes than his own country.

— HOMER

Respect and educate them or force them to pick up a gun.

Those were the two paths of Palestinian resistance that emerged in the immediate aftermath of the 1967 War. Tawfik and Siham Ramadan put their lives at risk in choosing the former. The Palestinian resistance movement, meanwhile, felt it was left with no choice but to escalate a campaign of armed resistance against Israel.

There was no questioning the passion and commitment of either cause. But it was only a matter of time before one side would capture the attention of the Arab world. That date was March 21, 1968. The place was Karameh, which housed Old Karameh and emergency camps No. 1 and No. 2. The trio of camps were across the street from one another, about thirteen miles northwest of Amman on the Jordanian side and within half a mile of the occupied West Bank.

Tawfik had worked hard to become the healer he promised to be under conditions few physicians could endure. He was literally trying to save lives one at a time. Figuratively, he was doing his best to keep things ticking because those refugee camps where he served were the pulse of the Palestinian nation.

"This particular situation of the Palestinian is very difficult to understand unless you go to the roots of it," he says. "It was the people in those camps in the 1950s and '60s who became symbols of this tragedy and, along with UNRWA, have kept the issue alive. This tragedy that has been perpetrated upon Palestine by the Israelis goes on today."

Like Tawfik, Arafat, who grew up under the spiritual shadow of Jerusalem and studied at Cairo University, spoke out in support of the Arab Nationalist Movement and opposed the 1948 creation of the State of Israel. But Arafat was seven years older than Tawfik, and when the war started, he believed Israel's refusal to negotiate gave him no choice but to fight alongside the Muslim Brotherhood. He was already someone who did not want to be pushed around and was not reluctant to raise his stature to defend his principles.

Then there was Siham. She was not trained to carry a physician's bag or fire a weapon. But she was good at learning and caring, and Palestinian children in refugee camps were in great need of both. Her original plan was to attend college and major in education, but the 1967 War made the decision for her.

Israel attacked on the day she was scheduled to complete the national exam that twelfth graders must pass before they graduate. What was most important about that day is it confirmed in her mind and heart that Palestinian refugee children needed her more than she needed college.

At the same time, Tawfik was scrambling to reopen his after-hours clinic outside the Karameh refugee camp as part of UNRWA's frantic effort to relocate thousands of Palestinian refugees overnight.

Yet their paths were starting to merge. Karameh was the place, and the period from June 5, 1967, to March 21, 1968, marked the incubation period of a Palestinian love story.

There was a UNRWA recruiting office not far from where Siham lived with her older brother and his family. Upon receiving word she had passed the national test, Siham walked into the office and said she wanted to volunteer. "I thought at the time that while I was only a high school graduate, I could still teach first graders," she says. "This was my decision and my duty."

A couple of weeks later, a UNRWA representative called with the news that she had been accepted into the program. Because phones were scarce, the only phone number Siham knew to provide them with belonged to the grocer and butcher not far from the building where she lived. The grocery store was essentially the command center for the cluster of surrounding multistory apartments and buildings.

In essence, the whole neighborhood got to celebrate with her as the good news was relayed to other residents of the building, one flight of stairs at a time. "I was really excited in every way. I was not thinking of all the chaos and all the mess that I would experience. The excitement inside me was that I was going to get to be of help to someone. I would be able to hold a child's hand and comfort him or her and put them back at their school desks."

On her first day at "school," Siham woke up before dawn, got dressed, and rode in a taxi full of strangers to the bus station in the center of Amman, where she caught an UNRWA bus that was filled to capacity with teachers assigned to various camps. The male teachers stood, holding on to a bar above the aisle. One of two emergency camps near Karameh in the Jordan Valley was her stop.

After an hour or so of traveling, Siham stepped off the bus into a spate of locomotion. She stood in awe as a city was being constructed before her eyes. While men scrambled to erect rows of tents, women transported baskets of food and buckets, leaving red dirt trails in their wake. It was a moment straight out of the Oklahoma Land Rush of 1889. The sound, well, the sound could have drowned out Niagara Falls.

"Everyone was helping one another to establish some sort of residency."

Somehow, it all came together without any sense of choreography. As for her part, Siham was one of a hundred teachers waiting for direction from a single administrator.

Eventually, she was directed to a tent filled with parents and their young children. "There was no teaching that first day," she says. "I didn't have any materials to work with. I left that day thinking that I would go home to a place where there was electricity, a refrigerator, a bed and a place to wash my hands, while these students had none of that. . . . They had so little to work with. Maybe not even a notebook and a pencil. Inside, it made me more determined to give them hope through education."

Karameh is where Siham caught her first glimpse of the one who was known to everyone as Dr. Ramadan. "He was in a position of leadership," she says. "He was taking care of the health of the camp and the school system, the health of the students, and he had started his own clinic to help support himself and his family. I remember him when he came to the camp I taught at. His sister taught there as well, and I developed a close friendship with her."

At Karameh, the tent under which Siham taught was anchored to the ground by heavy ropes. Even so, when it rained, everyone seemed to get wet. "But, you know, they say 'where there is a will, there's a way.' That was the challenge," she says. "That was everybody's challenge. I did not do it for money. There was no money to begin with. When the children left the tent where I taught, they went home to another tent, one with only a kerosene lamp. But the next morning, they would come back to class and show me that they somehow had managed to study the night before."

Arafat was accused of having an interest in teaching men in the camp a "trade" as well: the Israelis said he wanted to recruit terrorists. To Palestinians, the men were freedom fighters, known by some as the fedayeen. An Israeli raid on Karameh in February 1968 reportedly uncovered a large fedayeen base consisting of about a thousand men and Soviet-made machine guns and grenades.

Acquiescing to Israel's accusations, the Jordanian army surrounded the camp and ordered the fedayeen to withdraw in order to prevent further Israeli attacks into Jordanian territory. While some Palestinian fighters retreated into the hills, Arafat took the Alamo approach – he urged his forces to hold their ground and send a message to the Israelis, who had a huge advantage in firepower and manpower.

At dawn on March 21, 1968, a large Israeli force attacked, supported by fighter jets, under the assumption the Jordanians would not intervene. To their surprise, they were met with heavy artillery fire, while the fedayeen mounted a counteroffensive.

Again, war was raining chaos down on Tawfik Ramadan, who was the only medical officer on call and who was supported by one male nurse, one ambulance driver, and limited medical supplies. Before Israel's major assault that day, the three Karameh camps had been the targets of several Israeli air raids.

"We would wait until it was over just hoping they would still be alive," Tawfik says. "Then I would go out with the nurse and try to find the casualties.

"We had to go through a very difficult decision-making process of determining which person to transport to the hospital. I had to take the ones who I thought were going to survive because we had very limited medical supplies. Those who were injured badly, we had to leave to die. That was very painful for me to make those decisions with almost no time to think about it."

All he had time to do was improvise. For example, he converted the slats from wooden boxes used to pack tomatoes that grew in the nearby fields into splints to immobilize the fractured arms and legs of the wounded.

Having been tipped off that the Israelis were about to strike, Dr. Ramadan and many of the camps' inhabitants and UNRWA personnel, including Siham, had already fled by the morning of March 21.

It wasn't until a decade later that Tawfik learned that the outside world was led to believe he died that day. "When my father visited us in 1982, my cousin, who had been living in Canada for several years, came to see my father. He told him how he had been watching the Israeli attack on Karameh on television when he saw an Israeli tank completely drive over a mud hut at the camp and then saw a sign on the ground that read '*Dr. Tawfik Ramadan's clinic.*' He thought right then that I must be dead."

By the time the Israelis withdrew late in the day, they had suffered an unexpectedly high number of casualties: twenty-eight killed, sixty-nine wounded, plus four tanks and four other heavy vehicles destroyed. An Israeli jet was also shot down.

Though billed as a military victory by Israel, the battle was perceived by many as an Israeli setback and a triumph for the Arab world as it marked the first time since the June War that Israel did not prove invincible against the outmanned Palestinian resistance movement.

Although Jordanian soldiers, tanks, and artillery played a major role in the battle, Fatah immediately seized upon the battle to portray it as an example of Palestinian steadfastness. Accordingly, the fedayeen's prestige in the Arab world immediately skyrocketed as thousands of young men volunteered to join the Palestinian resistance. What mattered more was that Arafat had escaped, cementing his stature as Palestine's loudest voice.

It went without saying that Karameh represented the Palestinians' greatest moral victory at that point in time. Donald Neff reported for the *Washington Report on Middle East Affairs* in 1998: "The battle of Karameh sent a surge of optimism through the Palestinian community and established the Palestinians' claim to being a national liberation organization. Karameh also was a forceful refutation of the claim by some Israelis that Palestinians did not exist."

"Arafat, whose troops bore the brunt of the fighting, said: 'What we have done is to make the world . . . realize that the Palestinian is no longer refugee number so and so, but the member of a people who hold the reins of their own destiny and are in a position to determine their own future.'"

After the battle, King Hussein of Jordan proclaimed, "I think we may reach a position where we are all fedayeen."

Here is how the *Palestinian Journeys* website grades the showdown between the Israelis and Fatah: "The huge growth in Palestinian forces in Jordan after the battle, and the confidence that the 'victory' had given the leadership of the Palestinian guerrilla organizations, inspired further attacks by Fedayeen based in Jordan against Israeli positions. These prompted further Israeli raids and a sense that the Palestinians were not subject to the authority of the Jordanian regime or were even in open rebellion against it.

"Ultimately, this led to the fierce fighting between the Fedayeen and the Jordanian army in September 1970, known as Black September. Thus, the battle of Karameh changed the course of history for the Fedayeen, the PLO, and the Palestinian national movement."

Neither Tawfik nor Siham's future was altered much by what transpired at Karameh. Her crusade to help Palestinian children simply moved on to Baqa'a camp. Tawfik, meanwhile, set up a clinic in the Souf refugee camp. As luck would have it, Tawfik made weekly visits to Baqa'a, too.

CHAPTER 17

LOVE AND WAR

Love is the emblem of eternity; it confounds all notion of time; effaces all memory of a beginning, all fear of an end.

— MADAME DE STAEL

Tawfik Ramadan was never meant to have a nickname. As a kid, he was already too grown up for one, and then came college, medical school, and doctor status. But if he had been given one, the "Rock" would have fit because Tawfik is someone who does not flinch.

By definition, "unflinching" is the simple one-word adjective form. It is close to fearless but suggests that even if the person is concerned or afraid, he or she is nonetheless not reactive and does not show this concern or fear. "Oblivious" implies the person is completely unaware of these events (and hence unreactive).

After the attack on Karameh, Tawfik demonstrated unflinching resolve. He had been bombed and napalmed out of his camp by Israelis in the 1967 War; had treated the wounded as the Karameh camp was mostly destroyed around him; and had to start over yet again at Souf, an emergency refugee camp that was established overnight to shelter many of the same refugees who were making their third exodus since 1948.

If ever there was a time to pack it in, that was it.

"The lot of the refugees during this long period of dependence on relief has been one of hardship and disappointment," said Selim Yafa, chairman of the Advisory Commission for UNRWA, in 1960. "Opportunities for living normal independent lives have been non-existent for most of the refugees, and their life of enforced idleness has inevitably affected their outlook and morale." His statement should have been long outdated, yet here it was, more applicable than ever.

In 1948 a not-unsympathetic writer, T. R. Feiwel, wrote of the "wordless wish" saying: "The history of Zionist policy towards the Arabs is that this illusion, but an illusion frantically upheld, (that) the Palestine Arabs *do not exist,* at least not as a separate nation with its own aims for national survival which would have to be reckoned with . . . Increase in wealth, numbers, economic, and social possibilities has helped the Zionists to reach an astonishing degree of autarchy, to ignore their Arab neighbors even in mixed cities like Haifa or Jerusalem, and to prolong the illusion of an empty country."

So, it was only natural that this desperate flock would look to Dr. Tawfik Ramadan for help when he walked into his clinic at Souf, located thirty-one miles north of Amman and near the famous Roman ruins of Jerash. The only thing Souf had going for it was that it was not across the street from the Israeli lines.

The terrain favored Tawfik; logistics did not. UNRWA's mission was more compromised than ever: the camps were swollen by the latest wave of refugees from the 1967 War; funds were drying up; and relationships with host countries Jordan and Lebanon were strained.

The head of UNRWA reported that "the bare minimum was bestowed on a population living in dwellings which are unfit for human habitation: some in dark cellars, others in crumbling tenements, others in grossly overcrowded barracks and shacks . . . camps are extremely overcrowded with five or more persons living in one room. They lack adequate roads and pathways, and many camps are deep in mud in winter and dust in summer."

Emergency camps were challenging in other ways, particularly on days when the temperature reached triple digits and refugees were sleeping on sand floors with no way to cool off. Hardships were plentiful for the doctor, too. The situation was similar for Siham Alzaben, who, like Tawfik, moved with the caravan of refugees to resume her teaching. "I was compelled to be there and determined that I needed to help. This was not their fault, and they didn't deserve to be in that situation."

In following her heart, Siham made the difficult decision to leave home and family to support Palestinian refugees. She was able to find a new family inside the camp and, along with Tawfik, felt responsible for the almost one million uprooted Palestinians.

"The values of Arab culture are unique and often mysterious to Westerners," Tawfik says. "Even the word 'Arab' can be unclear because people presume Arabs are a single race. However, the term Arab refers to culture and language rather than lineage. Just as Americans are of mixed race and ethnic backgrounds, so are Arabs.

"For example, my father took care of many things for our family at the time because I had to concentrate on my position as a physician. He would go to the market and do all the shopping and bring everything for the family. But that does not explain the real role he played."

In the Middle East, respect for one's elders is endless and runs deeper than most Americans could even comprehend. As an adult, for example, Tawfik would not dare smoke a cigarette in front of his father, nor drink coffee before he gave his father a cup. The list marking the respect he held for his father is long.

The Institute of Middle East Understanding explains the importance of family this way: "As in most largely rural cultures, the family is the most important unit in Palestinian society. The Palestinians' political experience and reality have served to further strengthen family ties. With no real government-sponsored social safety net, and with the lack of a functioning economy or enough independent government institutions or even enough banks to provide home or student loans, Palestinians have had to rely on family and neighbors to fill the gaps."

The importance of family in Palestinian culture became clearer to Tawfik with time. "I had never seen a case of child abuse or drug abuse for the fifteen years I was in practice in the Middle East," he says. "If anything happened between the wife and the husband, the extended family would come together and solve the problem because it was not just the father and the mother raising the child. What is important to know is that any member of the family has the whole tribe behind them reassuring him or her."

By the time she began teaching students at her third refugee camp, Siham's definition of family also had broadened considerably. "In the camps, it was not entirely the responsibility of one's extended family to help," she says. "The way that people were mixed together and the circumstances that they faced, everybody was trying to thrive, to survive. And with the close proximity to each other – first you are living in a tent and then you graduate from the tent to a mud house – you could not escape getting to know your neighbor. The longer each of you are there, the closer you become. You are helping me; I am helping you. We are in it together."

The word "together" would soon take on a new meaning for her, and Siham would be the last one to recognize it.

Tawfik's responsibility for managing the camp's health and environmental conditions extended to the classroom, including the school tents at Camp Al-Baqa'a, where Siham taught. Siham still recalls how the faculty and staff looked forward to his arrival.

She was young and inexperienced compared to her more seasoned peers, most of whom Tawfik knew well. Before he arrived for the school inspection, Siham could see and feel the excitement everyone had knowing they were about to present their progress for the week to such an important man.

"Picturing the whole thing, the environment, in a way it's like, yes, writing a romantic story when we describe how I went from Amman, the capital, to the camps to teach, and of the chaos and fear," Siham says. "And meanwhile, you feel there is another aspect of it. Part of your heart goes to the children, and part goes to Dr. Ramadan when I see him. His name resonated in my mind."

While Siham was slow on the uptick, others quickly envisioned a romantic connection between the respected doctor and the attractive teacher. The first person to make the connection between the handsome physician and the beautiful young teacher was Tawfik's good friend, Imran Al-Tarsha, the UNRWA superintendent of education.

"One day he came to me when we were still at Karameh and said he had found me a wife," Tawfik says. Tawfik was curious because Siham had already caught his eye.

The two men proceeded to hatch a plan. First, Al-Tarsha called the principal at the camp where Siham was working and told him he wanted to meet her. When Siham arrived for the meeting, Tawfik just happened to be standing nearby.

"I probably would not have been interested in him if I had known about all that then," Siham says in all seriousness years later. "But I do know everyone at the time thought it was time for him to get married."

Tawfik said he knew she was the one for him the minute she walked into the room.

Fortunately, it is acceptable for the rules of courtship to be discarded in war, as evidenced by the courtship of Tawfik and Siham. In rural areas of Palestine, marriages had always been arranged by parents. The women of the family often played a key role in introducing the couple, and daughters would be asked if they accepted a potential groom before proposals were extended. Courting in larger towns and cities differed slightly in that it was common for couples to spend more time getting to know each other, usually with a family chaperone in attendance.

A thirty-two-year-old bachelor was far from the norm in Palestine, particularly a handsome and well-educated one. There was a simple explanation. Tawfik had chosen education over matrimony. The voice of his father reverberated within: *Education, education, education. That is your future.*

"I felt at that time if I got married, I wouldn't proceed with my education. I looked at marriage at that time as an obstacle in my way. I told my parents, told everyone, I was not ready because I had goals to achieve. 'When I achieve my goals, then I will tell you I'm ready,'" was his reasoning.

The plot thickened when Tawfik's sister, who was a close friend of Siham's and a fellow teacher, encouraged her to take her ailing mother (who was visiting Siham at the time) for a check-up at Tawfik's after-hours clinic. There was a brief encounter between the two: Tawfik told Siham her mother's allergies were flaring up and was in no danger. Then she was gone.

Two months later, they were married.

This was how the dating game rapidly evolved in a land where tradition had been usurped by war. "You could not go home to your family and say, 'Well, I am bringing my girlfriend to meet you today. This is who she is.' You know, you couldn't do that," Tawfik says. "Still, the man must take the lead in this. He must make the decision. And this is what happened to me after that meeting. I had to go and talk to my parents and my sister and I said, 'I think this is the right person for me and the proper time for me to be married.' My sister, who knew Siham well, helped me present her character to my parents, which is part of the traditional measures. Then we contacted her family and said we would love to come and ask for her hand."

Deep-seated feelings seldom make their way past the Adam's apple in Tawfik's throat. He is so accustomed to focusing on others that he has difficulty talking about himself, even when it comes to the love of his life. His quiet, gentle manner runs counter to the grain because the Palestinian people reveled in love songs and love sonnets long before they became famous for Palestinian poems of resistance.

And nothing personifies Palestinian romance better than the courtship and marriage of a Palestinian couple in love. In the *Cultural Atlas*, Nina Evason writes, "Palestinians are generally quite conservative in their ideals of marriage and dating, reflecting traditional Arab and

Islamic values. People are quite protective and paternalistic with regard to women especially. Casual dating is often strongly disapproved of among Palestinian society. In the Palestinian Territories, it is common for a couple to be introduced by families and spend time getting to know one another before deciding whether they want to marry or not."

As such, Siham would have preferred a traditional courtship. "With the war and everything, there was no time to write each other and spend time with each other or with each other's family," she says.

Interestingly, the man who had long shunned marriage did not want to wait a minute longer. "I wanted to do things fast," Tawfik says. "So, I, my father, and two friends, both relatives, went to her brother's house in Amman to introduce ourselves to her two brothers. First, we drank coffee. Then my father spoke, out of respect for our elders, and said he was there to ask on my behalf for their sister's hand in marriage."

Tawfik sat calmly, wearing his customary suit and tie. It could have been one of those rare occasions when the highly composed physician might have displayed a flash of nervousness, but he was not on edge, perhaps because his father had told him a long time ago that a well-dressed man would gain the respect of other men.

Later that evening, Tawfik was notified that Siham's family would like for him to return to formally propose. "After the first meeting, I didn't say yes or no," says Siham, who, according to Palestinian tradition, was not allowed to attend the meeting.

"I felt as a family we still had to discuss this by ourselves, and I wanted to talk to my mom. It was a hard decision to make, and it was confusing to me. First, I was brought up as the little girl in the family, and my mother was everything in my life. I had been hoping to go off to college and do something to make her proud so that I could help take care of her, or at least bring in some income for her and the rest of the family. And my brothers wanted to make sure Tawfik would be the right husband for me. A husband is not just for the woman; he is for the whole family, so he had to be accepted."

During that interval, Tawfik asked his sister to arrange a meeting with Siham. "I wanted that meeting to happen before I proposed in order to tell her what I believed in and what I had planned for my life, so that she knew something about me before she made her final decision."

He was not taking for granted that she would instinctively want to share her life with him, and he wanted to be honest about what their future might entail. As a physician during wartime, he had obligations that could take him away from home any hour of the day or night. He also shared with her his plans to develop a more specialized practice and the steps he might have to take to reach professional goals.

The prospective groom and his family returned a few days later to be greeted by the elders of the bride. Cups of coffee warming on a tray held the answer to his anticipated proposal of marriage. After the coffee was served, Tawfik waited for Siham's oldest brother to make the next move. If he did not raise the cup to his lips, it meant the answer was no.

"That meant it would not have been God's will for this marriage to happen, so then we would have gotten up and left the coffee behind," Tawfik says. "Not a good thing, but it was a very polite tradition because to have Siham's elder to have spoken the word 'no' would have been considered offensive in Arab culture."

With the coffee still warming, Tawfik, his father, and the other elders in his family reintroduced themselves and formally explained the nature of their visit. His father read a short verse in the Qur'an that pertained to marriage, chapter 30, verse 21, which was intended to be a formal proposal of marriage:

> "*In the Beginning: And among his signs is that He has created for yourselves, mates that you may incline towards them and find rest in them, and He has engendered love and tenderness between you. Surely in this are signs for people who reflect.*"

Taha responded to the proposal Za'al had extended on the part of Tawfik's family with the words Tawfik was waiting to hear: "Your request is welcomed."

The men then extended their hands and opened their palms in acknowledgment that the proposal had been accepted by all. Taha then asked them to join him as he read Al-Fatiha (The Opening), the first chapter of the Qur'an. At the conclusion, Taha picked up the tray containing enough cups for everyone in attendance and began to serve the coffee, first to the groom's side, and then to his family. "Then we drank the coffee and shared a happy moment," Tawfik says.

Their courtship did include some actual meetings between the pair, which was a break from traditional norms. "We got to know each other some," Siham says. "And if I had decided he was not for me, I would have stood my ground and said that I won't marry him because at that point we had the freedom to make those decisions."

Their engagement was formalized on November 17, 1968. Soon after, the couple made a trip to a jewelry market in the center of the city to pick out engagement rings and wedding bands. Given the unrest in Jordan at the time, the wedding ceremony was set for six weeks later on January 1, 1969, in Amman.

The wedding was coordinated by both sides of the family. Siham's family hosted the ceremony, while his family organized the wedding party. Had Jordan not been war-torn at the time, the celebration would clearly have lasted longer than it did.

Clearly an Al-Maliha wedding would have been something to see. Festivities would have lasted as long as a week leading up to the ceremony and would have involved the whole village. The only way to describe them is to say they are elaborate and large, involving much food, music, and dancing. There is Henna Night on the eve of the wedding, which is strictly for women on both sides of the family as well as the bride's friends. The highlight is the henna (a plant dye) itself, in which older women decorate the skin of the bride and her guests with intricate designs that often take hours to complete. Other traditions include the *dabke*, the traditional dance of Palestine, and the *zaffa*, a wedding march where the groom is carried on the shoulders of family and friends.

A Palestinian wedding is not complete without a feast. On the day of the wedding, the women of the groom's family busily prepare a huge quantity of food to feed families of the bride and groom and invited guests. *Mansaf* is a traditional dish served at all large gatherings in Palestine, especially weddings. Made of lamb cooked in a dried fermented yogurt sauce, *mansaf* is typically served with rice or bulgur on top of a thin piece of *shrak* bread. The name *mansaf* originates from the term for "large tray," which accurately represents how the dish is served. The tray, typically around thirty-six inches in diameter, is spread on top of white sheets on the floor, around which six to eight guests are seated in a circle. Each guest eats using their right hand and only takes the portion of *mansaf* that is directly in front of them. Tradition demands that immediate family members of both the bride and the groom not serve themselves until all the guests have eaten.

Music always sets the tone. Some songs are associated with preparation of the food. There are old Arabic songs of sadness and happiness for the bride who must leave her family, and there are songs that celebrate the bride's journey to her new home. Some songs are earmarked to accompany the groom's family when they take sweets to the bride's family as part of the Henna celebration.

Although the times were somber, Siham's wedding was like a rose among thorns. "The ceremony happened between my family's house and his house. By the time I was dressed and ready, all who were invited on his side drove up in cars, got out, and made a big circle in front of our house and started singing and clapping, the men walking ahead of the women. My brothers were holding my arms up from both sides, and my mother and the rest of my family were beside them.

"After the ceremony, we all went back to the cars and went to his house for the wedding night and celebration," she says. "There was enough dinner for everybody, whether ten people or five hundred showed up." Following dinner, there was a night of music, dancing, and increased happiness.

After their honeymoon in Cairo, the plan was for the couple to remain in Amman, where Tawfik had established his after-hours practice in a house near the camp, and begin having children. For Tawfik's family, this moment had seemed to have been forever in the making. As for Siham, she was still spinning inside. Life was moving fast for a nineteen-year-old.

Despite their best efforts, things did not go as planned. Very seldom do Palestinians get to choose.

CHAPTER 18

THE COURAGE OF MOTHERHOOD

When we choose to be parents, we accept another human being as part of ourselves, and a large part of our emotional selves will stay with that person as long as we live. From that time on, there will be another person on this earth whose orbit around us will affect us as surely as the moon affects the tides, and affect us in some ways more deeply than anyone else can. Our children are extensions of ourselves.

— FRED ROGERS

Siham could hear the sound of bombs and feel the reverberation of the walls as she crouched in the dark in the corner of a tunnel below the hospital where she had given birth. With her two-day-old baby girl clutched against her chest, Siham Ramadan had a decision to make. Would she stay and be buried alive, or would she run into the street where fellow Arabs were killing each other?

It is hard to imagine that anything in life could have prepared her for this moment. But this was not her first taste of war, and, in Palestinian years, Siham was now twenty-three years old going on triple figures based on the amount of life experience she had gained.

A lot had happened to her in a short amount of time. First, she had left home as a sheltered teenager to get an education; next, the 1967 War upended her future; then came a proposal from a highly respected man, followed by marriage six weeks later and the interruption of her teaching career.

The first three months of marriage to Tawfik had been like a dream, punctuated by a romantic two-week honeymoon in Cairo in early January 1969. The couple flew from Amman to Cairo, harkening memories for Tawfik of the flight he made from not far away in Jerusalem to Cairo fifteen years earlier to pursue a medical degree, and stayed at the stately Semiramis Hotel on the banks of the Nile.

In Cairo, Siham and Tawfik took a scenic riverboat ride and dined at the Tea Island, a famous restaurant at the Cairo Zoo, where their server happened to be the same man who had cooked for Tawfik and his roommates in their apartment in the Al-Manial neighborhood.

"I took Siham to many other places I had memories from: Cairo University Medical School at Qasr Eleini, the Groppi Café, the Heliopolis where I lived when I first arrived in Cairo, and other places such as the main train and metro line where the Statue of Ramses stands tall and huge," Tawfik says, his eyes sparkling. "We also visited the Pyramids and Sphinx in Aljeezah south of Cairo, where Siham rode the camel owned by one of our tour guides."

Their new life together in Amman brought its own sense of fascination for Siham as Tawfik provided a new second-story home they would share with his parents, and an adjacent building to serve as a clinic for him. The two structures were separated by a narrow alley, and both were near the Al-Wehdat camp in Amman where Tawfik served as chief medical officer.

Once they were settled, countless family, friends, and well-wishers dropped in to congratulate the new couple.

For a getaway, the couple drove Tawfik's new Mercedes 250-S to Baghdad for a memorable vacation, which came with the added dimension of Tawfik's cousin on his mother's side, Moosa Ishaq Alhawari, in the back seat. "He had just finished secondary school and wanted to complete his higher education in Baghdad, so we took him with us in hopes of getting him a scholarship," Tawfik says.

Tawfik called it a "nice, enjoyable ride." To him, that meant nice cars and high speeds because part of the road to Baghdad also doubled as an airport runway. "I think our speed reached ninety miles per hour, but I could not really feel it."

Tawfik went to Baghdad in search of a vacation. As a secondary benefit, he hoped to secure a scholarship to the School of Science at Baghdad University for his cousin by capitalizing on the relationships he had formed in Cairo with fellow Palestinians.

"Some of them were working in Baghdad on behalf of the Palestinian cause, so I hoped they would speak in support of my cousin," Tawfik explains. "To my surprise, they asked me to join a Palestinian delegation that was on its way to the presidential palace to meet with the president of Iraq, Ahmad Husan al-Bakr, who died in office of unknown causes and was replaced by his deputy Saddam Hussein. I remained silent at the meeting, but my cousin got his scholarship and Siham and I resumed our tour."

First, they visited and prayed at the sacred Shi'ite Mosque in Karbala City, sixty miles southeast of Baghdad. The mosque is huge and decorated with gold-plated doors, domes and minarets. Siham and his friend's wife, who had accompanied them, had to put on head covers and long black robes, as tradition required.

The next trip was to Al-Hindiya Dam, or Barrage, on the Euphrates River south of the town of Musayyib in Iraq's Babil Governorate. From there, they spent two days at Al-Amarah city southeast of Baghdad and finally ended up in Samarra, where they saw the remains of the historically significant city, the original capital of the Abbasid Caliphate. It is the only remaining Islamic capital that has retained its original plan, architecture, and artistic relics.

Baghdad was a welcome respite because life in Amman always conspired to pull them apart. If they weren't feeling the tug of family and friends, Siham was growing insecure as it was not unusual for a female admirer of Tawfik's to call to see how he was faring. In addition, he was bombarded with patients, both at the camp and at his home office. Keeping a vow he made to himself to never treat a patient the way his grandfather had been treated, it was routine for Tawfik to end a long day with a few house calls.

Tawfik was always happy practicing medicine, but, given her young age, loneliness and some insecurity on Siham's part were bound to follow. "I think when we got engaged, we were envied," she says. "I was envied by so many people, especially from the people in the education field, and probably some other girls who were more mature, who were more educated than me. They were looking at this young man who is rising up, he's coming all the way up, and they're trying to understand why he chose me."

Other challenges arose: "I had never been subjected to this kind of environment and this kind of responsibility, of being a wife for someone who is known, and at first, I did not meet that challenge. I had been the baby of my family, the one who was being taken care of."

Now she was living with his family, including his parents, a sister, a brother (who was often away in the army), and his wife and daughter. It was a welcoming family, but it was not her own family. "They loved me so much, but still, because of distance my mother could not see me any time she wanted. We barely talked on the phone," Siham explains. "It was very hard, and at certain times I used to cry a lot."

Then she lost the baby she was carrying. "Siham had a hemorrhage, and she actually required blood transfusions in order to recover," Tawfik says.

The loss of their baby was the biggest challenge of all.

"I decided I was compelled to meet all the challenges," she says. "In Arabic, there is a saying that when you reach a certain point, it's like the hair that broke the camel's back. All my life, even when I was very young, still, I was not too emotional. I am a thinker. When things come, I do not react too fast. I think things through. So, I had to sort it all out."

She came to a simple conclusion: "I either make it or not make it, you understand? And I decided to be more supportive, more understanding, to get to know his family better and become more comfortable in the social environment I was in."

There is something miraculous about how Siham wound up in the tunnel of a hospital with a life-or-death choice to make. The decision was hers, but the circumstances in which she found herself were not of her making, as is often the case with civilians during wartime.

Not only did the Nakba force Palestinians from their homes in 1948, but it also tore families apart much the same way the American Civil War pitted brother against brother. Tawfik says it all came to a head in what the Arab world mourned as "Black September."

Also called the Jordanian Civil War, the conflict was fought in the Hashemite Kingdom of Jordan and involved King Hussein and the Jordanian Armed Forces (JAF) on one side; Yasser Arafat and the Palestine Liberation Organization (PLO), the Popular Front for the Liberation of Palestine (PFLP), and many other resistance movements on the other; and the Palestinian and Jordanian populations in the middle.

Naturally, Tawfik was right there in the middle too, stationed at the Al-Wehdat refugee camp, a popular recruiting ground for Palestinian freedom fighters. This time, Siham was with him in the middle of the oft-repeated chaotic history that defines the Holy Land. However, it was not the history displaced Palestinians had envisioned when they fled in exile, primarily to the West Bank, the Gaza Strip, Lebanon, Syria, and Jordan, where UNRWA established temporary refugee camps to house them.

Everything about the Jordanian camps was temporary as the Arab League instructed its members to deny Palestinians a chance to gain citizenship to avoid dissolution of their identity and protect their right of return to their homeland. Refugee status was also passed to their descendants, who were denied citizenship in Arab states other than Jordan.

"No matter what papers we were given, we were still Palestinians," Tawfik says. "And the important thing to remember about the refugee camps is that many of the young Palestinian fighters grew up there and were driven by two things: one was the emotion and desire to liberate Palestine and return us to our homes; the other was that many of the young people did not have work, so they joined the freedom fighters."

The PLO eventually came to be seen more and more as a state within a state in Jordan as its grassroots support grew among Palestinians. Discipline within the different Palestinian groups was poor, and the PLO had no central power to control them. They drove noisily around Amman in jeeps with loaded weapons, like an army of occupation. Many Palestinians, however, welcomed their presence. Women would spontaneously donate jewelry they were wearing in gratitude. Meanwhile, others claimed that the PLO was extorting citizens. "Their very presence in Amman, far from the battlefield, seemed like a challenge to the regime," is how an observer in Amman reported their presence.

The Jordanian king had a problem: If he used force to oust the Fedayeen, he would alienate himself from both displaced Palestinians and the Arab world. However, if he refused to strike back, he could lose the respect of Jordanians and, more importantly, the army, which was the backbone of his regime and was pressuring him to act. To compound the situation, by 1970 two-thirds of the Jordanian population was Palestinian, and they were growing disenchanted with Hussein's attempts to balance his interests in preserving peace with Israel.

The stakes increased in early 1970 after Hussein and Nasser supported a ceasefire in an undeclared war of attrition with Israel in hopes of dislodging Israeli troops from the Sinai Peninsula. In response, George Habash, the PFLP leader, promised that "we will turn the Middle East into a hell," while Arafat told a cheering crowd of 25,000 in Amman in July that "we will liberate our land."

With war at the doorstep, Tawfik's brother and brother-in-law, who were a Jordanian army officers, were among the many Palestinians put in the tenuous position of having to choose between being loyal to a king or supporting a Palestinian rebellion. Jordan's king, after all, was the one who had sheltered Palestinian refugees.

"Here we are talking about Palestinians and Jordanians when, really, all of us are Jordanians," says Siham, who still holds a Jordanian passport.

Her brother Taha, for example, went off in the morning dressed in his army uniform and swore loyalty to the king. While his loyalty never wavered, as a Palestinian it was natural for him to question how the fate of Palestine would fare in the end. Generally, Palestinians had the same questions, especially in the big cities where the lives of many Palestinian and Jordanian families intersected daily.

Equally troubling to Siham was the us-versus-them attitude that was emerging among Palestinian and Jordanian organizations that had been united against Israel. Tawfik and Siham soon found themselves literally caught in the crossfire.

On top of that, Siham was pregnant again.

A last chance to avoid a full-scale civil war between the PLO and King Hussein fell apart after Egyptian president Gamal Abdel Nasser suffered a heart attack and died following an Arab League summit on September 28, 1970.

"He had invited King Hussein to Cairo to try to solve the problem with Yasser Arafat, but Nasser suffered his heart attack while the king was in the air on his way home," Tawfik says. "Nasser was very stressed because Arabs were fighting each other when he supported unity. He was the hero. He was the hope."

A telephone call Tawfik made to a high-ranking officer and friend in the Jordanian army confirmed their fears that a battle was brewing. "I had taken care of him and his family at my clinic, and I called him and said, 'How is it going?' He did not want to tell me anything on the phone. Finally, he said, 'The eye is red.' That was the message to me that the situation is bad."

Things were no better when it came to Siham's pregnancy. She was carrying the baby well and receiving prenatal care from an obstetrician who was a friend of Tawfik's. But with another war about to break out, the doctor escaped to Syria, leaving Siham without care.

When she finally went into labor on September 10, they were down to one option: the Jabal Ashrafieh Hospital, a Jordanian state-operated facility in the hills of Amman and a ten-minute drive from their home. Tawfik took her to the hospital and went back to treating the injured. Siham's family visited her the first day, but Siham spent the next three days in intense labor. Finally, on the afternoon of September 13, 1970, she delivered a daughter, who was named Salam, which means "peace" in Arabic. Knowing his wife did not like hospital food, Tawfik brought Siham homemade chicken soup the next day. They were beginning to feel like a real family.

Unfortunately, the war, well, it was right on time, too early actually, as fighting broke out that night in the area separating the PLO and the Jordanian army. On the morning of September 15, Siham was with Salam in her hospital room and Tawfik was about two miles away at his sister's house when heavy artillery shelling erupted. One of the targets of the Jordanian army was Al-Wehdat refugee camp, which the PLO was using as a staging area for its assaults. The PLO responded by directing its firepower at the Jordanian artillery positions near the camp. As fate would have it, the two buildings occupied by the Ramadan family got caught in the artillery crossfire and were partially destroyed.

Tawfik's father became trapped inside, which was only the beginning of the Ramadans' problems. By midday the hospital was under attack as an artillery shell struck the water tank on the roof, sending its contents cascading down the hospital walls outside Siham's room. In turn, most of the hospital staff fled the building along with the patients who could crawl out of their beds and walk. Siham was among the few who were not well enough to travel.

"There was terror in the air, and it was then I realized that I was in an actual war with people going in all different directions. Some had vehicles, and some ran. There was no food, no water. And there was no one to take care of us. I am in my room listening to the bombs drop and moving my baby's crib from one side to the other to try to protect her."

There was one place left to go – the tunnel beneath the hospital. That evening, one of the two remaining physicians helped move her and her baby to the tunnel where Siham would be left on her own.

"Everybody was praying that she would be safe at that time, but there was no way that we could go to the hospital," says Tawfik, explaining his sense of helplessness. "It was not easy because it was a choice between life and death, and where she was, there in the hospital, we thought she was more or less safe. If I drove my car there, there was a 100 percent chance I would be shot."

The shelling resumed at daylight the next morning, bringing with it a new threat as frightened civilians began to storm the hospital doors seeking safety in the tunnel where Siham and her baby had spent the night with the other remaining patients.

"They came in crying and carrying their babies. Then they started screaming. A lady who was in labor was among them. Other than a few drops, there was no water for the physician to scrub his hands with. But he delivered her baby by C-section on a stretcher under a kerosene lamp."

Although that baby lived, Siham, sitting only a few feet away, feared more than ever for her own baby's life: there was no food or water, and it was becoming hard to breathe in the tunnel, where people were getting crushed to death.

Fearing for her baby's life if they remained, Siham looked at Salam, wrapped her tightly in a blanket, put her in her arms, and ran out on the street and into gunfire.

All Siham could think about was going home to Tawfik. But she had no way of knowing that Al-Wehdat also was being shelled by Jordanian artillery forces.

She ran until a man stopped her. "Sister, sister, sister, do you need help?"

"Yes, brother, I need help."

"Where are you going?"

"I'm going to my house; it is that way. I'm going to the clinic of Tawfik Ramadan."

The man reached for her baby. She had no idea who he was, but she handed Salam to him. They ran together, dodging gunfire, for about three miles until they arrived at the camp's entrance. After risking his own life, the stranger handed the baby back to her.

Siham could not see her house, but she could see that Tawfik's black Mercedes was parked in the alley. There was only one more street to navigate. She started to cross it when she heard another man yell, "Sister, don't cross the street. It is filled with land mines."

She looked at him and replied, "I have to cross."

Siham doesn't know how, but she made it across the street, past Tawfik's bullet-ridden automobile, and to the front door of her house. The heavy metal front door faced a side street, and when she reached it, Siham pounded on the door, calling for Tawfik.

A voice shouted back, "Who's knocking on the door?" It was Za'al.

"It's me, Uncle; it's Siham, and I have the baby. Open the door."

In his excitement to know she was alive, Za'al could not find the key to the door, even though it was ten times the size of a modern door key. Za'al cried out in frustration, "I'm looking. What can I do? I cannot find the key."

"Okay, but where is everybody? What happened to the rest of the family? What happened to Tawfik?" Siham asked.

They all had fled, taking shelter at the house of Tawfik's younger sister, he replied. Unfortunately, the house was along the same dangerous route Siham had just traveled. "I just turned around with the baby in my arms and crossed that same street, which was the road to the city of Madaba."

This time, no one was there to help her, so Siham ran until she reached a red house at the end of an alley. Tawfik happened to be standing outside the door with his hands in his pockets, praying that his wife and baby were safe in the hospital.

"I saw him, and I started screaming," Siham says. "At first, I don't think he realized it was me. I think he thought I was dead. Finally, he saw me and came running to me and grabbed the baby."

Tawfik had gone to his sister Hamdah's house because both the refugee camp and his house were being shelled. Not long after he arrived, some people came to the door and said there was a lady next door who was pregnant and had gone into labor.

"The house was deserted. No one was there when this woman came along and went inside to deliver her baby by herself," Tawfik says. "It was after she delivered the baby that someone ran and said, 'Please come see this lady.'"

Tawfik obliged. He found the woman on the floor and her baby by her side with its placenta cord still attached. Tawfik had a lighter on him so he found an old razor nearby, heated it with the lighter and cut the cord.

Tawfik, Siham, and Salam were among ten family members crammed into his sister and brother-in-law's two-bedroom house as they waited for the fighting to cease. There was another addition along the way as Tawfik and Siham delivered Hamdah's baby boy, who was born in the same bedroom where Salam slept on a blanket on the floor.

Mounting pressure from Arab countries (such as Iraq) and a stalemate in his assault against the Fedayeen and Syrian-backed fighters led King Hussein to sign an agreement with Arafat to regulate the Fedayeen's presence in Jordan in October 1970. However, nothing was settled until the summer of 1971 when badly outgunned Fedayeen fighters surrendered to the Jordanian army in a forest near Ajloun, restoring Hussein's sovereignty. The Fedayeen was allowed to take up its cause again in Syria, and Palestinian refugees returned to even harsher conditions at Al-Wehdat as Jordan was in no mood to open any more refugee camps.

Naturally, Dr. Ramadan went with them.

CHAPTER 19

LIFE HANGING BY A KIDNEY STONE

Though nothing can bring back the hour of splendor in the grass, of glory in the flower; we will grieve not, rather find strength in what remains behind . . .

— WILLIAM WORDSWORTH

The stunning city of Amman, Jordan, was built on seven mountains that encircle the markets, museums, and historical sites that comprise the city's original commercial and cultural center. Amman Mountain, for example, had all the accouterments of Paris in the 1960s. Occupants of another affluent section where the bannisters were layered with thin sheets of twenty-one-carat gold looked down upon the plight of the poor inhabitants of Al-Wehdat, the stubborn Palestinian refugee camp that would not die. Ashrafieh Mountain is where Siham gave birth, got trapped, and outran death.

She lost her last sense of innocence in her flight. With it came the certainty that her children, her husband, and her family were now the absolute priorities in her life. "What I reflected upon after being trapped like that was how human beings get affected by sudden changes in their life. What are the consequences of making a decision that can cost the life of someone you love? There was lots of responsibility and lots of pain and fear and terror in me. And it changed me overnight."

Black September changed everything and nothing all at once. King Hussein's problems did not disappear with Arafat's expulsion. Most of the 300,000 Palestinians displaced by Israel's occupation of the West Bank were still housed in refugee camps, casting a harsh shadow over Jordan's hope for a much-needed economic recovery. Wealthier Palestinians who had backed the insurgency against the monarchy could afford a do-over by moving to Lebanon.

The bulk of the Palestinians living in Jordan were trapped. The situation was particularly dire for residents of war-torn Al-Wehdat as well as their chief physician. But Doctor Ramadan managed to rebuild his private clinic outside the camp and located another home for his wife and daughter that was large enough to accommodate his parents and other family members. Money was tighter than ever, which meant Tawfik would be working more than ever, as if fourteen-hour days were not enough.

Black September had cost them almost everything they owned. It was bad, and it would get worse because they would soon lose the extended family's only breadwinner.

Adjusting to the unexpected had become the underpinning of Tawfik's philosophy on life, and it gave him the uncanny ability to bounce back higher each time he got knocked down. He viewed setbacks as opportunities, hardship as gain, and new lessons from which to profit. He could shift as quickly as the desert sands when quick feet and a sharp mind were needed to address a problem, but when it mattered the most, he was the rock. Siham became the glue whose single-minded determination to keep her family together rivaled Tawfik's quest to find his true calling as a physician. Then came the day the "Family Rock" was crushed by a pebble not much larger than a chickpea.

Kidney stones are hard deposits made of minerals and salts that form as the kidney filters waste from the blood and produces urine. They generally pass through the urinary tract unnoticed. But if they break loose and push into the ureters, the narrow ducts leading to the bladder, stones that measure approximately five millimeters or larger may cause intense pain.

The one Tawfik had did more than that. "We were just starting to have some normalcy in life where Tawfik could come home from work in time to enjoy dinner and being together with his family when he started having health problems," Siham says. "He got very, very sick. It was painful, and he couldn't get rid of it."

The pain was much worse than a toothache; kidney stone pain is the worst pain you can imagine, Tawfik says.

As he was taught to do, Tawfik plowed ahead. Finally, when the pain became so unbearable he could not work, a urologist friend of his decided to open him up and remove the stone, which by then had migrated from the kidney through the ureter, where it had become trapped.

Removing it required delicate surgery in those days, and rather than having the procedure performed in Amman, Tawfik chose the American University hospital in Beirut. It was his calculation that there were fewer random gunshots in Beirut than Amman that might send an anesthesiologist running.

"I wasn't sure I wanted to die on the table all by myself."

The director of health services for UNRWA also thought Beirut was a better choice and made all the arrangements. Tawfik rented a car and drove five hours from Amman through Damascus to Beirut with Siham early in 1971. The surgeon, Dr. Azar, who operated on Tawfik, was Harvard University trained and a "very good person," according to Tawfik. During the first operation, Dr. Azar removed the stone and inserted a catheter to keep the ureter open and promote healing.

However, there were complications after the operation. "I had severe diuresis (a process in which the kidneys produce extra urine to facilitate the body's removal of a substance). It was like the kidney had woken up and I began to lose fluids through my urine. Dr. Azar had to call a nephrologist to come and arrange to give me electrolytes, fluids, and an IV. In the meantime, I got a fever that developed into sepsis or urosepsis (a term used to describe a type of sepsis that is caused by an infection in the urinary tract that must be treated quickly)."

To treat the bacterial infection, Tawfik was given a new antibiotic on the market, Gentamicin, which he took twice a day for two weeks. Each vial cost one hundred dollars at the time. Although the infection was brought under control, Tawfik developed a fistula from the suprapubic cystostomy when an opening in his bladder created by the catheter's insertion did not dry up as intended.

One day, when he was still hooked up to two IVs and a catheter, Tawfik felt the room swaying. The Irish nurse who was on duty at the time rushed up to his bed saying the country was in the middle of an earthquake. She then apologized for having to leave him there while everyone evacuated to the basement. It was only a mild earthquake, which Tawfik surmised was better than bombs.

Entering the fifty-eighth day of his hospitalization, Tawfik's condition had not improved. That day he got a visit from Dr. Mohammad Sharif, the medical director of UNRWA, who referred Tawfik to a friend of his in Britain.

"Sir Eric Riches is one of the best urologists in the world and is a former classmate of mine," Dr. Sharif told Tawfik. "I will introduce you to him."

So much importance was riding on the trip that Tawfik did not realize that security agents at the Beirut Airport had forgotten to return his international immunization certificate to him. There had been an outbreak of smallpox in England in 1962 that had been brought in by a Pakistani child, and medical authorities were still concerned about the arrival of potential carriers.

When a nurse at the health station at Heathrow Airport in London asked for his papers, Tawfik realized his mistake. "I reached in my pocket to take it out but realized the certificate was not with my passport," he says. "I told her I was a physician and had been vaccinated."

Tawfik offered to reveal the scar on his arm produced by the shot. But the nurse responded, "Sir, if Her Majesty the Queen comes here without a certificate, she either goes into quarantine for two weeks or gets the immunization." Knowing his appointment with Sir Eric Riches, the inventor of the Riches cystoscope, was only three days away, Tawfik got the shot.

In what could be loosely described as a miracle, the opening in Tawfik's bladder mysteriously dried up and closed before he could keep his appointment. "The day I went to see Sir Riches, he said, 'What's the problem?' I told him what had happened, and he said, 'Well, there's no problem now.' On the way out, his nurse told me that he would not charge me for the visit. But I donated twenty-five pounds (equivalent to about $150 at that time) to his favorite charity."

Although he was free of his stone, Tawfik realized that as a Palestinian who had chosen the field of medicine, there would always be complications, challenges, problems, you name it. He also knew that he had been given a second chance in life and that he should not waste it.

His decision came with a set of risks. Siham, Salam, and his parents were still living in Amman. To complicate matters, Siham was six months pregnant with their second child. Then, there was his position with UNRWA as well as his private practice.

To Tawfik, the complications did not outweigh his belief that the environment in Jordan – from the politics to the practice of medicine – had made it difficult for him to see a future for his family there. His time at the hospital in Beirut had also convinced him that he wanted to enroll at the School of Public Health at American University in Beirut with a specialty in pediatrics. It was an intensive two-year program that would require additional sacrifices on everyone's part, especially Siham, who had not exactly been dawdling the whole time Tawfik was battling his kidney stone.

Once Tawfik explained his vision for the future, she knew there would be no changing his mind. Another thing became clear to her, too: Her husband was driven by a dry-mouth thirst for knowledge and a passion for medicine, and nothing could change that – not a kidney stone, not the Zionist movement, not the eviction from his homeland, nor a split between Arabs, not even marriage and children.

How she chose to "adjust and accept the situation" may not have been as painful as passing a kidney stone, but it was hard. Then again, it was not as hard as delivering a baby in the middle of a hot war and a no-crying zone where she alone had a life-and-death decision to make and somehow got it right while holding her three-day-old baby in her arms.

If Tawfik was born to heal others, Siham was made to serve others because that is how she spent her time waiting for Tawfik's kidney stone to pass and for all the other challenges that were yet to come. Her first child was only nine months old, and she was already six months pregnant when Tawfik first entered the hospital in Beirut. Salam and Suha, their second child, are eleven months and three weeks apart in age.

"My part of the story of Tawfik's kidney stone is that I had a baby and was expecting again in a few months, and, when his recovery got delayed, I found myself riding back and forth from Beirut and Amman in a taxi filled with four or five strangers," she says. "When someone was traveling back and forth between Lebanon and Jordan at that time, you really had to think about whether Jordan would let you back in if you were a Palestinian."

Tawfik's decision to continue his education in Beirut also meant that Siham would deliver her second child, Suha, without Tawfik by her side as he had been visiting relatives in Kuwait. Compounding matters, her mother had remained home to protect her investment and tend her fields.

Suha means morning star in Arabic. They say that there is one big star in the morning shining between four-thirty and five o'clock, and you can look up and see it. It is the morning star that marks the fading of night and the coming of the new light of a new day.

Darkness to light. One of the overlooked tragedies associated with the breakup of a whole country was how it left entire families in the dark, as if they had been blindfolded and led in different directions, never to meet again. The tighter Israel locked down the country, the farther apart Palestinians grew. Twelve miles of separation might not sound like much, but it might as well have been an ocean since there was no way to get there without assuming great risks. It happened with Siham and her mother, whom she missed terribly.

Her mother came to see her new grandchild for the first month after Siham had Suha but then had to go back to make more olive oil and harvest the figs, grapes, almonds, and vegetables that she grew.

"Thinking back on it now, I ask myself, 'How did I do all of that?'" Siham asks. "But then I think, 'What choice did I have?' I'm married. I have a husband who is not feeling good. And when he is gone, I don't have enough financial support to take care of myself and my babies. So, there is no other choice. I have to be there to support him and to make it work for my family. That is all I had. I do not think I have even ever complained about what I was going through. This is the way it was going to be until we could say we are fine.

"But meanwhile, I have hope in the future that something is going to evolve, and my life is going to be different. What helped me is that I'm not a person who acts out of emotion. Even when I am very upset about something, or I don't know how to feel, I don't go and act based on how I feel at that moment. So, I suffered for a long time without any support.

"When I think about it, I realize that's part of me. I am not bragging about myself maybe until now. We have family overseas, his sister, my best friend who calls me almost twice a week. She says, 'You work too hard. You work too much; just slow down, take care of yourself. You've been sick.' And I say, 'What's going to happen if I sit down? I have too many responsibilities.' To carry this responsibility wherever I need to go is a part of me. And I'm determined."

Tawfik faced his own sort of separation anxiety because severing ties with UNRWA was not painless. In an attempt to hold on to him, agency officials floated the possibility of transferring him to Gaza, but the potential offer was countermanded by Israeli authorities, probably because of his association with and his previous actions in support of the Arab nationalist movement.

In September 1971 Tawfik was back in the classroom sixteen years after he took the airplane from Jerusalem to Cairo to study medicine. As was the case then, he had no regrets. He did not know if this new path would lead him back to Jordan, but he knew that he did not want to remain in Lebanon. The answer would come in time.

Tawfik found an apartment in Beirut on Al-Hamra Street near the Mediterranean Sea and was soon joined by Siham and their two daughters. He had already taken a huge risk by quitting his job and turning his private practice over to another physician. Now, he was about to begin a two-year program with limited financial assistance from the university.

As part of his pediatrics residency, he worked in the poor and crowded neighborhoods of Beirut (Mareyagi) and the city of Sidon in 1972 and 1973. At Mareyagi, his interest in numbers expanded to "three" as in the triplets who fell under his care after their mother insisted on delivering at home rather than at the hospital. "We had a midwife there, and I was there when she delivered them," he says. "The little one was so small we suggested that we will take him and admit him to the NICU (newborn intensive-care unit) at the hospital. But the mother said, 'No, I can bring him every day to your clinic, but I will not admit him because if I admit him, he will die.'

"So, she used to come every day to the clinic for me to take care of him. The baby developed a hernia and, fortunately, we had a pediatric surgeon at that time who gave him ketamine and did a hernia repair. No one did it before in a premature baby. He said he wanted to operate out of fear the baby would die because his mother was refusing to admit him to the hospital. He did the surgery, and she took him home."

As enchanting as Beirut was in those days, this was no vacation for either Tawfik or Siham. "After the war (Black September), you've got to do something," he says. "You had to make a decision, and you didn't have a lot of time to think about it. So, I had to just be assertive and do it."

Likewise for Siham. "He was studying all the time being in school all day long, and just coming home in the evening to study some more. Then he would wake up, go to school all over again," she says. "I was doing everything else."

It appears the rocky road is the one road Tawfik knows by heart. "You see, all these experiences gave us more ability to adapt to the situation and make the right decision at the proper time," he explains.

But what if circumstances had been different? What if that one kidney stone had not come along when it did? Would the road have led to Beirut and on to London and back to Beirut to further his education? What would their lives be like today?

Tawfik is quick to reply: "I would have stayed in Amman, kept on working, and made the best of it. I would not have come to the United States."

"That is why sometimes when we say everything happens for a reason even though the reason is not understood at the time," Siham adds. "Later on, when the consequences have been determined, when whatever happens finally happens, then you often say, 'We are thankful.'"

Tawfik still bears three scars from the two operations to remove the kidney stone. "The first time, the surgeon removed the stone. When the opening did not close, he had to open me up and find out what was going on. He said he could not find anything, so he closed me back up. When I came to the United States, I had another surgery, but I did not have the complications I had before."

For centuries, immigrants from all over the world have sought the freedom America affords by any means possible. Few have come by way of a kidney stone.

CHAPTER 20

INTO THE KINGDOM

When our community is in a state of peace, it can share that peace with neighboring communities, and so on. When we feel love and kindness towards others, it not only makes others feel loved and cared for, but it helps us also to develop inner happiness and peace.

— DALAI LAMA

While few geologists shared his opinion, American Max Steinke, one of nine children of German immigrants, was convinced there was oil under the sands of Saudi Arabia. Who knows where the world would be now if he had been wrong? How would the economy and the environment be different? Would the United States have supported Israel as vigorously as it has? Would the Middle East have found real peace?

What is known is that Tawfik Ramadan would not have made it to America by way of Al-Maliha, Beit Jala, Bethlehem, Cairo, Jericho, Karameh, Amman, Beirut, Abqaiq, and Dhahran or any other way. The discovery of oil changed the world, including the world of Tawfik and Siham Ramadan.

To us gas guzzlers, oil seems to spew out of the ground and into the pump, so how complicated of a topic can that be, you might ask? Well, the story of how oil was discovered in the sands of the Arabian Desert and how Tawfik and Siham wound up in the middle of an oil field is not a simple matter.

The first chapter was authored by Abdulaziz bin Abdul Rahman Al-Saud, an Arab tribal, political, and religious leader who founded Saudi Arabia and served as its first king from 1932 until his death in 1953. He had ruled parts of the kingdom since 1902, and with his conquest of the provinces of Riyadh, al-Hasa, Nejd, and Hijaz, Ibn Saud brought stability to the region, which incentivized the search for oil.

In 1937 Steinke captured the gusher of all gushers, altering the fate of the world and signifying that the U.S. would have a looming presence in the Middle East for as long as its own national interests remained at stake. The chief geologist at California-Arabian Standard Oil Co. (CASOC),

Steinke overcame repeated setbacks and skeptics until the well known as "Dammam No. 7" filled the sky with oil in March 1938.

Previously, the consensus was there was little oil to be found in the Arabian Peninsula, although some oil had been discovered in northwestern Persia (Iran) in 1908. The prospects of a new discovery were bolstered in 1933 when Saudi Arabia granted a concession to Standard Oil of California (SOCAL). The arrangement led to the formation of the California Arabian Standard Oil Company (CASCO), whose name was changed to the Arabian American Oil Company (Aramco) in 1944.

A geological formation named the "Dammam Dome" in the eastern province of Al-Ahsa was the first target of CASCO and was investigated in 1933 and again in 1935 without success. But Steinke, who was appointed chief geologist in 1936, urged the drilling of "deep tests" in order to explore the porous limestone "Arab Zone" underlying impervious anhydrite. It was a costly and accident-prone undertaking. With the home office in California threatening to pull the plug, Steinke urged patience. On March 3, 1938, Dammam No. 7 struck oil in a big way at a depth of 4,700 feet and was producing to the tune of 3,000 barrels per day by the end of March. Two years later, the Dammam field delivered more than 12,000 barrels a day, and the political and social dynamics in the Middle East would be forever changed, as would life for the Ramadan family.

From 1973 to 1976, Tawfik was employed as a physician for Saudi Aramco, where he and Siham witnessed perhaps the most exhilarating and lavish times in the history of oil production, led by Saudi Arabia. Another war and the assassination of a Saudi king got thrown in for good measure because war seemed to be the one constant in Tawfik's life. As if additional drama was required, Siham seemed to always be giving birth to another baby girl, with the chaos mounting alongside every contraction.

This time it all began in Beirut.

Graduate school came easy for Tawfik, but supporting a wife and two children with one more on the way, plus his parents and relatives, was becoming impossible. For the first time, Tawfik could not simply outthink or outwork a problem. Their savings were exhausted, and school was demanding all of his time.

"When he first started school, we had a little bit of savings, so that took care of us almost for the whole year," Siham says. "But by the end of the year, we were running low. And then, during that time, I again was expecting with our third daughter, Shadin. She was born in Beirut on March 11, 1973, so at the beginning of that year, we were about to have another child."

The good news was Tawfik was in the same country, even in the same hospital, when it was time for Siham to deliver. The bad news was he wasn't in the delivery room. "At that time, I was on call in the nursery in the NICU of the hospital, where quintuplets, five babies, had just been received," he says. "Siham was next door in their delivery room, and I was in the nursery and could not leave.

"Let me back up: Before that, when she would go to the obstetrician, he would say, 'I am going to get a baby boy for you.' At that time, no one really knew, because we did not have the ultrasound and all that stuff. I was in the nursery, and when Shadin was born, the obstetrician came out of the delivery room into the hallway and called me, and he said, 'I'm sorry, I didn't get you a boy, I got you a girl.'

"I said, 'Why should you be sorry? Is she normal and healthy?' He said, 'Yes.' I said, 'That's all what I want.' That day, another baby was born in the hospital with a Harlequin ichthyosis, a fatal syndrome wherein the baby has severely abnormal skin. In contrast, I have a normal healthy baby. What more could I ask for?"

The other good news was that Tawfik would soon complete his degree in public health and was on track to start his residency in pediatrics at American University in the fall. Unfortunately, that degree only marked the halfway point in his education. "And the well started to dry fast," Siham says. "There was no more money to continue. We were paying rent and utilities and everything else, taking care of the family. And we were really between the rock and the hard place."

It was so bad that the hospital refused to discharge Siham and Shadin until the bill was paid. As a last resort, Tawfik borrowed $400 from a friend he went to secondary school with in Bethlehem so the hospital would discharge her and the baby.

Three months later, recruiters from Aramco were at American University looking for physicians to work in a hospital setting at its rapidly expanding, ready-made city in the rich oil fields of the Saudi desert near the Persian Gulf. No discussion was required. With his degree in public health in hand, Tawfik got on a plane bound for Abqaiq, the Saudi Arabian gated community and oil-processing facilities located about thirty-seven miles southwest of Dhahran. In many ways, it was preparation for his next stop.

"When they interviewed me, they said come for three months to see whether you like us and we like you. So, I went as a bachelor without my family and lived in a portable (building) with three bachelors."

It was an interesting mix of personalities. There was Bill. He was Welsh. There was a Scot and an Englishman from London. Each had his own bedroom, but they spent a lot of time talking in the common area. Tawfik stood out as the only Arab in the room.

"They did not even understand each other, much less me. They taught me to play backgammon and got upset when I started to beat them. All of them were petroleum engineers, and then there was me. Also, there were very few Palestinians in the whole compound of maybe 5,000 people in the American compound."

While Tawfik was living a tame version of the bachelor life, Siham progressed with what was beginning to come naturally for her – she was expanding her role as the lioness. Predictably, she makes it sound simple: "I went back to Jordan while he went to Saudi Arabia. I went to my mom's and my parents-in-law. At the time I had three babies, and I bunked with them for three months."

Aramco's probationary period having proven mutually satisfactory, Tawfik returned to Beirut to transport Siham and his three daughters to what might be described as suburbia on a sand pile. There was one bump along the way. Another war broke out while they were flying from Beirut to Dhahran. The Yom Kippur War, Ramadan War, October War, or 1973 Arab–Israeli War (Israelis called it the "War Where Jews Were Surrounded" by enemies), erupted.

Upon landing in Saudi Arabia, Tawfik and Siham found themselves in the center of another battle where oil was the weapon and the world economy was the target. Arab members of the Organization of Petroleum Exporting Countries (OPEC) retaliated against the United States for its decision to resupply the Israeli military and to gain leverage in the postwar peace negotiations, cutting oil production and implementing an oil embargo against the U.S. and other countries that supported Israel.

The embargo quickly brought the U.S. transportation system and the economy to a crawl as gas prices shot up 400 percent overnight in October 1973, creating shockingly long lines of cars at gas pumps across the U.S. The oil embargo laid bare one of the foremost challenges confronting

U.S. policy in the Middle East: balancing the contradictory demands of unflinching support for Israel and the preservation of close ties to the Arab oil-producing monarchies.

Aside from foreign policy ramifications that are still playing out today, the OPEC embargo recast the American way of life for decades and spiked Arab resentment in the United States. Daylight savings time was put into effect year-round, the national speed limit was cut from seventy mph to fifty-five mph to increase fuel economy, automakers and architects began to rethink their designs, and future U.S. presidents began to seek energy independence. On a much smaller scale, Oregon turned off all hot water in state buildings, snowy Alaska only plowed half of the parking lots, and some towns banned Christmas lights as part of a "Don't be Fuelish" campaign. And without merit, all Arabs fell under the microscope of blame, much the way the Chinese were condemned for causing the spread of Covid-19.

For the time being, though, life in Abqaiq (where Tawfik and his family were housed for about eight months) and later in Dhahran, Aramco's premier residential facility, was as good as it could get for the Ramadans. Dhahran, for example, mimicked a Starbucks lifestyle years before there was a Starbucks. It was Disneyland under a heat lamp. It was mail-order Americana. It is probably where Amazon founder Jeff Bezos drew his inspiration to bring the world to your doorstep.

"When I walked into the American compound in October 1973, it was just like you're going into an American city planted in the middle of Saudi Arabia," Siham says. "The streets looked the way they do in America." But it was even cleaner, shinier, and safer than any American street.

The best part was that since Tawfik was hired as a pediatrician assigned to the outpatient clinic in Dhahran and was considered a senior employee, he was eligible to live in the American compound and benefit from its five-star accommodation. Their three-bedroom house could as easily have been part of the Los Angeles sprawl, circa the 1970s. "We had two big living areas, a big kitchen, utility room," Siham says. "Everything was beautiful . . . the trees, the green grass, everything. Plus, the utilities were provided. The water was running all the time, the lights, the same thing. Everything was provided for, and if we needed something else, we had a commissary in the compound."

The American compound even held a parade in which the Ramadan girls got to ride and a fireworks show on the Fourth of July. Christmas caroling and Easter egg hunts were the other ways the Americans could ward off their isolation and get a taste of "back home." For the Ramadans, it was a preview of America.

"From the beginning, I didn't see myself or us as being different, you know," Siham says. "It was a big change, but it also allowed us to get into a normal life, a life with normal family stuff. We were with engineers and physicians, and the economical level was high. Again, he started making money, enough to send some to his family." The family living next door to Tawfik and Siham in Abqaiq were Americans. Sue showed up early on with a small tray of cookies, and Siham invited her in for tea. "Here we were all thrown in with each other. After that first meeting, Sue and I would be talking to each other every day and our kids would be playing together. I would go to her house sometimes with something I had cooked that I thought they might find interesting. That was our cultural exchange."

Siham says she was ultimately drawn to the openness and acceptance of the American people who, unlike those groomed for the Arab world, did not immediately eyeball her to see where she was from or how she dressed or whether she was adequately preserving the dignity of her family in public. If she stepped outside in a long dress, one that might resemble a house dress, none of her neighbors gave it a second thought. No one questioned her religion or her accent.

"We started having friends and socializing, and in the second year, Tawfik got transferred from Abqaiq to the Dhahran compound, which was a much bigger American camp and where the Aramco administration was headquartered. That was at the beginning of 1975. Then life got even better: we had some savings, and we were doing well. My oldest daughter at the time had recently turned five and had just started going to kindergarten, an American school, at the Dhahran compound."

For Tawfik, there were no malnutrition cases, although there was some suspense associated with occasionally having to treat members of the Saudi royal family in Dhahran. And when he was in Abqaiq, there was the time when the nearby oil fields erupted in flames with the drop of a wrench.

"That resulted in a fire that I still remember," he says. "There were people welding those big pipes, and apparently a spark flew and caused a fire. We could see that it was about 300 feet high. And the people who were in that area within three miles were completely charred. I know because they brought in some of the remains for us to identify. I remember one guy ... we identified him from his belt. We could not find anything else."

In spite of all he had seen and done, Tawfik was not immune to being impressed, and it was not long before three men of stature won his admiration. One was Frank Jungers, who oversaw momentous growth as chairman of the board and CEO of Aramco from 1973 to 1978. The second was King Faisal, a staunch ally of the Palestinians. And the third was Saudi geologist Ali Al-Naimi, who became the first Saudi president of Aramco and chief executive officer and later minister of petroleum and mineral resources.

Although he did not personally know them, Tawfik admired the first two for their vision. As for Al-Naimi, before he became somebody, he and his wife were the Ramadans' neighbors in Abqaiq when Al-Naimi was still a geologist. "About a dozen doctors and engineers and their wives would take turns hosting the group on the weekend, where the food and conversation was wide-ranging," Siham says. "We knew he would ultimately be high up in the company, but he and his wife were very polite and humble around us."

Jungers in many ways paved the way for Al-Naimi's advancement by initiating the construction of the Saudi Master Gas System, the consolidation of eastern Saudi Arabia's electric power grid, and the Saudization of the company workforce while ensuring that American shareholders profited.

"I remember when we first flew into Dhahran in the airplane you could see the whole desert lit up in flames (at oil extraction sites, flares are used to dispose of large amounts of unwanted associated petroleum gas, such as CO_2). Jungers was a patient man who made calculations that you could extract the sulfur from the gas burned from the oil, liquify it, and use it for other purposes."

Jungers held what *Fortune* magazine called "one of the most delicate positions in all industry." Known as an innovator, he became fluent in Arabic in order to better communicate with his Saudi workforce and establish the importance of developing shared values.

Jungers's achievements were directly tied to the special relationship he formed with King Faisal, who, according to Jungers, was very cognizant of Saudi Arabia's role in the Islamic world and in the Arab world. The plight of the Palestinians was chief among the concerns he expressed to Jungers, who described it this way:

> "He was a very gentle man; he was a quiet man, taciturn, sincere. But when it came to this issue, the Palestinian issue, he had very strong feelings," Jungers said in a 2003 interview recorded with PBS. "One time he got me in and lectured me a long time on this, and he finally said, 'I'm going to have to tell you, you're simply not doing enough. And I'm serious about this. And somehow Aramco has got to establish in the United States more of a clout to get this message across, the message that Palestinians have the right and that the Israelis were overstepping all of the agreements that were made in the United Nations and that we should do something about this to advise the American public of this injustice and of the unbalanced political movement in the United States.'"

Under pressure from King Faisal, a number of major American corporations issued statements that Palestinians had certain rights to the land that were recognized by the United Nations. "In fact, Standard Oil of California had riots outside their office building in San Francisco because the head of Chevron at the time did make some statements," Jungers said.

Jungers's attempts to shift support to the Palestinians did little to alter the narrative that Israel was in the right while oil-rich Arab countries were exploiting American consumers with their oil boycotts.

The 1975 assassination of King Faisal bin Abdulaziz Al-Saud at the hands of a vengeful nephew rocked the Middle East and hurt Tawfik deeply.

"Those who came after Faisal don't look at Palestine and Jerusalem the way Faisal did," Tawfik says. "Why Palestine? There was a religious reason for that, and it's what we call Jerusalem. The Qur'an tells us, and we believe that the Prophet Mohammad traveled to Jerusalem from Mecca and that he ascended to Heaven and prayed with all the prophets. And that night he went back to Mecca. He told everybody about what he saw, the other prophets, so Jerusalem was the first holy place for Muslims. Wherever you prayed in the world, you had to face Jerusalem. After so many years, it changed to Mecca. King Faisal had made statements that Jerusalem had to remain Palestinian and that he was committed to it."

It is not known whether one event was linked to the other, but Tawfik's future with Aramco took a different turn after Faisal's death as, once again, the past foretold the future.

The story follows the pattern Tawfik and Siham laid out for themselves all their lives – nose to the grindstone with him working long hours at the clinic and her raising the children. Their efforts always seemed to get acknowledged everywhere they went.

This time Dr. Jim Rhea, a physician from Atlanta, Georgia, and head of the department of pediatrics at the Aramco hospital in Dhahran, was the one who took notice. Rhea and his wife, Ann, were a special couple. On the Fourth of July in the compound, Dr. Rhea would wear a chauffeur's suit and cap and crank up the engine of the 1934 Rolls Royce. Ann would put on her countess's dress, sit in the back seat, and wave to the crowd as the Rolls paraded through the streets of the compound.

"How could you not like them?" Siham acknowledges. The feeling was mutual. Dr. Rhea was impressed with Tawfik's skills and how hard he worked. And it bothered him that Tawfik was only getting paid a fifth of what he earned (Tawfik got paid in Saudi riyals; Rhea in dollars).

One day Dr. Rhea approached Tawfik with an idea: "We need a neonatologist in the department of pediatrics. If we help you go to the United States to finish your residency in pediatrics and do a fellowship in neonatology, and then if you come back here in three years, you will be in a much better position. You'll be on the American payroll for a specialty and subspecialty."

It seemed like a great idea for all concerned. All Tawfik would need was a security clearance, and Dr. Rhea told him he would take care of that requirement. The details of the plan called for Aramco to sponsor Tawfik's enrollment in a pediatrics residency program at the University of Oklahoma Health Sciences Center in Oklahoma City, Oklahoma.

"We got very excited, and it came down to the point where we had to decide whether Tawfik should leave by himself or if we should leave as a family," Siham says. "We decided to go as a family after I said I was not going to wait in Saudi Arabia. We were going across the sea. This was forty to fifty years ago, and America seemed so far away, not like now."

Two weeks before they were due to depart, Dr. Rhea called Tawfik into his office. He was in tears and stumbling over his words. Finally, the purpose of the meeting became clear: Aramco had decided to drop its sponsorship of Tawfik's journey to America.

"Even if you go on your own and finish your specialty training, your position here will not be waiting for you," Dr. Rhea said. "You will be on your own."

"Why? Maybe because I am Palestinian." Tawfik said to himself.

There could be no other answer because Tawfik had passed the Educational Commission for Foreign Medical Graduates and apparently had the full support of Aramco officials, including the whole pediatrics department.

Tawfik believes the signs were there all along. "There was a third compound at Aramco where there was a refinery," he says. "One time an Indian pediatrician got sick, and they wanted someone to relieve him. So, they told Dr. Mona Mange, who was a pediatrician born in Jerusalem and a U.S. citizen married to an American, to go. When she got to the main gate at the refinery at Ras Tanura, the security guard said, 'Sorry, Dr. Mange, you are not allowed. You were born in Palestine. You cannot come to Ras Tanura.' So, she made the two-hour drive back."

To determine whether a Palestinian would likely be hired for an equivalent job in Saudi Arabia, Tawfik conducted his own experiment. After reading about an opening for a pediatrician on a military base in western Saudi Arabia, he called pretending to be interested in the position. He got a call back asking for a copy of his CV (curriculum vitae), a vita that would show Tawfik was born in Palestine. "After that, I never heard from them. I kept calling, but each time whoever answered the phone would say the person I had talked to was busy."

Tawfik's career was unraveling, but, predictably, he kept his composure. He submitted his resignation and thanked Dr. Rhea for his efforts. After all, they were like family.

By that point, Tawfik and Siham had sold everything they owned and had bought their tickets to Oklahoma City. Nothing was going to stop them.

CHAPTER 21

THE ULTIMATE TEST OF DETERMINATION

You cannot hope to build a better world without improving the individuals. To that end, each of us must work for his own improvement, and at the same time share a general responsibility for all humanity, our particular duty being to aid those to whom we think we can be most useful.

— MARIE CURIE

It is true that Palestinians want to go back to where they came from. So, how can it also be true that when their mind is set on something there is no turning back?

There's another way to look at it: Why would Tawfik and Siham want to cross an ocean without a life raft?

"Let me tell you why we did that," Tawfik says. He recounts a story about an important leader in Arab history named Tariq ibn Ziyad (after whom Gibraltar is named) who in 711 CE crossed the strait from northern Africa with his army of about 7,000 and embarked on the conquest of Hispania, establishing the foundation for a kingdom that lasted nearly a millennium. Facing an army of 100,000 upon landing, he ordered his army's own ships to be burned. In a speech to his men before the battle of Guadalete, Tariq explained why he had eliminated failure as an option:

> "Oh, my warriors, where could you flee? Behind you is the sea, before you, the enemy. You have left now with only the hope of your courage and your constancy."

Tawfik took it to mean if Tariq's army could not retreat, neither would he and Siham. Someone in charge at Aramco had burned all of Tawfik's bridges to the United States and back, but he preferred to look at the situation the way Tariq spelled it out to his men: There was only one direction to go, and that was forward. Sort of like how Palestinians continue living in refugee camps because they believe that is the only way back home.

If nothing else, Palestinians believe they have no choice but to stay the course. The Israeli government can cut off their electricity, detain and imprison them, confiscate their homes, and basically imprison them, but it will not stop them. "Quitting is not in our lexicon," he says. "We are a people with great determination."

But this time there was no fleet of boats, only a single airplane carrying Tawfik and Siham and their three daughters. They touched down in Oklahoma City, Oklahoma, about nine o'clock on a Thursday evening. Tawfik and Siham were carrying their green cards, some cash, and the opportunity to undertake a residency in pediatrics at the University of Oklahoma Health Sciences Center.

It was July 29, 1976, and already this Palestinian couple had their backs against the wall.

At least someone was there to greet them: Dr. Khader Hussein and his wife, Cecilia. The Ramadans had never met them, but the Husseins treated them like close friends on the basis that they had a mutual friend in Dr. Mohammad Ahmad, an Aramco pediatrician who helped Tawfik get the OU contract.

"Actually, they picked us up as a family of six because I was pregnant with my fourth daughter, Raniyah," Siham says. "And they brought us to this very nice apartment they had rented for us in northwest Oklahoma City and dropped us off. It had three bedrooms, with a living area and a dinette and a kitchen. She had rented furniture. The beds were made. The kitchen had groceries. Cecilia had even cooked a meal for us that evening. We will be thankful to the Husseins for the rest of our lives."

The next morning, Dr. Hussein drove Tawfik to an auto dealership where he plunked down $6,000 in cash for a new Chevrolet station wagon. His next purchase was a console television. Again, he paid cash.

"A few weeks later, I went to see a banker who told me I should have come to him for a loan," Tawfik says. "I did not understand what he was talking about because I had not heard of such a thing."

With his own car to drive, Tawfik told Siham that he would follow Dr. Hussein to work on Monday and after that would be on his own. This meant it was officially Monday Morning in America.

Tawfik had a successful first day at the office. He got where he was supposed to go on time, met the people he needed to meet, worked all day, and found his way home that night.

Siham had a different kind of "first day." "When Tawfik left and that door shut behind him, it felt like I was in Beirut again," she says. "I had to struggle to adapt, and two months later I had another baby."

Two weeks after landing in Oklahoma, Siham was feeling the weight of the world – a faraway world. She needed a car to take the girls to school, but she did not know how to drive one. Siham had studied English since the fifth grade but feared she would be mocked by Americans when she spoke, and she worried that Salam and Suha might fall behind in school because of it. "Salam learned her ABCs, numbers, and all that in kindergarten in Dhahran, but she had never learned how to speak English well."

A problem solver, she found a solution to the transportation problem, but it was tricky: "I walked the older girls and left my third daughter at home. We had a big window in the living room, and I would open the curtains and make her watch the kids playing outside. While she did, I told her that she was not to leave there until I came back. The walk to school took about fifteen minutes. Shadin never left her position at the window until I came back through the door."

Nothing was easy during her first year in America. Until Siham learned to drive, she could not even go to the grocery store without her chauffeur, Tawfik. The problem with that was he was hardly ever home. His work monopolized almost every waking hour, even on the weekends. As a result, he left early, came home late, and was always tired. Often, he would sit at the kitchen table, put his head down, and say, "Do you have something for me to eat or do I need to go to bed?" It was a rhetorical question because Siham always had food prepared for him.

One Saturday morning, Tawfik and Siham and their three daughters were picking out fruit in the produce section of the nearby Skaggs Albertson grocery store, when good fortune was there for the picking. Shadin was standing beside her mother. Her hair was curly, and she had on a green dress with white polka dots.

"All of a sudden, I see this lady with beautiful red hair and designer clothes," Siham says. "She had a daughter standing beside her. She picks Shadin up in her arms and is looking and talking to her. She had this happy face, and we started talking. We found out her daughter's name, what her husband does. We probably stood there talking for fifteen minutes."

Siham did not know until later that Shadin had stuck out her tongue at the woman, who then could not resist the child. The woman had a German accent and spoke with confidence. She told Siham to head to the checkout line and that she was going to take her home with her after

Siham had packed her groceries.

The Ramadans followed her home to what seemed like paradise. "She had a beautiful house. Shiny, clean, and a pond to go with it," Siham recalls. "Her husband was home, and they prepared all kinds of food and tea and we had a good time. After that she became like a sister to me. She was like an angel from the sky who came to save us."

Ursula Sklatz knew what it was like to feel like an outsider, having moved to the U.S. from Germany twelve years earlier. "I could tell she was having a hard time," Ursula says of her first encounter with Siham. "I asked her where she was from, and she said she had just arrived from overseas. We instantly talked woman to woman, mom to mom. She apologized for Shadin. I said no apology was needed, and, from that moment, we became friends forever."

Ursula had been in Siham's shoes – stuck without transportation and without a friend. "My instincts told me that this was my family right here," said Ursula. "Our different cultures had nothing to do with it. We are all human beings, and we should love each other and try to understand one another."

For the next year, Ursula would often take Siham to the store and drive the girls to school. She even taught Siham how to drive a car and coached her on how to get a driver's license.

Siham said that her chance meeting with Ursula in the produce section demonstrates how life is full of opportunity because forty years later Siham was on the other end of a similar chance meeting.

"I'm known for going to Walmart and pushing one basket and pulling another one through the store because of the big family we have," says Siham. "When I get to the cashiers, most of the time they are teenagers, and I start a conversation with them. One day I noticed this young lady, who's Nigerian, I think, and had an accent. I have an accent so that brought us together. I asked her what brought her here and was she going to school."

"Yes, I'm going to ECU (East Central University) and want to be a nurse, but I still don't speak English very well, and I'm having difficulties because I'm not smart enough to be a nurse," she said.

Siham interrupted her: "My dear, it's going to be your will. If there is a will, there's a way. If you want to be a nurse, don't listen to anybody. Don't let anybody put you down. You are not less than the others who are nurses or doctors. If that is what you want to do, it will happen."

The young Nigerian student took the words to heart, and her mind followed in turn. She remained in school, and Siham continued to mentor her: "I got her phone number. She would call me at certain times for certain things she had in mind. I kept encouraging her. Anyway, she went to nursing school and got involved in social work. She later got married and had a daughter, whom she brought to Tawfik's office."

Similarly, Tawfik put into practice what Siham preached. After logging sixty to seventy hours during the week, he moonlighted every weekend for below-average wages as an emergency room doctor at hospitals to earn extra money. He would pull out of the parking lot after making evening rounds at the Children's Hospital in Oklahoma City on a Friday, drive straight to Ponca City, work that night and around the clock Saturday and Sunday, before driving back to Oklahoma City in time to make rounds at seven a.m. on Monday.

"One time I was supposed to go to Ponca City but knew I couldn't make it on time," Tawfik says. "So, I was driving fast when a police officer stopped me and asked for my license. I told him I knew I was speeding but that I had to be in the emergency room at Ponca City because the other doctor was leaving and that there would be no one else to see the patients. He said, 'Okay, follow me.' Maybe he wanted to make sure I was going to the hospital. So, I followed him, and, you know, he still gave me a ticket. But when I called the judge and told him the story, he said, 'Don't worry, I'm going to wipe it out for you.'"

Two years into his residency, survival was still the name of the game, particularly since he had another two years to go. But Tawfik had a plan circulating in his head, no matter how far-fetched it seemed to others.

That is how Ada, Oklahoma, a conservative Christian town in the Bible belt and the headquarters for the Chickasaw Nation, became an unlikely landing spot for a rapidly growing Muslim family. No one was more surprised than Siham, who, after two years' time, was just becoming comfortable with her family's new life in Oklahoma City and maintained hope of one day returning to Jordan, if not Palestine. And if not Jordan or Palestine, then perhaps to New York City or Detroit or Los Angeles, where Muslims were not an oddity or perceived threat.

But in keeping with his mission to prioritize his patients' needs, Tawfik determined the children of Ada and southeastern Oklahoma needed him more than, maybe, anyone else in Oklahoma or the world, for that matter. To Tawfik, nothing was more important than the life of a child. Ada offered the potential for him to play a vital role in that life-saving process.

The NICU is a special area in a hospital where newborn babies in need of intensive medical care are often placed. Because few Oklahoma hospitals in 1979 had either the staff or the technology to adequately care for premature babies who were not only sick but also required specialized care, they had to be moved to larger hospitals in metropolitan areas, which could jeopardize their care.

It was a long shot, but Dr. Owen Renerett, chief of the pediatrics department at OU Children's Hospital, thought Ada needed both a pediatrician and a Level II NICU and that Tawfik Ramadan, who was entering the research and laboratory phase of his neonatology fellowship at OU, was the right candidate to open one. "After realizing that 6 percent of our admissions came from Ada, Dr. Renerett surmised that there was a problem there and that we needed to go there and open a Level II unit, which he wanted me to do as part of my fellowship," Tawfik says. Really, he had been preparing for this moment almost his entire life.

"In the Middle East, 50 percent of the population were children, which meant most of the patients were children," he says. "So, when I later went to Beirut and to the school of public health, I combined public health and pediatrics. I have always observed the difference between adults and children as patients. Children are honest. They get sick fast, and they improve fast." Tawfik, as it turned out, admires honesty and is results-oriented.

Dr. Ramadan likes to tell a story about the old man who comes to see the doctor and tells the doctor the medicine he gave him isn't working. The doctor steps away, looks at the man's medical chart, and discovers it has been ten years since his last visit. Little wonder the man was having problems.

"I was making rounds one day with Dr. Jim Rhea, who was chief of pediatrics at Aramco, and we were looking around when he said, 'Look at any one of those smiles. It means they are ready to go home.' He was a wise man because it is true that a child who is sick never smiles."

It's also true that Dr. Ramadan doesn't like to play God. "We should do our jobs as physicians, as doctors, as healthcare providers, and then hope for the best outcome," he says. "We should not talk about life and death here. That is not our duty, whether you believe or you don't believe."

To Dr. Ramadan, "doing his job" means taking the extra step, then another, and then another. "I will tell you about such a case involving an obstetrician in Ada and a lady who was in labor," he says. "Suddenly, they lost the heartbeat of the baby, so, they rushed her to get a C-section. They called me and I came immediately, but the anesthesiologist was late. So, we were in the operating room and Dr. John Siegle told the lady her baby was going to die unless he did the C-section with local anesthesia that would only numb her skin. She asked me what to do and I said, 'Do it,' and she said, 'Yes.' Then Dr. Siegle said, 'Dr. Ramadan is here and we will take care of the baby.' And in less than seven minutes, the baby was out, but he still had no heartbeat and was not breathing. But we worked with the baby – we put a tube down his windpipe, and we breathed for him. We gave him oxygen and put him on a respirator until he began to breathe on his own.

"And that lady never complained about the pain, which must have been enormous because Dr. Siegle had to cut through her abdominal wall and open the uterus before delivering her baby. She and Dr. Siegle were amazing, and I went home feeling I had done my job."

At the time, Ada had no clue what it would be like to get a Palestinian pediatrician with big ideas about transforming low-weight babies into healthy babies. The town also did not fathom how fortunate it was to find another pediatrician as dedicated to his patients as Dr. George Stephens.

"One day after I came to Ada, Dr. Stephens said he could now take a vacation and visit his brother, who was a retired internist in California," Tawfik recalls. "When he cut his vacation short, I asked him why. He told me that he could not tolerate sitting around with his brother watching TV and eating. He said, 'My hobby is to sit next to my phone and receive a call from a lady with a sick baby at two o'clock in the morning and then go to meet her at the emergency room to take care of her baby.'"

Several years later, Dr. Stephens was responding to one of those late-night calls with his wife alongside him when they were involved in a head-on collision. Upon impact, his wife threw herself on her husband to protect him. She died, but he lived to save more lives.

In similar fashion, Tawfik's contributions to the greater good have not been lost on Siham, who learned to practice the art of saving the day so her husband could be there for his next patient. Their decision to relocate to Ada, Oklahoma, meant Siham would be starting all over again for at least the fifth time (yes, she was expecting her fifth child, Deemah, at that point) in a place not exactly of her choosing.

"We moved to the United States on July 29, 1976," she says. "We moved three years later to Ada. So that means between July 1976 and July 1979 he spent two years finishing his residency in pediatrics and starting his fellowship in neonatology. So, meanwhile, the idea of going to Ada was to establish the NICU there and to help our financial needs and serve our growing family. And again, the need was there.

"Regardless of whatever I thought, Tawfik was committed to the idea that that's where he was going to go and was excited about the need or what he could do there. So, the decision was made that we are going to move to Ada and that our growing family would start all over again."

Naturally, there was nothing left to do but pack up the station wagon and head for Ada, Oklahoma, about 90 miles from Oklahoma City and 6,800 miles from Jerusalem.

CHAPTER 22

FULFILLING THE PROMISE

> *"We will certainly test you with a touch of fear and famine and loss of property, life, and crops. Give good news to those who patiently endure who, when faced with a disaster, say, 'Surely to Allah we belong and to Him we shall return.' They are the ones who will receive Allah's blessings and mercy. And it is they who are rightly guided."* (QUR'AN 2:155–157)

> *"Have no fear of sudden disaster or of the ruin that overtakes the wicked, for the Lord will be your confidence and will keep your foot from being snared."* (PROVERBS 3:25–26)

> *"He who gives attention to the word will find good, and blessed is he who trusts in the Lord."* (PROVERBS 16:20)

Faith is practiced in many languages, denominations, and far-flung places. Perhaps it should not be all that surprising, then, that Ada, Oklahoma, was the scene almost forty-five years ago of one of the biggest leaps of faith.

Ada is one of those in-between dots on the map, hardly big enough to be considered urban but not so remote that any mysterious light in the sky is as likely to be a UFO as it is a stoplight. While the Chickasaw Nation made Ada its headquarters in 1975, the tribe did not wield the influence at the time to underwrite a fancy makeover of Main Street. Besides, what country singer Merle Haggard said about Muskogee in "Okie from Muskogee" could just as easily have been said about Ada. When all was said and done, the welcome wagon in a town far off Interstate 35 was simply not prepared to serve the needs of a Palestinian family that practiced Islam. Of course, when children are involved, no risk is too great, no price beyond the pale. And so it was when Tawfik and Siham Ramadan and the residents of a southeastern Oklahoma town almost blindly put their faith in one another in the summer of 1979. Today, both the Ramadans and the town have much to show for their commitment.

This miracle did not exactly play out in either a blaze of light or a gust of wind. There was no reassuring voice from On High guiding that packed station wagon full of kids and lots of doubt into the foothills of the Arbuckle Mountains. For one thing, Siham was still not as proficient in English as she would have liked. Although their new neighbors on the cul-de-sac greeted them warmly when they arrived, Siham dreaded the painful assimilation process she assumed her daughters would face in a town not used to having Muslims around.

But she hid her fears until some years later when Siham did open up to her oldest daughter, Salam, who was in high school and facing her own demons, about the sense of doom she felt. Even then, Siham laid her feelings bare in order to comfort her daughter.

"She said the day that we drove into downtown Ada she had all of us in the car with the car packed, and a moving truck behind us, and she just cried and cried driving through downtown," Salam says. "She said it was a ghost town. We had come from places that were, you know, densely populated with lots of life and bursting at the seams. Even though some of it was in wartime, there was lots of culture, lots of stuff going on. And then they drive into this place. It was something she had never seen before, this quiet town with small structures everywhere, with not a lot of people. And she said she had never felt so disheartened in her life, even in the face of everything else she had been through. She said that was her lowest point. But she kept at it and held all of her concerns about this new world we were entering inside of her in order to be strong for all of us.

"When she told me what she had been feeling, I looked at my mom and realized she was a person just like me. Like she had all these feelings, like she was hurting inside just like we hurt inside because I had always looked at her as such a figure of strength. Like nothing could hurt her, even when I would argue with her as a kid or as a teenager. But when my mom told me that story, suddenly everything changed about how I felt about her. From then on, I knew I could ask her anything."

What they discovered that day is that both of them initially felt lost in Ada.

If there is such a thing, Salam was the one child who was born with "displacement syndrome," something akin to PTSD. It is not a feeling strictly reserved for Palestinians bound to a refugee camp.

"I grew up in a time when who we were as Palestinians made us a controversial subject for people in the United States to deal with," Salam says. "Nobody here even knew what Palestine was, so we were ostracized, isolated, and censored. Because of the stories my parents had told me and having been born in Black September, in my head I felt like I was in a Hollywood movie. You must remember my mom was the rebel in slippers with me wrapped in her nightgown who ran out into the middle of war with soldiers saying, 'Ma'am, ma'am, there's land mines everywhere.' But she went anyway because she was not going to die in that hospital basement."

From there, Salam recalls snippets of her life in Amman, Beirut, and Saudi Arabia: the emptiness of the apartment in Beirut while her father remained hospitalized, her grandmother's tears and the words "Why do you have to go?" at the airport as her family departed for America, and of being a little girl in the United States where to be Palestinian was to be ostracized. Quizzical looks and suspicious glances seem to follow Palestinians everywhere they go in the States.

"I had to fight back with the knowledge that I have because I had lived there (the Middle East)," she says. But raw facts – the true story of how Palestinians were driven from their homeland – was no match for perception, and it was obvious that Salam looked and dressed differently than her classmates.

"I remember in Oklahoma City, I was sitting in class, in the first or second grade. We had just come from the Middle East, so I was wearing a long robe called a *dishdasha* that my mother had bought us before we left Saudi Arabia. I loved mine. It had a blue stripe, and I wore it to school that day. But this boy came over and he picked up my desk and turned it over and made fun of what I was wearing. And here I thought what I was wearing was so beautiful and so great. I could not understand what he was looking at, but I guess it was new to him. And then I remember on the playground, I was scared to go to recess because as soon as I went out, they would start saying salami, salami, salami, and then the boys would come and push me down. So, I always had my knees scraped up."

The pattern continued in high school. In English class, the students learned about adjectives by describing one another. It always seemed she was the only girl with dark eyes and black hair. Because she stood out, Salam felt all eyes were staring at her when she walked through the hallways at school.

The pressure to assimilate reached a breaking point when she walked into the band room one morning and saw that everyone had formed a circle. Standing in the center was Jay, the youth minister. Suddenly, one of her friends grabbed her and pushed Salam toward Jay.

"You know, your friends care about you," he says. "Your friends are worried about you. You know, you're going to hell if you don't accept Jesus into your heart."

"I was stunned, and I never felt free again until I got married and we were on the way to Jamaica on our honeymoon," Salam says.

Time brought some clarity and understanding. "I don't think that you can stop these things that happen," Salam says. "And I don't think I could have said anything to anyone to change the course of how this went down, because we were the same age and had those short years of experience in life. It was not their fault. I came from a different world."

Tawfik had spent a lifetime darting in and out of traffic, so to speak, to get to a safe place. Along the way, he learned that timing is everything and that he had to wait for the right time to cross a busy intersection.

For example, the pediatric ward and neonatal unit that Tawfik envisioned for Ada were not something he could simply pull behind him in a U-Haul trailer. While he had the support of OU administrators and the Ada medical community, the Oklahoma Department of Human Services questioned whether it was wise to create a Level II neonatal intensive-care unit outstate, and there also was competition from McAlester and Shawnee for Level II accreditation.

As eager as he was to fulfill a dream, the best way to succeed was for him to simply plow ahead and put his patients first. That's how he met his guardian angel, Marilyn Highland, who gave birth to a premature baby at Valley View Regional Hospital on Tawfik's watch.

Marilyn (who died June 11, 2021) was an assistant professor at East Central University whose son Tyrone was delivered prematurely at twenty-eight weeks and was not expected to live. "The baby was blue, barely breathing, when he was transferred to Children's Hospital in Oklahoma City," Tawfik says. "We (the transfer team) had to intubate the baby, put him on a respirator, and rush him to the neonatal unit. The baby had bleeding in his lungs, his head, and his gut, all the major complications of a premature baby."

At that time, CT scan technology was primitive compared to today, relying on a Polaroid camera as part of the procedure. The neurosurgeon evaluated the scan and said, "I don't think we need to do anything about it but let him pass." The entire medical team agreed it was time to discontinue life support.

Tawfik had made a connection with Marilyn, so the team asked him to deliver the bad news. "When I talked to the father (Rick Highland), he said Marilyn would not agree to do that. And that's what she told me when I talked to her. She said she would accept her son no matter what condition he was in."

When Tawfik reported back to the medical team, he sounded as adamant as Marilyn in fighting for the baby's life.

Tyrone is now about forty-seven years old. He has a slight deficiency but functions well. He has even traveled to China on his own.

To express her gratitude, Marilyn became the driving force behind Tawfik's dream, using her son's recovery to create community awareness of how premature babies could benefit from having specialized care. Whenever there was a civic club audience to win over or money to raise, Marilyn was there, much the way Ursula had been there for Siham after their chance encounter in the produce section.

Within two years, Ada was home to the first Level II NICU and pediatrics ward in that part of the state. There was plenty of credit to pass around, starting with Dr. Stephens, who encouraged Tawfik to consider Ada as a home, and Marilyn, whose power of persuasion was unmatched.

Tawfik obviously was the backbone of the effort, but his most important contributions were made out of the public eye and came long after the limelight had faded. For example, five days a week for almost a whole year, Tawfik was pulling triple duty to ensure that the nurses for the new neonatal unit had the proper training. That meant he would get up at four a.m., make rounds at the hospital before driving two nurses ninety miles each way to Oklahoma City for training, before returning to Ada in time for him that evening to make nightly rounds before ending up at home well after dark. Sometimes he went two or three days at a time without seeing his own children.

Once the Level II NICU and pediatrics ward became operational, he played a pivotal role in adding another essential service: "When I arrived in town, there was still no ambulance service other than the funeral home, which carried some patients," he says. "I took care of the kids for one of the City Council members, so one day I told him from a medical point of view that we should have better equipment and trained personnel.

Another physician, David Ramsey, was interested as well, and within a year we had an emergency medical service in the town."

Dr. Ramadan came to Ada to serve others. Going in, neither he nor Siham realized that Ada would repay them with the most meaningful gift imaginable – a place of higher learning. Outside of family, nothing is more important to the Ramadans than a good education, and East Central State University certainly obliged them on that front.

Founded as East Central State Normal School in 1909, East Central University now serves about 4,000 students and offers degrees in seventy programs. Among its graduates are two governors, Robert S. Kerr and George Nigh; Bill Anoatubby, the Chickasaw Nation governor; and Lyle Boren, former U.S. congressman from Oklahoma.

"One of the best things for us was having East Central University available," Siham says. "Education means a lot to us. That is the way we raised our kids, and we kept telling them and insisting that they make education their first choice and everything else second."

Dr. Gerald Williamson, a longtime administrator at ECU who came to Ada about the same time as the Ramadans, first ran into Dr. Ramadan in a downtown Ada men's clothing store. "It was either the winter of 1979 or 1980, and there was a gentleman trying on a camel hair topcoat, so he just stood out to me," Williamson says. "He had such a distinguished look, and he was so meticulous about trying on this coat. It wasn't just that he put it on, but you know, he tugged at it like you should. And he buttoned it. There was just something that stood out about the gentleman trying on that coat."

Every time Tawfik's children encounter Williamson, they have a good laugh about their father and his trademark coat. "I hear he still has it, and the kids think it's my fault he bought it."

The more Dr. Williamson became acquainted with the Palestinian couple, the more he realized that while appearances mattered to both, neither had any interest in putting on a show. "There are so many things that the Ramadans do that people don't know," he says. "They don't make an issue out of anything that they do and are never seeking the spotlight, whether it is the homeless shelter where they donated the building or the services they have provided to ECU."

It began almost forty years ago with Dr. Ramadan volunteering his time to conduct annual physical examinations for the school's football team. It expanded when Dr. Williamson approached Tawfik to see if he would take over as the pediatrician for student health services. Tawfik agreed. He received some compensation for his services, but his wages did not come close to covering the cost of the additional insurance he was required to purchase.

"That's just who Dr. Ramadan is," Williamson says.

While Tawfik was managing a private practice, overseeing the neonatal unit, and providing his services to ECU at no charge, Siham was shepherding the education of her children while "moonlighting" in her own way as a student who obtained both her undergraduate and master's degrees at ECU.

Siham was seven months pregnant with Deemah when she told Marilyn Highland, who was in charge of the speech and communication department, she wanted to enroll in college. "I think she looked at me with surprise given my condition, but I assured her I wanted to go back to school."

Siham's first class that semester started at nine a.m., which meant she had to get the four older girls ready for their school day and drop them off at the various schools they attended. When Deemah was born, Siham only took ten days before going back to class.

She eventually took on as many as three classes a semester, even after Mohammad, her sixth child, was born in 1982. "One day this lady whom I had known because her son and Mohammad were playing soccer together was going to the library at the university for something when she stopped and looked at me."

"What are you doing here?" she said to Siham.

"Well, I'm taking classes."

"How many kids do you have?"

"Six," Siham answered. The two women departed, and several months passed before they again met on campus and struck up a conversation.

"You know what?" the woman said.

"No," Siham answered, a bit curious.

"I'm like you now. I'm taking classes."

"What makes you do that?"

"Well, after that day we met, I went home and thought about it and said to myself, 'If Siham has six kids to take care of and can still go to school while I only have one young child, I should be able to go to school, too.'"

The woman eventually obtained her college degree and became a teacher. "Every time she sees me, she says, 'All this is because of you.'" The one person Siham looked to for inspiration was her mother. "She is my role model in life because she sacrificed her life for her children, and for her home," Siham says. "I think, more or less, I'm the same way. Every day I did everything I could to make things better for my family: clean the house, go shopping, go to the office, then come home from school every night and prepare a big meal. Then I tried to study at the end of the day."

Then there was Tawfik, whose dedication to medicine set another example for his children. "I tried to instill in them that the aim of life is not to build wealth or gain authority. Rather, it is about how much you can give to people to change their life positively, whether it is spiritual or financial."

Although Siham went on to get a bachelor's degree in business administration and a master's of science and psychological services degree, her focus never strayed from her children's performance in school. Every six weeks, for example, she would call the school to request a parent-teacher conference, first for Salam and then for her other siblings as they advanced. School officials would tell Siham that she and Tawfik were the only parents who didn't want to wait for the regularly scheduled parental appointments.

It was not until much later that Mohammad realized where all this attention on his parents' part would lead. "He was always wondering why the teachers were giving him more work when he was already the best one in class," Siham says. "Yes, we were telling the teachers to do that, but the teachers also did it because he was ready to be challenged."

In many ways, the Ramadans and Ada were like one of those arranged marriages once popular in Palestine, perhaps more akin to the mail-order bride category. Either way, both the family and the town grew closer over time. Or it could be said that the harder the Ramadans worked to adapt to their surroundings, the more Ada grew to appreciate them.

"I tell you, the first two years we moved to Ada we had very little money," Siham says. "We had to go to the bank every three or four months and try to get our credit extended so we could take care of our household and pay the staff. All the while, Tawfik was working very, very, very hard day and night, almost twenty-four hours a day."

Tawfik's elementary school teacher in Al-Maliha taught him an important lesson about life. "He said that life depends on how you look at it," Tawfik says. "He gave us the example of two prisoners sitting in a cell in jail. One looked down and saw the mud and dirt on the floor and looked sad. The other one looked up at the sky through a hole in the ceiling and saw the stars and the sky and felt happy. You can make the bitter lemon juice of life sweeter by adding one teaspoon of sugar," he said.

"We had to prove ourselves early on in Ada, and I welcomed the challenge for us to make a difference in the life of the whole area there. When the neonatal unit started functioning, we had a set of twins from Purcell and we had babies that came from Ardmore, from Tishomingo, from all the surrounding towns, to Ada. We served a large community; the hospital was supportive; the administrator of the hospital was supportive; everyone was supportive."

CHAPTER 23

THE CHALLENGES OF EXILE

Only the mind cannot be sent into exile.

— OVID

By 1982, things were beginning to fall in place for the Ramadans. They owned a home, had good neighbors, and their children were doing well in school.

Somewhere along the way, Tawfik had discovered the benefits of borrowing money. The trouble was it had to be repaid. "We had a good life, but it took a lot of money to live the way we did," Siham says.

They were living the American Dream by day. Yet they were tossing and turning with Palestine at night.

For one thing, Taha, Siham's oldest brother and father figure, had been ill for a while, and Siham constantly worried about him. Knowing how hard it was for her to move to the United States and how much she worried about Taha, her mother and other brother kept the news of his death from her until after he was buried. Even then, she had to practically coerce the news out of her brother in one of the few phone calls she could afford to make.

"When I asked about my brother on the phone, there was silence," Siham says. "It was clear to me something was wrong. Finally, he told me."

Her family feared that if Siham knew Taha was on his deathbed she would ache all the more knowing she did not have enough money to fly to his bedside and that she had too many babies at home to leave for any length of time.

The horns of Siham's dilemma would get sharper and sharper as she struggled to keep her balance. "We now had this big family that we wanted to raise," she says. "We wanted them to be educated, and we wanted to provide them all the good things in life. Even if I'm not there, I go through the suffering that those who are in Palestine or in the camps go through. I still take it to bed with me every night all these years later. We don't have our home, we don't have our families, and cannot be with them in the good times and the bad. This is not just my feeling."

Say what you will, the one trait the almost 15 million Palestinians in the world share is an overwhelming sense of place and only one place on Earth, a special place on which many of them have never set foot. It doesn't matter where they now live, how rich or poor they might be, how sick or how lucky they have it in life, they carry Palestine with them everywhere they go. Their ears are on constant alert about news from Palestine. Their eyes tear up with every new Jewish settlement that swallows a Palestinian neighborhood. They are never at peace, not even amid the splendor of a glorious sunset or the comfort of a rocking chair.

So, when the Phalanges (an Israeli-backed Lebanese militia) only needed forty-eight hours to massacre between an estimated 1,500 to 3,000 trapped Palestinian refugees and Lebanese civilians in the Sabra and Shatila Massacre of 1982, Tawfik and Siham began living their nightmare all over again.

In contrast, few Americans cared about the civil war in Lebanon, which began in June 1982 with Israel's invasion of Lebanon and the siege of Beirut. Tawfik claims the bloody invasion made it easier for Israel to avoid scrutiny and invade the country in order to root out the PLO, which was launching attacks on Israel from southern Lebanon. The massacre came a week after the PLO withdrew from Lebanon with assurances from the U.S. and a multinational force that the remaining Palestinian refugees and civilians would be protected. However, Israeli defense minister Ariel Sharon was blamed for giving the Phalanges free rein to commence the slaughter of refugees and civilians.

But Americans cared deeply a year later when two suicide bombers detonated truck bombs inside a U.S. military compound in Beirut, killing 220 Marines, 18 sailors, and 3 soldiers as well as 58 French paratroopers and Lebanese civilians. A group called Islamic Jihad claimed responsibility, saying it wanted to drive the international coalition of troops out of Lebanon.

It was easy in the beginning to lay the entire blame on those labeled as terrorists, but Palestinians, having suffered immeasurably under Israeli occupation, say the real terrorists may not be who we assume they are.

While the Sabra and Shatila massacre left him in shock, Tawfik had no choice other than to keep treating the children of Ada and the surrounding area, sometimes as many as fifty a day. Siham had babies at home, two older girls in school, a household to run, and an overworked husband to tend to when he dragged himself home.

When they did get some free time, their minds automatically defaulted to the same topics – the heavy hand of the Israeli leadership and the plight of their fellow Palestinians. But in those days, worry-and-wait was their only recourse. Telephone calls to their relatives back home were carefully rationed because of the expense, and cards and letters never captured the whole story. Their agony was exacerbated by the news they got on television and in the newspapers, not to mention the way they felt the U.S. government sided with Israel over human decency.

All these years later, the United States' failure to make Israel suffer meaningful consequences for essentially orchestrating the massacre at Sabra and Shatila still angers even the most kind and patient man. For Tawfik, it was personal because he had treated Palestinian refugees, many of them children, at the Shatila camp only ten years earlier while he was in school at American University in Beirut.

The other important takeaway for Tawfik was that the Lebanon massacre reaffirmed his belief that Palestinians were being sacrificed in order for the U.S. and Europe to maintain a foothold in the Middle East through Israel.

"I don't think the U.S. policy is intended to pay much attention to the religious aspirations of the Jewish people," he says. "The policy is really designed to make sure Israel succeeds so the U.S. can have someone in the Middle East they can rely on in order to keep the oil flowing."

Tawfik's views are reinforced by history and highlighted by personal experience. He attributes much of the suffering of Palestinians to the expansion of colonialism after the fall of the Ottoman Empire in the early 1900s, when he says the U.S. and Britain could have done something about the foothold the Zionist movement was gaining in Palestine.

"They knew Palestine was being flooded with Jewish immigrants, and they knew what was going to happen," Tawfik says. "But part of me believes they wanted the Jewish people contained in a certain place because their actions and their presence often created a strong backlash." The West's strategy failed in 1973 when Israel could do nothing to prevent the Arab oil embargo from taking a heavy toll on the U.S. economy. President Jimmy Carter took on the thankless job of attempting to find some middle ground between Egyptian president Anwar Sadat and Israeli prime minister Menachem Begin in a historic meeting at Camp David, Maryland, in 1979. The Camp David Accords produced a framework for peace between Egypt and Israel, but its full implementation was undercut by friction within the Arab ranks and by Likud, the newly elected ruling party in Israel, which was staunchly opposed to sacrificing any land that it had confiscated in exchange for peace with the Palestinians.

By mid-1982, Israel had broken a ceasefire with the PLO, which had set up military operations in war-torn Beirut in the aftermath of the Black September conflict with Jordan. Next came Israel's invasion of Lebanon with the aim of destroying Fatah, the dominant military arm of the PLO, and neutralizing Arafat. While Arafat was granted safe passage to Tunisia, the refugees in Shatila were not as lucky as the IDF guarded the entrances and exits of the refugee camps with troops and tanks while Phalangist Christian Arab militias killed thousands of those trapped inside.

"As usual, the Palestinian people were ill-informed and unprepared," Tawfik says. The only way he and Siham could fight back was by putting their best foot forward one day at a time. On August 16, 1982, the two of them were sworn in as citizens of the United States in a ceremony in Muskogee, Oklahoma.

CHAPTER 24

THE PALESTINIAN INTIFADA

Darkness cannot drive out darkness: only light can do that. Hate cannot drive out hate: only love can do that.

— MARTIN LUTHER KING JR.

The Zionist movement and what followed broke Tawfik Ramadan's heart. "First of all, they took my home from me, a home that I cannot go back to and live where I was born or be buried there."

At the same time, he blames the Israeli government for what came next: the responsibility he felt to devote ten years of his life treating patients under the harshest conditions in Palestinian refugee camps, followed by his brush with death in the 1967 War and the civil war in Jordan, capped off by his struggles in Beirut and Saudi Arabia to provide for a family and pursue his dream of saving lives.

"Perhaps I could have had a normal life if I had been allowed to have one," he says. "So, yes, I am bitter."

America afforded him the rewarding life he enjoys today, but it came with a price. "What really bothers me is that many people here in the United States and the world talk about the suffering of the Jews, but they don't say anything about how the Palestinians have suffered. There are two exoduses: the Jewish Exodus from the bonds of slavery in Egypt and the Palestinian Exodus of 1948. Yet they are different because the Jewish people are perceived to be the Chosen People while the Palestinian people are not the chosen people."

Tawfik is careful to differentiate his regard for Jewish people as a whole and the political and military factions of the Zionist movement. "Let's go back to the Holocaust," he says. "Most of the people that were taken in the Holocaust were Jewish. They were not Zionists. The Zionist movement used the Holocaust as an instrument to get into Palestine. But a lot of the grandchildren and sometimes children of the survivors of the Holocaust, they're standing up against Israel and saying, 'Do not do this in our name,' because when our families left the Holocaust camps they said, 'Never again in our name.'"

His perception of one of history's most egregious double standards again hit him square in the face in 1987 when he felt Palestinians were left with no choice but to rise up in protest as they had done in 1936, the year he was born.

My, how history seems to repeat itself when it comes to punishing Palestinians for simply living where they were born.

As was the case in the Great Revolt of 1936 against the British Mandate, the first Intifada, or Palestinian uprising, was a mass, civilian-based, unarmed resistance movement involving thousands of people of all ages and status across every geographic boundary. Like many transformational events in history, it occurred almost randomly as a result of a so-called traffic accident.

But it is important to tug at the roots to get the whole story of the Intifada, and Palestinian roots of suspicion run deep where Zionists are concerned. Those roots have been nourished over time by an evil rain that began falling across the Arabian Peninsula with the birth of Zionism. And by the early 1980s, another storm was brewing, sown by dark clouds fueled by a "cruel, deceptively 'liberal' settler-colonial occupation, difficult economic conditions and the politicization of the Palestinian people, who saw the PLO as their sole leadership." In addition, Palestinians had nothing to show for the Camp David Accords other than less territory in which to maintain their existence. And other than some condemnations of Israel and a few apologies, the atrocities committed at Sabra and Shatila had done nothing to diminish U.S. support for Israel.

Therefore, it was a given that fate would intervene at some point, and it did in late December 1987. The actual flame of Palestinian resistance was the result of a traffic accident in Gaza when an Israeli military truck smashed into two vans carrying Palestinian laborers, killing four of them. Palestinians believed it was a deliberate act of revenge for the stabbing and death of an Israeli a few days earlier in Gaza.

Demonstrations broke out on December 9 in Jabaliya, the largest refugee camp in Palestine, resulting in the death of a teenager who was shot in the heart by an Israeli soldier's bullet. Other protests quickly spread through the Gaza Strip, Jerusalem, and West Bank refugee camps, villages, and towns.

The first Intifada is also known as the "Stone Intifada" and for good reason. In the face of Israel's land expropriation, rapid settlement construction, and oppressive measures taken by the IDF in response to the civil disobedience, Palestinians, who had few weapons at their disposal, had been reduced to throwing stones at Israeli tanks as a last resort.

While violent at times, the early stages of the first Intifada were largely a peaceful movement that the Israel military responded to with its so-called "Iron Fist" policy. It used live ammunition against unarmed protesters, jailed demonstrators, and imposed punitive curfews and closures. Tears appear in Tawfik's eyes as he describes the stories he was told of how Israeli soldiers would break the arms of boys who were caught throwing stones.

Both sides did show some pragmatism. The resistance movement avoided using firearms and made attempts to find a middle ground. As a basis for the start of negotiations, Arafat accepted UNSC Resolution 242, which called upon Arab states to accept Israel's right to live in peace within secure and recognized boundaries. With the Intifada proving to be detrimental to Israel politically and economically, in 1992 a new Israeli government was elected with orders to negotiate for peace.

A year later, secret talks between Israel and the PLO under the mediation of the Norwegian government resulted in the Oslo Accords, whereby the PLO reaffirmed Israel's right to exist in exchange for Palestinian self-governance of its remaining territory.

Regrettably, the ultimate goal of achieving a two-state solution was in jeopardy from the beginning. The PLO was being challenged internally by Hamas and the Palestinian Islamic Jihad, which turned to suicide bombings and attacking Israeli targets to build a following. Far-right Israelis also opposed the accords to the extent that Prime Minister Yitzhak Rabin was assassinated in 1995 for signing them.

The tinderbox containing Israel and the PLO, two of the most flammable objects on earth in 1987, lay in sharp contrast to the tranquility of Ada, Oklahoma, with one exception.

While most Americans did not care what happened in the Middle East as long as it stayed in the Middle East, there was plenty to contemplate inside the Ramadan household, where Tawfik and Siham were deeply concerned about the fate of Palestine and the future of their children.

The Ramadans had six children at that point, a much larger home with a well-stocked pond and a prayer room, and still more work than there were hours in the day, given that interest rates on loans had climbed to 16 percent.

Yet there was always time for more schooling, whether the topic was the importance of an education or their Palestinian roots. Palestinians have a saying that Tawfik often recites: "Because of our situation about the colonization, we say, 'They can take your land; they can take your house; they can take your job; but they cannot take away your education.' So, whenever you have made that investment in yourself, this is something that nobody can take away."

The advice sank in – their six children have received a combined total of fifteen undergraduate and advanced degrees. Clearly, each child has scaled the high bar set for them by their parents.

Salam obtained a biology degree from East Central University, a master of public health degree from OU, and went on to become a dentist.

Suha received a bachelor of science and chemistry degree from ECU and both her master's degree in public health, epidemiology, and statistics and her medical degree from OU Health Sciences Center, and completed her pediatrics residency at the University of Illinois in Chicago.

Shadin holds a BS in accounting from ECU and a master's degree in international finance from Oklahoma City University.

Raniyah received a BS in psychology from OU, a master's degree in public health from OU, a PhD in neuroscience from OU, and her postdoctoral training at Case Western University in Cleveland, Ohio.

Deemah earned her BS in interior design from Oklahoma State University and a master's degree in business administration from OU.

Mohammad received a BS in mechanical engineering from Johns Hopkins University and his medical degree with a specialty in urology and robotic surgery from OU.

Salam calls it "setting the standard." It was an open-minded, nonjudgmental approach on their parents' part where the expectations were delivered with the touch of a masseuse instead of forced down their children's throats. "There is a standard, but it's not because they expect you to do it," she says. "It's because they expect it of themselves. And now we hold ourselves to a standard and hold people around us to a standard, although we don't judge people."

And given the tenor of the times, it also was more important than ever for them to educate their children about Palestine. For one thing, Tawfik and Siham knew their love for Palestine would not automatically transfer to their children, whose viewfinder was tinted red, white, and blue and who were constantly being exposed to the prevailing theory in the U.S.

that Israelis were the victims and Palestinians were their tormentors.

It made for a difficult balancing act for Siham, who was grateful for the freedom and opportunity America afforded her children but who also worried that her Palestinian heritage would be lost over time, the same way Palestine has disappeared from modern-day maps of the world.

While the Ramadans credit the public school system in Oklahoma for providing an excellent education, they realized it was their duty to "home school" their children when the subject turned to Palestine.

To that end, about every two weeks, when everyone was at home, Tawfik would call out to Mohammad, or "Mo," as he was known when he was still a little boy.

"Go call your sisters to the living room," Tawfik would say. And Mo would begin his search down the hallway for his sisters, who were scattered around the house.

"Guys, come on, guys," he would say. "It's lecture time. Come on."

A lecture is not what their parents had in mind, although it might have seemed like one to a six-year-old. "Basically, we wanted them to learn about this whole, wide world, not just what it was like to be here in America, the good as well as the bad," Siham says. "So, we used to work with them by getting everyone to sit in the middle of the floor and talk about life, about the world, about our culture and what we were doing here."

Tawfik and Siham wanted them to know more about Palestinians and the Palestine from which they came – a country that taught them the importance of family and being courteous to others, and showed a willingness to accept people of different faiths. Basically, they wanted them to see a side of Palestine and the Palestinian people that was not reflected on television or would likely be found in a school textbook.

They had a dream: If only they could get Americans to identify with the "Palestine Standard," with its emphasis on family, faith, and education, then perhaps it would be possible to bridge the divide created by differences in religion, politics, and culture.

What troubles Tawfik and Siham the most is that they have seen with their own eyes how they are right on the facts yet have had difficulty getting Americans to accept them.

The Ramadans, all of them, have frequently butted their heads against this wall, as illustrated by a story involving Deemah. "I think she was a sophomore in high school at the time," Siham says. "The summer before we had been overseas so the girls could see their cousins and the boys and girls they used to know, and to see all the education that was going on. At the universities, boys and girls were going to the same classes, and some girls were going sleeveless, wearing shorts, wearing regular clothes. Others were wearing long skirts, long sleeves, and headscarves. They were teachers, engineers, and doctors from both genders.

"When Deemah got back to school that fall, she was in a social studies class where they spent ten minutes watching a program called Channel One that talked about different cultures, different religions. It happened that they were talking about the religion of Islam and Muslim women, and the teacher was explaining to the students about how oppressed the ladies in Islam were because they cannot leave their homes and what they had to wear and what they were not allowed to do."

Deemah became agitated and raised her hand to explain she had recently visited the Middle East and did not feel like she had been oppressed. The teacher did not call on her no matter how many times Deemah raised her hand. Eventually, she told her mother what had happened.

"Okay, don't worry about it. We'll take care of it," Siham said.

The next day Deemah came home in tears. She said, "They were talking about the Qur'an, and he was saying untrue things. I raised my hand, and he would not allow me to talk."

"You are not inferior," Siham said. "You are like everybody else. You have the right to be answered."

That was the final straw for Siham: that night she told Tawfik to make his hospital rounds early so they could walk in together at the high school to meet with the principal, whom they had known for many years, from Salam to Suha, to Shadin, Raniyah, and now Deemah.

The principal was very responsive and set up a meeting with the teacher for the next day.

"Why would you say those things?" Siham asked the teacher.

"I get my information from CNN and Fox," he said.

"Look at me. Look at me. You see what I'm wearing now," Siham said to him. "I'm like everybody else, like every American. Tomorrow, I'm going to come back to school and I'm going to be wearing my long dress, my long sleeves and a scarf will be covering my head. Today, I look well educated and when I speak to you, you answer me. If I come back tomorrow, are you going to look at me and say that I look ignorant because I'm dressed differently? Is this the way you judge people from other cultures, other nations?"

Although Siham and Tawfik made their point and the teacher apologized for not allowing Deemah to challenge his opinion with her on-the-ground observations of daily life in parts of the Middle East, Palestinians and Arabs, in general, have been viewed far more skeptically than Israelis.

It holds true even when they see a Palestinian child throw a stone against an army.

CHAPTER 25

THE UNTOLD PALESTINIAN STORY

Many of life's failures are people who did not realize how close they were to success when they gave up.

— THOMAS A. EDISON

Shadin Ramadan was too young to remember her uncle, the dashing Arabian military officer whose looks were cast right out of *Lawrence of Arabia* and who actually played a small part in the film.

But she remembers the day her uncle Taha died at the age of fifty-nine. "My mom got a telephone call, and the next thing I know she is sitting there in the recliner of what was our new home in Oklahoma City, sobbing and sobbing," Shadin says. "She could not stop."

That was in 1977, and the tears still fall. Collectively, Palestinian sorrow is a true heartbreaker. They are not the first because suffering starts around the margins and works its way inside of you. You can ask who and for how long and get no shortage of answers, starting with members of the Jewish religion and going forward to the Indigenous people of North America, 20 million refugees in Africa, Myanmar's Muslim minority, and on and on.

On the outside, Tawfik wears his own pain as if it were nothing more than a furrow in his brow. Inside, it is another story. "When my father got sick, you know, I could not go to see him before he passed away," he says. "That was hard on me, and it was hard on me to lose my parents without being able to be there. This is something that is very important to our culture; when our parents get old, they don't go to a nursing home. They stayed in their home. We hired a person to stay with them all the time. They would not even move to my brother's house; they wanted to stay in their own house."

Although they could not speak English, Siham's mother, Aysha, and Tawfik's father, Za'al, navigated their way to America on separate occasions, strictly out of desire to see their children and grandchildren than a need to see the country.

Tawfik's father came for a visit in 1982, around the time his first grandson, Mohammad, was born. He could not read or write, but somehow he navigated his way through airports in Amman, Frankfurt, and Houston to reach Oklahoma.

"We took him to the history center in Oklahoma City so he could understand more about the history of Oklahoma and the West," Tawfik says. "He was happy to see that, but the most important thing for him was the kids."

Za'al's next priority was his son's vast expanse of lawn and an adjacent pond in Ada. "He would wake up early in the morning and pray and then go outside with his saw and start trimming the trees," Tawfik says. "He planted so many trees for us, and he worked and worked all the time."

It was like Za'al was re-creating a scene from the Al-Maliha hillside for his long-ago displaced family. But Za'al didn't stop there. "Those big road cement blocks outside our home in Ada, well, the previous owner of the house had left them in a heap, so he decided to put them alongside the pond," Tawfik says. "I rented a forklift to move them, but he said he would not use it. 'Bring me two crowbars and a piece of wood,' he said. He then rolled those big blocks about fifty yards by hand on the grass and the driveway down to the pond. The forklift I paid for sat there unused for two days. But those blocks are still there where he placed them."

To come to America to visit her family, Siham's mother went far out of her comfort zone. In 1983, Siham's mother spent almost three months in Ada, a lot of it standing in front of the stove. Every day there was a different meal and a different meat. On top of that, she made homemade bread that the kids could smell all over the house when they got home from school. And when the children were doing their homework in the evening, she would constantly ask them if she could prepare some hot tea or a snack for them. It was wintertime in Ada, not exactly frigid but not balmy Mediterranean weather either, so Aysha went about making tailor-made blankets for each of her six grandchildren.

"It made a big difference in my children's concept of what a family is and what it means to have a grandmother," Siham says.

A city of any size, much less a country as big and as far away as the United States, was a daunting prospect for Aysha. "She was well respected in her small society and had never been away from her own home except to visit her two brothers who lived in Ramallah and Jericho," Siham says. "To me, it looked like she was willing to put herself through the unknown and unexpected to make her daughter, son-in-law, and her grandkids know that the possibility is always there."

Best of all, her mother brought Palestine with her when she came.

"For one thing, she provided stability and calm at home for Tawfik and me," Siham says. "She gave our children memories that have stayed with them, whether it was the freshly baked bread they came home to or the way she would reward them with snacks while they did their homework."

Now those brief flirtations with their once-upon-a-time fairytale lives are all that Tawfik and Siham have left as time and distance have extracted a heavy toll. Tawfik's mother and father died six months apart in 1994. Za'al resided in Jordan at the time of his death, so close, yet so far, from Al-Maliha. Aysha, meanwhile, was still tending to the farm in Siham's village. Neither were able to attend their parents' funerals.

That's not to say Tawfik would not have gone home for good if he could. "A Jewish person who was born in New York City, whose ancestors came from New York, who has lived there all his life, and has never even seen the Holy Land is allowed to go back to Israel, gain citizenship, and own a house," Tawfik says.

Meanwhile, Tawfik, who carries a U.S. passport in one pocket and his aging Palestinian passport in another, is lucky to get past a West Bank Israeli checkpoint without being harassed by an Israeli soldier.

It is Amnesty International's contention that "since the establishment of the State of Israel in 1948, successive governments have created and maintained a system of laws, policies, and practices designed to oppress and dominate Palestinians. This system plays out in different ways across the different areas where Israel exercises control over Palestinians' rights, but the intent is always the same: to privilege Jewish Israelis at the expense of Palestinians."

Though they are 6,800 miles away, Tawfik and Siham can almost feel the knock of the Israeli government on their own front door – their connection to Palestine is that strong. Their children hear it, too.

Shadin describes her attachment in the simplest of terms – the quiet simplicity of the land, the preeminence of family, and the importance of respect. Shadin is the child who over time has taken up her mother's cause as the family's worrier-in-chief, while still reserving a place in her heart for the plight of the greater Palestinian people. As a typical teenager, she resented her parents for restricting her freedom. She soon learned that not wearing shorts or not being allowed to spend the night at a friend's house was minute compared to the way Palestinians had to live their lives under Israeli occupation.

"We'd go back every two years to Jordan, not necessarily Palestine, but still just to see our relatives and everything. We went to Palestine in 1990, '94, and '96, I think," Shadin says. "There is so much history, more than just the Jewish side of history, which is better known to people. The Palestinian side seemed to have been kept under cover. On one trip, we went to Jerusalem and Bethlehem, where my aunt lived. It was so nice to see her and become more connected. But there was sadness, too, because I remember one time my aunt was going to get groceries and she took a gas mask with her. 'Why do you take that?' I asked.

"You know, at the time I didn't understand the degree of the conflict and how bad it was. She said she took the mask because the Israeli soldiers were very young, having joined the military at the age of eighteen. To her, they were kids, but she said she had learned to wear her facial covering to the market because sometimes as a joke those 'kids' would gas the whole market."

It is impossible to say how Tawfik and Siham Ramadan would have fared had they not boarded that plane to Oklahoma in 1976. At that point, they had no other choice. Aramco officials had pulled their financial support for Tawfik's medical training in the States along with the promise of being able to return to his old job. And the political winds were blowing against Palestinians worldwide, limiting career opportunities, even those of a qualified physician.

What Siham does know is that she is thankful to be here. "I am thinking this has all been in God's hands. But what I worry about is that two generations from now, will our families still have connections with our family overseas and with Palestine?"

There is reason to worry. The scrutiny on Palestinians living in the U.S. has been intense. They know their first responsibility is to their children and grandchildren, but they worry equally about the fate of their relatives overseas as well as the hundreds of thousands of Palestinians they don't know, who are either living under Israeli occupation or warehoused in refugee camps. They are outnumbered 50-to-1 by the Jewish population in America, lack the political backing that Israel enjoys, and are anguished over the fact that they don't believe their side of the story gets represented fairly.

This is why Tawfik, after a twelve-hour day at work, sits like a sponge in front of his computer devouring and then forwarding to his contacts every bit of relevant information he can about what is happening on the ground in Palestine and in the Israeli government. Age has not diminished his passion for the Palestinian cause or extinguished the flame deep in his soul that will light the way home for Palestinians everywhere. To be Palestinian is to both wander in uncertainty through life and, instead of sleeping at night, lie awake wondering what you can do on behalf of the Palestinian people.

Tawfik is in good company. Though more than ten years younger than Tawfik, the story of Dr. Eid Mustafa, a plastic surgeon who was born in Deir Ballot in the northern part of Palestine and eventually established his practice in Wichita Falls, Texas, is similar to Tawfik's, as is his devotion to Palestine.

Eid's father was a very successful farmer in Haifa who lost everything when the Israelis took his land as a result of the 1948 War. "My father had become a farmer without a farm, so by 1950 he was asking, 'How am I going to support this family?'" he explains. "So, he ventured out to make a living. He liquidated every asset he had at the time and bought a one-way ticket on a ship that sailed from Beirut to Venezuela in South America."

Dr. Mustafa's father had an older brother who had immigrated to Venezuela in the 1920s, and he joined his brother as a farmer in a new country.

In time, Eid's father learned to speak Spanish and transformed himself from a farmer into a businessman. He started going door-to-door selling fabrics. Eventually, he started carrying his goods on a bicycle, then a wagon. Finally, he had a store in downtown Valencia.

It took thirteen years, but his father eventually saved enough money to go home to Palestine and his family. "I was a year old when he left, and I had never seen him until he came back," Dr. Mustafa says. "When he got back, he said he had saved enough money to send each of us children to college, or as high as we wanted to go and still live with dignity."

Dr. Mustafa's father viewed school the same way Tawfik's father did – there was no substitute for a good education. "Looking around at that time, this was in 1967, the only people who were able to quickly overcome the trauma, and their refugee status, were people who had a degree that could be carried with them wherever they went," Eid says. "Those people became engineers, professionals, and teachers. Material possessions you could lose very easily; knowledge would travel with you. So, yes, the Palestinians became focused on education as a way of resisting the loss of their very existence."

Education and the field of medicine saved Dr. Mustafa, just as they saved Tawfik, but it pains him to this day that the hole in the heart of occupied Palestine has grown larger with time. "Palestine was supposedly governed by the internationally recognized ways and laws of dealing with occupied territories and occupied people. But, of course, Israel has never followed those rules," he says.

And the price the Palestinian population in Gaza and the West Bank has paid made it worse. According to Dr. Mustafa, Palestinians have been victimized for too long, while Israel is treated as if it is above the law. "They can kill and get away with it. They can steal (Palestinian property) and get away with it. They can abuse people. They can impinge on their human rights and get away with it. Every day in Palestine, a Palestinian is killed on camera in broad daylight, and the killer gets rewarded instead of being punished," he claims.

It is a painful atrocity to ponder and to feel helpless in the process. Even so, it is impossible for Eid not to think whimsically of the country he once knew and wants back: the simple and peaceful existence that Palestine once offered.

"Things were very basic, you know. The longer I'm gone the more I realize what a wonderful life it was before occupation," he says. "I miss the cuisine, the walks at sunset. There was absolutely no crime. Things were safe. We ate organic food that grew in the backyard. We had fun as a village every time there was a wedding or a graduation or a circumcision, or whatever. It was a party. It was stress-free and wide open for the imagination."

From the time he started volunteering his medical services in Palestine twenty-five years ago, Dr. Mustafa has not seen a reduction in need for those services. He has treated children who have been shot. He has worked under conditions that any hospital in the U.S. would not tolerate. He has seen Israeli soldiers storm into the hospital and take patients he had just operated on off the gurney as they came out of the recovery room and dragged them out of the hospital "to God knows where." And his direct way of calling it like he has seen it over the years when it comes to callous medical treatment of Palestinians has put him on the wrong side of Israeli officials, who will allow him to enter the West Bank but have barred him from entering Jerusalem.

Dr. Mustafa is not looking to make a statement. "I know that I'm doing a little bit, you know, that will help some people. That's rewarding to me," he says. "If I flipped the coin, I would probably hate myself to know that there are people I could help and I declined to do so."

He is no different from Tawfik, who from 1962 to 1967 volunteered at one of five clinics founded by a group of physicians in Jerusalem in the 1950s and helped raise money (much of which came from Kuwait) to build Al-Maqasid Hospital to serve Palestinians. Tawfik went on to become a board member of the Jerusalem Fund, a charitable, humanitarian, educational, and cultural organization that supports community development and relief efforts for Palestinians, with the support of Dr. Subhi Ali and Dr. Mustafa (the president and vice president, respectively, of the Jerusalem Fund). Founded in 1977, the Jerusalem Fund initially provided scholarships to Palestinian university students before expanding its activities to educate the U.S. public and policymakers about Palestine's past, present, and future as well as support humanitarian efforts within Palestine.

On the outside, Palestinians are proverbial wanderers, searching for a way home. Inside, they all are wondering if they have done enough to help the cause.

CHAPTER 26

RANIYAH

I am too far away from what I love and my distance is without remedy.

— ALBERT CAMUS

If Palestinians could paint a portrait to clear up the misperceptions pertaining to their passion and their motives, Raniyah Ramadan would be the one to sit for it.

Educated. Confident. Personable. Attractive. Caring. Determined. Loyal. Thoughtful. Optimistic. Anyone who knows her would say as much or more.

In Arabic, she would be described as the *Wasitato el-Ekd*, or "the decorative part of a necklace." It is no coincidence that Raniyah means "gazing" in Arabic, and to "fix the eyes in a steady intent, often with eagerness or studious attention."

It is a definition that describes the Palestinian movement as well as any one word. Without a compass, Palestinians are stargazers using the heavens to light their way home. And while they cherish and honor the past, their gaze is fixed on the future because with it comes hope, and Palestinians live for hope.

Raniyah was the fourth daughter born to Siham and Tawfik and their first child of Oklahoma. It was a far-flung geographical mix, but, boy, did she get results.

"For every occasion, she was the first one," Tawfik says. "For instance, if we had a holiday or a birthday, she was the first one to call me early in the morning at six o'clock, 'Dad, happy birthday.'"

Raniyah's mother got equal billing. "She was the first one to call in the morning, 'Good morning, Mom, how are you?"

"There is a saying in Arabic when someone is like this, who gives more of herself to and for everybody than she chooses to receive, we say it's like the rose of the garden," Siham says. "When you want to pick out a rose, you look for the best rose. When there's someone like that, we say that you have the feeling that she is not going to live, she will be the first to go because she is the rose of the garden, and God is going to choose her first."

As much as we educate ourselves about our children, parents sometimes are left in the dark. Not when it came to Raniyah; everyone seems to have a Raniyah story.

One woman says she and her husband found each other through Raniyah. "She introduced us and thought we would click," she says. "We are now happily married."

A friend says he would not be where he is today without Raniyah. "When I had graduated from college, I didn't know what to do with my life. Then it happened that I met Raniyah, and I was telling her that I didn't know what to do with my life, but that it was my dream to be a pharmaceutical representative. She just looked at me and said, 'Are you serious?' I said, 'Yes.' She said, 'Okay, I'm going to connect you with somebody.'"

And she immediately took out her phone and put him in contact with someone who could help him. "Well, I got the job. When I met her, I didn't know if I would have a penny. Now, I'm making $100,000 plus because of Raniyah."

While the objects money could buy mattered to her, money could not buy her a family, and family is what mattered most to Raniyah. She demonstrated its importance in countless ways, and she was not shy about spreading the gospel of family.

Tawfik and Siham were not the only ones to take a financial hit in the dot.com stock market crash of 2000 when, after peaking one month earlier, the NASDAQ composite suddenly lost 34.2 percent of its value. The hasty sell-off of technology stocks and the Federal Reserve's shift in how it regarded equity prices cost investors $1.7 trillion in losses. Besides the Ramadans, one of those who also had a lot of eggs in that basket was their neighbor and friend, Dr. Mahmoud Shakir.

One day something happened to his car, so Dr. Shakir (which means "thankful' in Arabic) picked up the phone and called Raniyah, knowing she would take him to work if she were home.

"Good morning, Uncle."

"Raniyah, I want you to come and take me to work now."

"Okay. I will be there in a few minutes."

They were driving along talking when Raniyah turned to him and said, "Uncle, I know you are very, very sad and you are very upset about the money, but look at you. Look, you are still here with your family. You are still working; you are making money. You are living life. Where is your faith? I know you have a strong faith." In recounting the story to Tawfik and Siham after Raniyah's death, Dr. Shakir said as soon as the words came out of Raniyah's mouth, "I just slapped the front of my head with my hand, and I said why has nobody else told me those words? Why must it come from a young girl who is twenty-three years old?"

That was Raniyah, who was born on September 30, 1976, six years and two weeks after her oldest sister. Salam was born in Amman in the middle of a civil war. Raniyah was born to play catch-up in double time. There was no stopping her. But the remarkable thing is that she never left anyone behind in the process. And everyone followed because Raniyah brought universal joy and acceptance.

"She had the most beautiful personality, was brilliant, and was easy to raise from the time she was three years old," Siham says. "She loved going to school." Raniyah was about to turn three years of age when the family arrived in Ada right before the start of the school year in 1979.

After a year in preschool and another year in pre-kindergarten, Raniyah was more than ready for kindergarten. But kindergarten was not ready for her. School district rules stipulated that a child must be five years of age by September 5 to enter kindergarten. Unfortunately, she was three weeks short of turning five. "The school would not take her. They said she is too young and wanted her to repeat pre-K," Siham says. "But she already knew a lot more than what you learn in pre-K. She could have been in the first grade at that time."

Taking a play from Za'al's playbook, Siham paid the school principal a visit. "I told them, 'I think this little girl, she can do more than repeating this (pre-K).' The principal told me the state would not pay for her education for the first year because she had missed the cut-off age date. She said I would have to pay for it and she would have to be tested first."

Money was not an issue. Neither was the test. Raniyah got up one morning, got dressed for school, and went in by herself to be tested. She passed and started kindergarten at the age of four. Each semester Siham wrote the school a check for $475.

Raniyah's love of knowledge was only exceeded by her exuberance for life. More than joy, life was a celebration to Raniyah. She liked a good party. She liked to travel and dine out. She liked to dress up and look beautiful but could pull it off in a way that never signaled any intent to say, "Hey, look at me."

Somehow Raniyah managed to keep one eye on her friends and the other on the laboratory because scientific research was her calling. After graduating from high school in Ada, she received a BS degree in 1998 from the University of Oklahoma, followed by a master's degree in public health from OU in 2000 and a PhD in neuroscience from OU in 2007. Her research attracted the attention of Case Western Reserve University in Cleveland, Ohio, where she was awarded a postdoctoral research fellowship in ophthalmology and visual sciences.

In 2008 she was attending a neuro-ophthalmology conference and job fair in Florida when another world opened to her. One of the companies recruiting on-site was Regeneron Pharmaceuticals, a biopharmaceutical company founded only twenty years earlier. Raniyah saw something special in Regeneron, and the feeling was mutual as a few days later she got a call from the company saying they were interested in hiring her.

"She actually had two offers and wasn't sure which one to take," Siham says. "I told her to go wherever her heart told her to go."

Raniyah chose Regeneron and New York City or, more specifically, nearby Tarrytown in Westchester County, the site of the company's headquarters. Later, Shadin, whose husband was completing a residency in medicine in nearby New York City, ran into one of Raniyah's bosses at Regeneron who told her what impressed him about Raniyah: "When your sister came to us, we didn't take her for her education. We did not take her for what she knew. We took her for the personality she presented to us."

By the end of 2008 Raniyah was feeling on top of the world. Her research in neuro-ophthalmology with Regeneron Pharmaceuticals was on track, and she was living in Manhattan, the city of her dreams.

In June 2009 she accompanied four of her siblings and her parents to Morocco and Spain on a family trip. Shadin missed the outing because her husband, Abdullah, was about to begin his residency in Boston. Raniyah's desire to get the family together for her father's sake came with an awful twist of irony.

When September rolled around, Raniyah's parents, siblings, and friends were deep into planning for Raniyah's birthday, as they hoped to give as good as they got. Remember, Raniyah prepared for other people's special occasions better than Hallmark.

There was a glitch. The family vacation seemed to have tired her out, and Raniyah never got tired.

Next came a phone call to Shadin. September was now almost half over. "My legs have been swollen the past few days, really swollen," she told Shadin. "I don't know what it is. But don't call mom and dad. Just ask Abdullah (Shadin's husband who is a physician) what I should do."

Abdullah told Shadin to tell her to put her feet up. He then advised Shadin to call her father over Raniyah's objections. "I said that of course I was going to call my parents and tell them what is happening," Shadin says.

The next day Shadin was sitting with Raniyah in the waiting room of an internist, a friend of her husband's family. Suddenly, Raniyah did the unexpected.

"I'm scared," she said. "My friend, Savannah, just died of breast cancer. Everyone used to call us twins. Her name was Savannah Sandman, and mine was Raniyah Ramadan, so everyone said we went together . . . and she just passed away. Now, I don't want to die."

It was not like Raniyah to be anything other than upbeat.

The ultrasound revealed something of concern, so the doctor ordered a CT scan. "Abdullah called me and told me to go to my sister-in-law's house," Shadin says. "Then he called my dad and everyone. He said she's got cancer in her liver." The heartache everyone felt was unimaginable. The denial was absolute.

Having regained her positive outlook, Raniyah had only one thing to say: "I'm going to work tomorrow."

"Maybe you need to relax and take it slow," Shadin said.

"No, no, no, I feel fine," Raniyah answered. "I got this. I have all this stuff to do." Tawfik, meanwhile, was fixated on scheduling the CT scan.

"We went to the ER and waited for hours until the CT got done," Shadin says. "When it was over, Raniyah said she was going out with her friends that night. She got dressed. She looked amazing. And she went out and celebrated with her friends and did not tell one person that she had cancer."

The next day, Raniyah went back to work at the lab. In the meantime, her mother and Suha arrived in time to accompany her to Sloan Kettering Hospital in search of a second opinion. Raniyah was healthy and happy. She could beat this, everyone thought.

None of that impressed the doctor, who told her she had maybe two weeks left to enjoy life. He didn't even want to try to paint a happy picture.

Tawfik could not abide such a dismissive attitude from a doctor, from the time he was a boy watching his grandfather suffer. The pain of hearing Raniyah addressed in the same manner was unbearable for him.

A few days later, she got some more bad news about her liver from another physician. It was later determined that he had misread a report, but the damage had already been done. "She had a strong mind, but these people constantly were saying... it was fatal. Then, her body started swelling and she went downhill," Shadin says.

Tawfik and Siham brought Raniyah home to Oklahoma.

"She couldn't walk so she had to sit in a wheelchair at the airport in New York and was holding a bottle of water in her hand like a security blanket," Siham says. "I couldn't process what I was feeling to see that I am the one who is pushing my daughter, who is less than half my age, in a wheelchair. That was not the role I ever saw for myself. She was not even thirty years old."

Fall was on the march by then, projected by the experts to be followed by a bleak winter. There were too many doctors in the Ramadan family to not know the score. And Raniyah was a scientist who could diagnose herself better than any doctor. But no one was giving up.

An interventional radiologist, Dr. Kenneth R. Stokes at Baptist Hospital, performed a chemo-embolization to shrink the tumor in her liver and better target the malignant cells.

The results were miraculous. She felt normal again. "Not long after that, we had a wedding for one of our friends, and she came to the country club and spent the whole night dancing and singing," Siham says.

Raniyah was soon making life better for everyone around her and predicting a complete recovery. That's not to say she didn't grasp the importance of every minute.

One of her dreams was to own a Mercedes, so her parents bought her one.

"I think she knew what was coming, but she was at peace," her mother says.

There were more chemo treatments, a liver chemo-embolization, and the hope of a clinical trial. By the middle of 2010, Raniyah began getting severe headaches. She returned to New York with her parents to see a top oncologist.

After they arrived, Raniyah suggested they all go to the opera. The next morning they had brunch with a friend/colleague from her lab, but as Raniyah stepped out of the restaurant to flag a taxi, she stopped in her tracks. "I am seeing double. I have a retinal separation," she said without hesitation.

Her self-diagnosis left her shaking.

Raniyah and her parents returned to Oklahoma City, where an MRI revealed a tumor in the back of her head. Siham says the only time Raniyah told her that she would not want to live was if anything happened to her brain. Otherwise, she was always optimistic that she was going to beat cancer and then find a cure for cancer.

A cure could not be found. Cancer was spreading throughout her body.

Siham had a dream after Raniyah got sick in which she saw a pink snake coming toward her. Pink happened to be Raniyah's favorite color. The snake emerged from one of the dining room windows in their home in Ada and started growing bigger and bigger. Somehow, Siham found herself pressed against a china cabinet as the snake drew closer. Then she saw the snake had two heads, both as pink as pink can be. Then the dream was over.

"After that, I always saw snakes but never the same snake. They got smaller and smaller, and they always escaped me," Siham says.

It was analogous to the miracle cure that escaped her daughter. For example, Tawfik and Siham had made all the necessary preparations to take Raniyah to a highly recommended clinic in Germany that offered a form of treatment and medication she could not receive in the U.S.

"We bought the tickets for her and for us, and our suitcases were ready to leave the next day," Tawfik says. "Raniyah was at Shadin's house getting her ready when she called me and said, 'Dad, come right now.'"

Raniyah was having a seizure and had to be hospitalized that night. The trip to Europe had to be postponed, never to be rescheduled.

Raniyah died soon after that, in July 2011, but not before she had exhausted her last ounce of resistance.

"The psychologist came to see her and told her she was going to die, just like that," Siham says. "She told him that she was going to live and that she was going home.

"We took her to Shadin's house, and I made a big plate of spaghetti. I'm not sure she ate much, but she was talking to us; she was doing very well. All of us went to sleep, and sometime after midnight she asked for each of us to come to her room and she told us everything would be okay. We went back to sleep, and around five o'clock in the morning we had to call an ambulance. She was admitted to intensive care because at that point she was septic. They intubated her, and that was the end."

Raniyah remained on life support for a week, at which point Mohammad gathered the family together.

"We were all at the hospital, and then Mohammad left wearing his scrubs," Siham says. "He went home to change his clothes, and a couple of hours later he came back dressed in a black suit and white shirt and black tie. He took us into a dark room they call the silent room. He looked at all of us and said, 'Mom, Dad, sisters, my sister Raniyah, I don't think that her spirit is with us anymore. I think her spirit is with God.' We had to accept that. Then the plan was to remove the tubes and see if she could breathe on her own."

Her dad was the one who had to sign the papers authorizing Raniyah to be taken off life support. The physician whose one goal in life had been to save others now faced the unimaginable – he would have to sign the order allowing his daughter to slip away as if by the stroke of a pen.

Tawfik signed the papers and cried.

It was not any easier for Siham. "Even in the afternoon when they pronounced her dead and we walked in to see her for the last time, although she was cold, she had the warmth in her cheeks," Siham says. "I touched her and felt that she was not in pain. She seemed asleep. I had tears. I told her goodbye, that God would take good care of her, and that I would see her in Heaven."

Siham kept her composure at the funeral, focusing on how beautiful and peaceful her daughter looked. Siham found strength in something Tawfik had told her before the service began: "In Arabic, he told me today is Raniyah's wedding day."

It wasn't until a week later that Siham woke up buried under an avalanche of grief. That's when Siham started thinking in Arabic.

"I had never written poetry, but that's when a poem came to me," she says. She pulled out a yellow tablet and wrote the first of four poems titled *Farewell*. In the second poem, 'The Hour Is Near,' Raniyah is sitting up in bed, her back straight and strong, and her head leaning on a pillow. I'm describing the moment when Raniyah woke up at two o'clock in the morning at Shadin's house, a few days before her passing. She had been sleeping in a room with Suha, who came to us when Raniyah woke up and said, 'Mom and Dad, Raniyah wants to see you.' The whole family came, too.

"In the poem, she was looking at each one of us and telling us farewell, or goodbye, in a beautiful, soft voice. She was saying, 'Mom, it's okay. Dad, it's okay. Salam, it's okay. Suha, it is okay. Shadin, it is okay. Deemah, it is okay. Mohammad, it is okay.' I am asking her what was okay, but she did not answer. I interpreted it as she was saying goodbye."

Raniyah's death, in a way, marked the death of the family as it was constituted. "I think that every one of us felt like we failed," Suha says. "I think the thing that was the hardest was to see my dad, who never admits defeat, experience that kind of pain. As a physician and a healer, I know in my heart that he feels strongly about not giving up."

For Deemah, the sight of her father so steeped in grief that he could not utter a word broke her heart, too.

Aside from the obvious, what was it about Raniyah that made her special? If the number of people she encountered in her life totaled ten thousand, then there would be ten thousand different answers to that question. "She was amazing because she had a special connection with each one of her siblings," Shadin says. "I think every single one of us will tell you, we were very close to her. Every single one of us. She was literally the glue."

There is a lot of Al-Maliha in Raniyah. Her father's village was a place of joy, laughter, and family. And Raniyah was one who loved lots of company. That is one reason Tawfik has never recovered from her death and why the term "closure" will never apply to either the descendants of Al-Maliha or the family of Raniyah Ramadan.

Mohammad says as much: "This has been difficult for all of us. We all are still probably suppressing it a little bit because Raniyah was the best mix of all of us. But as much as she has brought us together, it is hard to be together in her absence."

Siham, the nurturer, the protector, the fighter in the family, felt what Mohammad felt, but she knew as the matriarch of her family, she had to summon the courage and the strength that her own mother had demonstrated all those years ago.

"The pain is still in my heart," she says. "Raniyah lives inside my subconscious, and sometimes I ask myself how I can live all these years without Raniyah. But then I must reply to myself, 'What else is there to do? What is my choice but to be here and take care of the others? We are still a family.' As my daughter Suha told us, Tawfik and I had already lost one, and now we were not seeing that the other five are still here. Think of this family."

It took time, but the Ramadans – all of them – came together as a family in the best of ways. They could not save Raniyah's life. But they could ensure that her intellectual curiosity, personality, and work ethic lived on through others.

That is how the Dr. Raniyah Ramadan Center for Undergraduate Research & Learning at East Central University came into existence, fueled by grants from Tawfik and Siham and their children and the Native American–Serving Nontribal Institutions Program with the support of the Chickasaw Nation.

ECU president John R. Hargrave, a good friend of the Ramadans, called it an "exciting project which will enhance the hands-on learning experiences of our students involved in our research-learning programs. This generous gift from the Ramadan family will have far-reaching benefits to the teaching and learning environment here at ECU." A more appropriate way to honor Raniyah could not have been found.

At Regeneron Pharmaceuticals, she worked on ocular disease models and initiated the protocol for an animal model of an ocular infectious disease that affects about two million Americans and conducted the histology analysis for the company's uveitis models in rats and mice.

Raniyah was as excited about the research of others as she was her own, which is why ECU's undergraduate research center, where a student's appetite for research takes flight, reflects Raniyah's priorities so well. Long the realm of graduate students on large college campuses, research opportunities were rare for undergraduate students at ECU, although Dr. Duane C. Anderson had been advocating for such a facility for years.

The Ramadan family has also funded a scholarship for an upper-class science student and an undergraduate internship every summer for an ECU student at the lab group where Raniyah worked while she was at the University of Oklahoma. Tawfik and Siham were especially proud that the first internship was awarded to a Jewish student because it reflected their daughter's love for everyone. The family also sponsors a distinguished lecture series given by an eminent neuroscientist at the OU Neuroscience Department, sponsors a PhD student's attendance at a national conference, and funds an outstanding neuroscientist's presentation of his or her research in memory of Raniyah. In addition, they have endowed a scholarship at Oklahoma City University (OCU).

"We didn't know what to do with ourselves after she passed, but when we talked about how to memorialize Raniyah in a way that would capture her essence, we thought about how she had always loved school and learning," Siham says.

The Ramadans did not stop there. Over time, Raniyah and her parents had become close friends with Zaineb Shams and her mother, Faridah, who was a faculty member at Oklahoma City University. In the course of their conversations, Faridah had mentioned that some Muslim students who attended OCU often had a hard time finding a place on campus to pray during the weekdays. Tawfik and Siham did not forget this particular point after Raniyah's death, which led them to find another way to keep their daughter's spirit alive.

"Robert Henry (OCU's president at the time) thought it might not be appropriate for a Christian university to build a mosque on campus, but the idea of having an interfaith center where any student, no matter their religion, could come for reflection and meditation no matter what time of day appealed to all of us," Siham says. The Dr. Raniyah Ramadan Interfaith Prayer Center in the Kramer School of Nursing opened in 2014.

It is not surprising that Tawfik and Siham put so much stock in helping others find a "home" when they have spent most of their lives longing for their true home. And so, when Siham had lunch one day with a friend in Ada who mentioned the idea of creating a home for the homeless, it was a natural fit for Siham. "The lady asked Siham if she would be on the board, and Siham said yes," Tawfik explains, taking up the story. "At the first board meeting, they were discussing the need for a building and how hard it was to find one big enough in town. Siham did not say anything at the meeting, but when she got home, she asked me what I thought about a building we already owned. I said, 'Let's give it to them.'"

The homeless shelter was named Mama T's B&B (Bread and Blessing) in honor of Mother Teresa, who dedicated her life to serving the less fortunate of God's children, regardless of their faith or lack thereof. Its goal is to transform the lives of those who enter its doors so they may leave the shelter as quickly as possible, prepared to lead independent, healthy lives as productive members of the Ada community.

None of us, including me, ever do great things. But we can all do small things with great love, and together we can do something wonderful.

— MOTHER TERESA

It was this quote that Salam saw when she opened Raniyah's phone shortly after her sister's death. Mother's Teresa's words were also similar to the goal Tawfik set out with as far back as 1962, when he was a young medical officer tending to a displaced Palestinian population that, everyone felt, would be going home soon. It does not matter whether you are a perpetual refugee or someone temporarily swept up in the chaos of life; the importance of home can never be discounted.

The Hour is Near

SIHAM RAMADAN

TRANSLATED BY IBTISAM BARAKAT

Raniyah, my daughter, sits in her bed selflessly.
Her steadfast back is defiant and upright.

Her eyes circle the room politely, affectionately,
Bidding each one of us, the final farewell.

She speaks softly; with a voice not frail:
Beloved Mother, father, Salam, Suha, Shadin,
Deemah, and Mohammad, do not mourn
For I am bidding you farewell
And my heart is fulfilled.

The day of the great separation
then arrived soon.
everyone who loves Raniyah arrived
for the goodbye procession.
All are bleeding tears of sorrow and confusion.

Tawfik, Raniyah's father, faces me announcing:
Listen, Siham, Mother of Raniyah,
Today is Raniyah's wedding celebration.

Yes; I reply.
She is beautiful in her white gown
As her soul travels to the home of eternity.

Mohammad, Raniyah's brother now appears
dressed in a suit. His necktie
the color of midnight darkness.
His white shirt glows as the
snow caps of Mount Herman.

Only Siham, his mother, detects his hidden tears.
Oh does a man have enough tears for the
waterfalls of mourning to run down his cheeks.

Mohammad gathers the family and leads us
To the quiet, hidden room for a painful resolution.

He holds his mother tightly within his arms
He glances at his father with great affection:
Father, sisters, the hard hour is approaching, he begins.
We are a learned family, of many physicians.
Oh, how bitter this matter.

He then says:
The unbearable moment is now upon us.
A trial of the soul, beyond utterance.
This is Allah's will that fulfills destinies.
Let us be content with Allah's choices.
My sister was called to the other world by Allah.
She answered her creator's call.
I feel that she is now a sacred soul
in the big mystery.

Now Salam, Raniyah's sister, speaks
She is pale, afraid; trembling as she laments:
Raniyah, to whom I would confide my soul and my secrets!
You have left me alone — Without you,
and without my happiness.

Suha's voice then remembers:
Raniyah. I am your doctor sister,
the scientist and researcher.
Near your bed in the intensive care unit, I stand
In all circumstances of your need, I am at hand.
I supervise every pill you take
I observe the spoons, the tubes,
to save you from the throbbing pain.

Shadin then shares her deep sorrow:
Everything in my life is halted so I can prolong your life.
East and West I roamed searching for the cure.

Deemah is silent with a wondering mind.
She suddenly questions loudly:
What may be an answer to such painful crises?
What must I do when I come home and announce:
Raniyah, dinner is ready!
Upon hearing no answer, I then run
to your room and find no one...
The ember of the reality
Of your loss slaps in my face.
I am about to fall down, and kiss the ground,
and I refuse to lose my strength.

I stand and speak to you, Raniyah.
I am going to conquer the world
And live to the fullest, and use all my talents
In your name, Raniyah
Because I can.

Because of that early morning
When we were sleeping in the same bed.
You told me: Deemah, never be lazy.
Go to work my sister.
And do the work passionately.

Now these words that came from your lips
are my daily compass.
They wake me up and inspire me to work
every morning like a moral boss.

For you, Raniyah, with these words,
And Allah's willingness
I shall honor your memory,
Overpower any reluctance
And accomplish beyond dreams.

CHAPTER 27

THE OTHER SIDE OF THE STORY

Believe you can and you're halfway there.

— THEODORE ROOSEVELT

There are always two sides to a story. If it's a complicated story, there can be many sides, as indicated by the startling number of subplots that mark the Palestinian–Israeli conflict.

Historians, scholars, and religious and governmental leaders have spent entire lifetimes dissecting one of the world's most hotly debated topics – the Holy Land – including how it came to be and what should become of it. In their pursuit, they have produced endless volumes of books, archives, theories, documentaries, and recordings of all kinds to support their various conclusions.

Which side should you believe?

If you live in Boston or Budapest, it's an interesting theory that might affect your belief system but probably won't impact your daily routine. So, you make a cursory judgment based on your leanings and move on. But when one is stuck on Ground Zero, so to speak, there isn't much time to debate who belongs where when a bomb is about to go off on top of your tent in the middle of a refugee camp on the floor of the desert.

That's where the debate recently landed, leaving the world to finally realize that, well, what's the point of continuing to keep the debate going given that the Israeli government, with the tacit support of the U.S. government, is well on its way to eliminating any remaining Palestinian presence in the country.

A theological, geographical, and humanitarian discussion of worldwide importance has been supplanted by a military operation focused on taking more Palestinian land and humiliating the Palestinian people in the process. It would seem to call for an honest debate based on the recent death count on both sides. But we shall see.

Palestinians view Israel's apparent need to drive them into the ground is a strategy that was conceived long before Hamas-led militant groups launched a deadly surprise attack on Israel on October 7, 2023. Palestinians say they have seen it coming for years and have sounded the alarm to no avail.

After 1948, Palestinian refugees started a "Hey, We're Here Too Movement," hoping the world would care as much about them as they did Holocaust victims. Many of their descendants are housed in those same camps today.

Failing to capture the world's attention, Palestinian resistance leaders switched tactics in the 1970s, using airplane hijackings, abductions, bombings, and demonstrations in order to be heard and gain some leverage at the negotiating table, assuming negotiations were even feasible.

The first Intifada in 1987 came in direct response to Israel's rapid expansion of illegal settlements and an oppressive and illegal crackdowns in all aspects of Palestinian life. Under the Oslo agreement of 1993, an independent Palestinian state was foreseen by 1999. Rather than ceding land and control, Israel went on quest for more, increasing the number of Jewish settlers from 76,000 in 1990 to 203,000 in 2000, excluding the Old City and East Jerusalem.

With another broken promise on the horizon, Palestinians launched the second Intifada in 2000. And once again it was Ariel Sharon who struck the match by barging into the al-Aqsa Mosque compound in East Jerusalem with more than a thousand heavily armed police and soldiers over the objections of Palestinian leaders and the advice of his American allies.

For the most part, the early days of the uprising were largely nonviolent, as had been the case in the first Intifada. Again, the Israeli military responded with excessive force, firing about 1.3 million rounds of ammunition in the first few days, killing 47 Palestinians and wounding 1,885, the majority of whom were bystanders. Five Israelis were killed by Palestinians in the same time frame.

It was not a surprise to Tawfik Ramadan that the uprising would spew over into an armed rebellion. Palestinians in the West Bank had their backs to the wall. In Gaza, their backs were up against the sea. In between, they were being treated like the dogs some Israeli policymakers said they were.

Could Israel have prevented the second Intifada by stepping back until the uprising wore itself out? Maybe not, because Gaza or the West Bank might have eventually exploded on its own. But Tawfik thinks

Israel had more sinister plans. He thinks it was possible that Israel intentionally sowed the seeds of a rebellion by confiscating more land and indiscriminately imprisoning droves of Palestinians to pick a fight, in order to demonstrate to the world that Palestinians still posed a grave threat to its lawful existence.

Whether it was by hook or crook, Israel achieved its goal of getting the arms and the money, including $9 billion in loan guarantees in 2003, that it would need to take on its enemies.

Israel got something even more important for the future – two things, really.

One, the Bush administration, citing Israel's security concerns for Israeli citizens, broke from recent presidential tradition by declaring future Israeli—Palestinian peace negotiations would not hinge on a complete return to the armistice lines of 1949, meaning Israel could continue to build settlements on Palestinian land without any consequences.

Two, the mainstream media in the U.S., with few exceptions, continued to report on the two Intifadas as if they were merely public address announcers at a football game, confined to only announcing who carried the ball, who made the tackle, and how much yardage was lost or gained. Any context regarding the underlying issues, or the wide disparity in the death count, apparently would draw a penalty. For example, it was not mentioned that the Israelis fired their football out of a bazooka while Palestinians brought a nerf ball to the game.

Huwaida Arraf, a Palestinian lawyer and human rights activist, offers one explanation why, in the critical battle of public opinion, Israel often gets a pass: "This dismaying reality is an inevitable result of perhaps the biggest shortcoming of international law – that adherence to it and its enforceability depend largely on voluntary state consent and compliance. In other words, absent the political will to make state behavior comport with the law, violations are the norm rather than the exception. In this case, Israel is certainly not interested in sacrificing its colonial agenda to comply with international law, and with the unwavering political and economic support of the United States, thus far it has not had to.

"What's more, even though the UN has repeatedly recognized the right of an occupied people to use legitimate armed force in the struggle for 'liberation from colonial and foreign domination,' and has specifically applied this to Palestine, Palestinians have had to endure decades of being labeled as 'terrorists,' while the terrorism perpetuated by their occupiers and oppressors has been labeled 'self-defense.'"

The blame game that dominated the long-standing Palestinian–Israeli conflict had been usurped by a game of semantics, and Israel was winning. Terrorists. Jihadists. Suicide bombers. The words were bandied about so frequently and carelessly that, before long, every Muslim and Arab in America fell under suspicion. Adding to the stigma were the wars the U.S. was conducting in Iraq and Afghanistan. On the nightly news, an already agitated American audience grew more appalled at the thought of Israeli men, women, and children getting blown up each time a Palestinian took Israeli lives with him or her on a crowded bus or at a railway stop.

Israel was winning on the streets of public opinion, and it was winning on the optics. "Hadn't their people suffered enough in the Holocaust?" was the principal question of the day. Likewise, why did Hamas intentionally attack civilians when Israel only made "targeted" attacks against Hamas designed to minimize the loss of civilians?

Some things in life are simply too difficult to comprehend without a deep dive into history and the facts, and perhaps this was one of them. But not for Tawfik. Israel had the planes, the tanks, the weapons, and a well-trained army. The Palestinians had a cause and a lot of conviction and not much else to fight with. Penned in on all sides by the IDF, Palestinians were in no position to take the moral high ground. They were not going to win, but they could make a statement to the world: "We are still here."

Three years in, the unexpected happened. Sharon proposed that Israel unilaterally disengage from Gaza. The plan, which was implemented in 2005, called for the demolition of twenty-one Jewish settlements and the removal of Israeli troops and more than 8,000 Jewish settlers. Did he finally bow to public pressure in Israel, or did he finally gain some compassion?

It is clear to Tawfik that Sharon did not foster the idea in the name of lasting peace in the Middle East or to appease Palestinians for what he did to them in Beirut in 1983 or in the two Intifadas. Historian Avi Shlaim believes Gaza and its 1.4 million residents were getting too dangerous and too expensive to police. Israel's withdrawal was "aimed to undermine the Oslo peace process by freezing the political process and indefinitely delaying discussions about a Palestinian state," he wrote. The higher Palestinian birth rate also posed a "demographic time bomb" that would threaten the Jewish majority in areas claimed by Israel, according to Shlaim.

To elaborate, Sharon's senior adviser, Dov Weissglass, explained Sharon's reasoning this way: "You know, the term 'peace process' is a bundle of concepts and commitments. The peace process is the establishment of a Palestinian state with all the security risks that entails. The peace process is the evacuation of settlements, it's the return of refugees; it's the partition of Jerusalem. And all that has now been frozen. . . . What I effectively agreed to with the Americans was that part of the settlements would not be dealt with at all, and the rest will not be dealt with until the Palestinians turn into Finns. That is the significance of what we did."

Any celebration Gaza felt it had coming was squelched by the fine print in the disengagement plan, which ultimately allowed Israel to totally isolate Gaza and essentially imprison its inhabitants.

Political economist Sara Ray describes the disengagement from Gaza as completing the separation and isolation of the Gaza Strip from the West Bank. Whereas the period before the disengagement featured increasing dependence on the Israeli economy and that of the West Bank, the period after the disengagement is characterized by Gaza's economic, social, and political isolation. She describes the disengagement as normalizing the occupation in the eyes of the international community, despite the expansion of the occupation and the lack of any "safe passage" between Gaza and the West Bank.

For more than two decades, Israel has controlled Gaza's airspace and territorial waters by blocking the reopening of the airport that was made inoperable by the IDF in 2002 and by preventing Palestinian authorities from building a seaport. Israeli authorities also determine who gets to cross the overland route from Erez to the West Bank. The availability of water and electricity has become another form of punishment employed by the Israelis, although such necessities also have been impacted by infighting between Hamas and the Palestinian Authority. Israel claims its security measures were implemented to prevent Gaza "terrorists" from setting up shop along the border between the West Bank and a heavily populated Israeli sector after Hamas took political control of Gaza in 2007.

The blockade performed as intended because by 2015 more than 80 percent of Gaza's 1.8 million people received humanitarian assistance, while unemployment reached 45 percent. Hardly anything or anyone was moving in Gaza; about the only work being performed took place below ground, where Palestinian armed groups used construction materials to build tunnels they used to launch rocket attacks into Israel.

The Politics of Humiliation vs. Coordinated Acts of Defiance has been the main event almost each night for years in Gaza, only the eyes of the world weren't watching. If they had, Tawfik believes the demolition of Gaza might have been avoided.

"A psychiatrist who was treating young people in Gaza told a story about how the young ones live in a constant state of anxiety and fear at the hands of the Israelis," Tawfik says. "They are humiliated in their homes when the IDF comes to kill their fathers or take them to prison. They are humiliated at checkpoints where a gun is pointed to their head. They are humiliated in the streets if they get out to demonstrate against oppression. They live with constant humiliation, and they have nothing in their hands to defend themselves."

What Tawfik heard next from the speaker should surprise no reasonable person: "Because there is nothing worse for a young person than to be humiliated, that is how suicide bombers are born."

Ramzy Baroud of the *Jordan Times* writes that when Zionist militias, using advanced Western arms, conquered ancient Palestine in 1947–48, they expressed their victory through the deliberate humiliation of Palestinians. "Much of that humiliation targeted women, in particular, knowing how the dishonor of Palestinian females represents, according to Arab culture, a sense of dishonor to the whole community," Baroud explains.

The affronts Palestinians who live, work, and travel to Israel range from the degrading to the deadly and are delivered with the subtlety of a blast from a firefighter's hose.

"On one of our visits, we were in Ramallah when Israeli security wanted to arrest a man who was in a building across the street from the hotel we were in," Tawfik says. "With the loudspeaker, they called him out and told him to come down. So, he did. Then, they told him to take off his clothes in the middle of the street until he was completely naked. After that, they came and handcuffed him and put him on his knees before they took him away. It was done to humiliate him."

It happens all the time in Palestine, out of sight of the world.

In 2006, shortly after the end of the second Intifada, Tawfik was traveling with another delegation from the National Arab American Medical Association (NAAMA) and Physicians for Peace when a female obstetrician, two nurses, and the secretary of NAAMA were stopped because they were carrying medical supplies into the country.

"The Israelis confiscated all the supplies and held the American lady all night for interrogation," Tawfik explains. "She finally got to call the American embassy in Tel Aviv to tell them she was an American and needed their help. You know what they told her? They said, 'Welcome to Israel.'"

The lesson she learned was that nobody was going to stand up to the Israelis, not even the American government, which supports Israel financially and militarily.

Palestinian children are another story. About five years ago, Israeli forces were barreling through a Palestinian West Bank neighborhood with orders for residents to vacate their home in thirty minutes or stay and watch the house be demolished over their heads.

While her parents rushed to clear out their most valuable possessions, their daughter, a first-grader, took one item – her school backpack. What will she think about Israelis if one of them confiscates her backpack one day at a checkpoint, tears up her textbooks, and throws away her pencils? Tawfik says sometimes this is the case.

Siham, meanwhile, can't take her eyes off the children of Gaza and what they must be feeling. "Israel wants to keep the war going and going until it eliminates Hamas. But think for a moment: how are they going to do that for everyone who already has nothing?

"They have already killed more than 72,000 people. How many of them are fathers and mothers, how many of their children do you think are still living? Just think of the little boy or girl who lost their mother or their father, or grandfather or brother or sister. What's that little girl or boy going to be in twenty years? What's he or she going to do? It won't matter if you call it Hamas or something else; they are probably going to fight Israel."

CHAPTER 28

A PEDIATRICIAN'S LEGACY

The soul is healed by being with children.

— FYODOR DOSTOYEVSKY

Some people go by the book. Tawfik Ramadan goes by a list.

He has a list for every occasion, one compiled after careful contemplation. A man who can take time to make a list and then follow it is seldom rattled and certainly not prone to losing his way. And Tawfik always has been as steady as steady goes, except, of course, when confronted with the prospect of losing Raniyah.

His ability to keep his eye on the prize while combating the complexity of the moment is something he was wired for, as far back as that promise he made to himself to become a physician with perseverance.

And, so, sometimes to a level beyond belief, Dr. Tawfik Ramadan has driven home this point at every medical stop he has made on a sixty-year-plus journey. An odyssey is more like it because it did not exactly go by the book as it waffled between fairy tale and Greek tragedy.

Yet, as the time comes for Tawfik Ramadan to take stock of his life, his tendency is to boil it all down to a list: "I have a summary to finish with," he says. "I think there are five points to be made if my story is told.

"First, there is my narrative as a Palestinian, based on history versus the Israeli narrative that is based on a big and nondocumented historical point of view from the Bible. My narrative is that Palestinians existed there before the Israelis, will continue to stay, and one day will go back.

"The second point is a reflection of all Palestinians who lost their homes, were uprooted, and lived under different hardships, whether in refugee camps or outside refugee camps or immigrated to different countries. This is what I call the new Exodus, the Palestinian Exodus. This is quite an experience that should be emphasized.

"The third point is our experience as a family. How we managed to raise successful children and how we were able to get over all the challenges. We managed to raise those six children and help them achieve their goals in life and to be successful. They have become citizens who have accepted their role in this society and now help people. They bring positive changes in people's lives.

"The fourth point is that despite the many crises we went through, those moments did not break us. Although we felt the pain and were depressed at times, we got through the hard part.

"Then, there is our commitment to paying something back to the nation, the state, and our local community. And there is the payback to our original homeland, starting with the Jerusalem Fund and the generous contributions they have made to create diabetes centers, scholarships, and centers for education."

Just as Tawfik's life would not have been complete without Siham by his side, neither would his list. "I have one more thing to add, please," she says. "What resonates in my mind right now, again, and probably it's for every other immigrant from anywhere in the world who's come to America. There is the unsettling feeling there all the time for me, besides my family. I know my family are Americans and proud to be Americans, meaning I, too, am proud and thankful to be an American who came from one end of the world to come here."

For Palestinians, the challenges do not end when they step on American soil. The difficulty lies in putting their past behind them so they can live in the present and dream about the future.

"What we experienced as adult immigrants is identity recognition," Siham says. "We live what we call a hyphenated life, hyphenated cultures, American-Palestinian, or Palestinian-American, so we live in two camps. But it makes me more determined that I am American more than I'm not an American. To me, this is part of the challenge."

Tawfik agrees that Siham's own experiences have mirrored his in every way. "One day I was talking to a lady from the American Academy of Pediatrics in Washington," he says. "I was asking her a question and she said, 'Where are you from, doctor?' I said, 'I'm from Ada, Oklahoma.' She said, 'Oh, is that overseas?' I said, 'Yes, it is overseas. You're right, 100 percent.' Because of my accent, she assumed I was coming from a different world."

What Tawfik and Siham learned is that if they build a bridge instead of erecting a wall, then despite the differences that tear society apart – whether it's language, religion, culture, whatever – they will have an easier time finding a path to common ground.

More than forty-five years ago, the Ramadans and the townspeople of Ada, Oklahoma, began such a journey. The road was steep and rocky in places, but as they got to know one another, the fear of what could be lurking around the next corner gave way to acceptance.

To mark the occasion of the construction of the bridge between two worlds, the townspeople of Ada, friends, and family gathered to celebrate Dr. Ramadan's sixtieth year practicing medicine and his eighty-fifth birthday on August 22, 2021. Sixty years of service would seem to warrant some time for personal reflection on his part. But typical of the man who has spent practically his entire life asking everyone, "How are you feeling?" Tawfik seemed hesitant to talk about how he felt beyond delivering gratitude to his family and to the people of Ada for welcoming him and his family forty-two years ago. His poignant words were delivered in the respectful manner he has always exhibited.

Instead of reflecting on his life, Tawfik wanted to talk about some healthy steps the rest of us might consider in our own lives. To be sure, he had a list to mark the occasion, a list verified by the doctor himself and softly delivered with love for all. Here is what he said:

- Nourish immediate and extended family, friends, and community – because they are guardians of the future generations.
- Education, Education, Education. With education, you can change your life and even the world. Your education stays with you wherever you go, and it is the passport for success in life. Reading books is good food for the brain.
- Live healthy lifestyles: maintain a balanced diet, exercise, and have adequate sleep for a healthy body and sound mind. Throughout my sixty years in medicine, I learned an important lesson: that practicing prevention in all aspects of life (especially health) is vital. Vaccines are one of those preventive measures. They are one of the major human accomplishments against deadly infectious diseases that mainly affect children. Vaccines prolong one's lifespan. When I was in medical school, there were only two vaccines; now we have more than two dozen. Practicing these preventive measures may touch on individual freedom and liberty, but we should understand that liberty has boundaries regulated by social responsibility, especially when it comes to family and public health. One suggested that since we have a Statue of Liberty on the East Coast, we should have one for responsibility on the West Coast.

- Upgrade yourself: Drop bad habits and strengthen good habits. This promises more chance of a successful and healthy future.
- Establish yearly reflections of your accomplishments: Praise your successes and learn from your failures.
- Unload your stress, especially when it affects personal health. Don't worry about small things; let it go. Take a loss if needed and walk away. Losing a deal is better than losing a mind. As a pediatrician, I suggest that we, as children and adults, need to cut down on the time of exposure of our eyes and brains to all electronic screens – there is evidence now that the impact of prolonged exposure harms the growing brains of children. We need to practice moderation and discipline for this matter.
- Leave behind something good to humanity, good deeds and ongoing charity. The Prophet Muhammad was reported to have said: "When a person dies, his deeds are cut off except for three: Continuing charity; knowledge that other people benefit from; and the righteous child who supplicates for him." The main meaning of life is how much positive impact one can bring to other people's lives.
- Laugh and laugh and laugh loud: Laughter will bring vitality to your life and keep your heart young and happy.

It is not by happenstance that family, friends, and community ended up number one on Dr. Ramadan's recipe for a good life.

His son, Mohammad, validated everything his father believes in with his own remarks that day. After requesting a moment of silence for his late sister, Dr. Raniyah Ramadan, speaking for his family, Mohammad expressed his gratitude to the audience for turning out to honor "the real Dr. Ramadan," a running joke in what is a family of doctors.

"To know Dr. Ramadan, one must know that he is a learned man," Mohammad says. "He believes in the meaning of the history and the root of things. "So, let's take the word 'doctor,' which is derived from the Latin word *doceri*, meaning to be taught or teacher. I think back on almost every moment I spent with him observing him or discussing things with him and others. And he's always been the teacher. He's interested and even invested in not only his family, friends, and especially patients, but also the people he casually knows. He has a passion for it, learning about people and, when appropriate, imparting his knowledge to them to help them. As any teacher will tell you, a great teacher must be a great learner, and this would be an understatement for him. He has always been an avid reader, consuming multiple books at a time for his entire life.

"He's not only a teacher. He's a physician, a healer. He comes from the time when to be a medical doctor was not an occupation. It was who you were. It was not a nine to five. It was a calling and an honor, no matter the time or place.

"I have learned many things from him. And as I grow older, I have learned deeper and deeper lessons from his words and his life example. More recently, I have come to truly appreciate his dedication and sense of community. And that is why today is being dedicated in his honor."

As authenticated by Mohammad's tribute to his father, Tawfik Ramadan's "Life Reflections" were not a list generated from WebMD or someplace else on the internet. It is a list that has been time tested and put into practice by the doctor himself. Will it guarantee sixty years of fulfillment doing a job that you love as it has for him? Probably not. But that's one other thing that makes Tawfik Ramadan unique. When you throw in that much of the first third of his medical career was spent treating patients under the most primitive conditions in Palestinian refugee camps, it gives credence to the fact that Dr. Ramadan's advice is worth heeding.

A number of experts in their own right stepped to the microphone on a hot afternoon in the Chickasaw Business Center on the ECU campus to point out how often Dr. Ramadan has been proven right and how lucky the town has been to host him and his family.

There was Bill Anoatubby, governor of the Chickasaw Nation, who acknowledged how wonderful it has been to know and call Tawfik a friend for a number of years and to witness his dedication to children and families throughout the area. "I thank you for your selfless service and extend our deepest gratitude," Anoatubby says.

Tawfik's calm demeanor often overshadows the depth of his resolve. Brenda Ware, CEO of the Central Oklahoma Family Medical Center, provided a classic example. "The story has been shared about Dr. Ramadan's arrival at Valley View Hospital (now Mercy Hospital) years ago, when he quickly realized there was not a designated pediatric unit within the hospital," Ware says. "It was at that time that Dr. Ramadan took a moment, located a large piece of cardboard, wrote pediatrics on it, and promptly declared that area the pediatric section in the hospital. What a perfect example of a leader recognizing a need and taking action."

As Dr. Charles Mettry noted, numerous students apply for medical school each year, but only a small percentage make it through to completion because few of them know and understand the struggles of being a physician. "Doctors invest a great deal of time in their work. And the profession is not subject to a regular schedule," Dr. Mettry says. "Emergencies and illnesses do not lend themselves to an eight-to-five day. A physician is on at all times. Dr. Ramadan's legacy will be one of a physician whose patients, peers, and community hold him in the highest esteem."

A good friend and fellow pediatrician, Mettry reinforced how Tawfik's singular vision for quality medical care in rural Oklahoma has saved untold lives and enriched the whole community. "When he and Siham arrived on July 29, 1979, there was no pediatric ward at the hospital and no expertise, equipment, trained nurses, and logistics to provide for sick babies," Dr. Mettry says. "I can only imagine the time and energy he spent in rectifying that situation. He knew he could not do it alone. So, he marshaled citizens of Ada and surrounding communities to assist in this great endeavor. I arrived a few years later and was able to enjoy the fruit of his labor. I had not been here very long when Valley View Hospital hosted a birthday bash in the neonatal intensive-care unit. The room was filled with parents and patients for whom he had provided care. The testimonials from grateful parents seemed endless. Who knows how many of those critically ill babies would not have survived without his care?"

The mayor of Ada, Dr. Tre' Landrum, is among the thousands of children who have grown up under Dr. Ramadan's watch. The mayor went on to become a physician himself, and it is not lost on him that without Dr. Ramadan's pioneering medical advances, he might not have chosen to return to his hometown to practice medicine. Confessing that his mother remains a bit of a pack rat, Dr. Landrum, who is an ear, nose, and throat specialist, said not long ago he ran across a bottle of ear medication Dr. Ramadan prescribed for him as a child and that his mother had saved. "I thought that was very fitting," Dr. Landrum remarked. But he said the real reason he was in attendance was to say "thank you" to Dr. Ramadan.

Dr. Landrum added that being a medical student is something he aspired to become from the time he was a child and a patient of Dr.

Ramadan's. "What I always said is I wanted to come back to a community like Ada. I wanted to connect to a small town, but I wanted to come back to a small town that demands a higher level of medical care.... And it is a wonderful, wonderful thing, but a high level of care is something that I've always looked at in the Ada medical community. And there's a lot of people as I look around here that I absolutely said, this is the type of person and doctor that I want to be. There are several around here, but today I get to do something that's even a little bit more special because as I mentioned, I'm also mayor of Ada, and I have a proclamation for Dr. Ramadan."

With that, the mayor proclaimed it "Dr. Ramadan Day in Ada," a day to both celebrate Tawfik for his sixty years of service in the profession and to wish him a happy birthday.

Others struck a similar note, alluding to his skills as a doctor and to his compassion for his patients and the town he serves. Doctor Katricia Pierson, president of ECU, acknowledged that it was the university's turn to give back to Dr. Ramadan and his family. "When I think about what you've given to the university, what you've given to the faculty, staff, students, especially, the students, one word comes to mind – generous," she says. "You are generous beyond belief. The generosity you and your family have provided to this university cannot be measured."

But their contribution has already been measured in a way that means everything to Tawfik. Dr. Pierson summed it up best when she revealed that because of the undergraduate research facilities the Ramadan family helped provide, the three-year average for the acceptance of ECU students into medical school had risen to 93 percent.

The legacy of that Palestinian boy who was called to serve as a physician on the bleakest day of his young life in a country most Americans know little about will now live on, thousands of miles away. A healer knows no boundaries.

CHAPTER 29

AND THE LAND SHALL BE CALLED PALESTINE

Our freedom is incomplete without the freedom of the Palestinians.

— NELSON MANDELA
upon his release from South Africa's Verster Prison

Should the Bible be the final word on history?

Is one diaspora more unacceptable than another?

Have the Jewish people become what they have been shown throughout time?

For seventy-plus years, Tawfik Ramadan has been left with no choice but to debate those questions. To a lesser degree, so has Siham, the less idealistic of the two.

In *The Bible and Zionism*, Nur Masalha writes that the "conviction held by Westerners and Zionists (both secular and religious) that God and the Bible have given the 'Jews' Palestine (the 'promised land') in perpetuity is one of the underpinnings of modern political Zionism and Israeli colonialism in Palestine.

"A scrutiny of the language used in the Old Testament in relation to the emergence of political Zionism from the late nineteenth century onwards shows the way in which a secular European conquering ideology and movement mobilized the figurative language of the Jewish religion into a sacrosanct title deed to the land of Palestine signed by God. Very little is said about the actual genealogy and provenance of Zionism, especially its European settler-colonial context of the late nineteenth century from which Zionism drew its force; and almost nothing is said about what the creation of the State of Israel entailed for the indigenous inhabitants of the land."

Writer and researcher Nicola Denzey Lewis also warns readers that the Bible sometimes gets things historically correct and other times not. "For instance, the author of the Gospel of Luke tells us that although he was not around during Jesus's lifetime, he sourced his information from eyewitnesses and that he has worked to write it down accurately (Luke 1:1–4). Nevertheless, there are historical inaccuracies in its account of Jesus's birth.

"Did ancient writers like Luke seek to write history as it happened? Probably not. The point of many of the writings in the Bible – probably most of them – was to strengthen people's faith. This is different from writing a factual account."

In a 2021 *New Yorker* article, the author Masha Gessen surmised that a central political question of our time is not so much where or how to draw the line, but when. "All over the world, we see regimes that are following clear trajectories away from democracy, justice, and freedom. As we watch them move inexorably along these disastrous paths, we wonder: When do we decide that the thing we feared would happen has happened already?"

B'Tselem, a leading Israeli human rights organization, addressed the question by documenting human rights violations in the occupied Palestinian territories since 1989. In January 2021 it issued a position paper announcing it has decided to draw a line. The paper is titled "A Regime of Jewish Supremacy from the Jordan River to the Mediterranean Sea: This Is Apartheid." B'Tselem made the same charge again in 2022.

It is not lost on Tawfik and Siham how much the Jewish people have suffered and deserve a home. But because they were not wanted anywhere else, why is it acceptable for a Jew to simply take a Palestinian's home and then continue to act like they are the persecuted ones and Palestinians are the terrorists?

"Land expropriation" is the preferred term of the Israeli government in characterizing its seizures of Palestinian property in the occupied West Bank, possibly because it carries the weight of judicial authority. In what is a win-win for Israel, for every Palestinian home that is demolished, a nonsanctioned Jewish settler builds a new one.

A report summarized in an article by Human Rights Watch in May 2020 described how the Israeli government has created more than nine hundred "Jewish localities" but none for Palestinians other than a few villages created to house Palestinians displaced from other communities. In 1900 Palestinians owned virtually all of the land in Palestine. By 1967, they held 22 percent of the land. Today, they own less than 12 percent of what is known as Israel.

Tawfik knows the story firsthand dating back to 1948, when his family lost all it owned. Some of his relatives wound up in Bethlehem. Not far away was one of UNRWA's first refugee camps, Dheisheh, which was established in 1949 as a temporary refuge for more than 3,000 Palestinians from forty-five villages west of Jerusalem and Hebron, including those from Tawfik's own village of Al-Maliha.

Seventy-five years later, Dheisheh remains a stark symbol of Israel's determination to erase any hint of Palestinian history. But Dheisheh also represents both the struggle and the hope of the Palestinian people. To them, Dheisheh is as revered as the Taj Mahal, the exquisite jewel of Muslim art in India and one of the masterpieces of the world, although the true beauty of Dheisheh lies in the faith of its inhabitants.

"I was a student in Beit Jala, in the seventh grade, when Dheisheh opened," Tawfik says. "I don't think anyone can imagine how primitive the conditions were and how hard it was to live in that environment. Despite a harsh winter in 1950 where snow was up to our knees, those people managed to stay in Dheisheh and resurrect their tents. They are still there in Bethlehem today, at least many of their descendants are."

Later that summer, Tawfik was invited by UNRWA to attend a summer camp at Dheisheh to learn carpentry along with a dozen or so other children. "I walked back and forth from my home to the camp every day for about two weeks. We had a very nice teacher who taught us how to hold the saw and cut the wood. I made a box that I took home."

Palestinians seek out the tender moments that can draw them home wherever they can find them. Tawfik found one then, and all these years later, Dheisheh's residents keep searching for theirs.

This is what writer Oliver Wainwright of *The Guardian* has to say about modern-day Dheisheh: "(Today) Dheisheh looks very little like how you might picture a refugee camp. When I visited in 2018, I found not rows of tents or shelters, but winding streets of multi-story concrete houses, a dense urban place of self-built structures that had evolved piecemeal over the decades. There are shops and schools, mosques and a community center, all packed into an area of less than one-fifth of a square mile. The only giveaway of its status is the occasional UN-branded garbage truck patrolling the narrow lanes.

"Walls remain bare and steel reinforcement bars poke from most rooftops, but there is a good reason why it all looks so unfinished. Dheisheh is the product of being forced to live in perpetual limbo, with the eternal hope of one day leaving.

"By refusing to go away silently into the night, refugees in all the Palestinian camps know they are preserving the light of the right of return alive, because over time humanity has become numb to the insanity of numbers as the Palestinian–Israeli nightmare gnaws on another century of lost opportunity."

But what is one more refugee in a crowded camp in a world numb to the numbers?

The Gaza death count by January 2026 had reached more than 75,000, including about 42,000 women, children, and elderly people, according to Lancet Global Health research. Israel's death toll from the October 7, 2023, attacks stood at about 1,200 people killed.

In contrast, about 20,000 Palestinian Arabs, 547 Jews, and 126 British soldiers were killed while Palestine was under the control of the British Mandate from 1918 until 1948.

The calculated removal of Palestinians from their homeland is also made clear by the overwhelming shift in ethnicity: In 1922 Palestine was home to 673,388 non-Jews and 83,794 Jews. In 1947, there were 1,324,000 non-Jews and 630,000 Jews.

By 1950, Palestine had been turned inside out as the Jewish population had increased to 1,203,000 while the non-Jewish population decreased to 167,000. The tale of the tape does not rival Nazi Germany where more than six million Jews were estimated to have been killed as part of Adolf Hitler's "Final Solution," but it is clear that a pattern has been established.

In 1970 there were 2,582,000 Jews and 440,100 non-Jews.

By 2000, the Jewish population increased to 4,955,400 while the non-Jewish population grew to 1,413,900. In a century, from 1922 to 2020, the number of Jewish people had risen from 17.1 percent of the population to 79.3 percent.

Why do the numbers not matter?

Well, numbers never cry. They never got a chill sleeping in a canvas tent all winter. They do not require clean water or food or an education. Numbers do not have memories, either long or short. They cannot have babies who need care. Numbers do not cause problems. When you add it all up, numbers are perfectly content being numbers that like to line up neatly in rows and tell a one-dimensional story.

Whereas politicians like to massage the numbers to suit their purposes, Tawfik sees inescapable faces.

Whoever was next in the waiting room at his clinic or at the medical station in camp became the one who got his full attention. But that was not a number sitting in his examination room. The heart he put a stethoscope to was beating in someone's chest.

And he thinks about that man with myasthenia gravis, a chronic autoimmune disease in which antibodies destroy the communication between nerves and muscle, who was among the refugees that fled the day the Israelis bombed his camp in Jericho amid the 1967 War.

"I stayed in the clinic in camp for the first four days of the war, trying to keep the people from running from camp into what could have been a massacre," he says. "I can still see people running across the bridge to the East Bank. That one man needed an injection every day to keep him alive, and when he told me he was leaving, I feared he was not even able to cross the river that day. He stands out because I knew he was going to die."

He had the same feeling that day in 1968 when Israelis attacked the Karameh camp. "One ambulance for all those injured people scattered around the camp. I cannot look at a human being's life and say, 'Well, you are dying. Goodbye. Let me go and pick out someone else who can live.' Even if I can help someone live another thirty minutes, a human life is a human life, and physicians are trained to keep people alive."

Yes, any diaspora is wrong, he believes.

Because he is Palestinian and still has family in the Occupied Palestinian Territory (OPT), it is as if Tawfik himself remains under Israeli occupation. In fact, he sees the Church of the Nativity, the oldest major church in the Holy Land, located in the center of Bethlehem, as clearly today as he did almost seventy years ago when he was attending secondary school not many blocks away.

"Today, it is often the center of demonstrations for Palestinians whose rights have been suppressed and who have been persecuted," he says. "I can see myself there as a boy, marching in the streets with students from my school. The Church of the Nativity is on a higher plane from the street below. Across the street is the house of my oldest sister, and it is now the house of her children."

Tawfik's heart longs for the Palestine he knew and aches for his sister's family and the hundreds of thousands of refugees who cling by a thread to hope. He and Siham assist his extended family financially and those living in the OPT by supporting the work of the Jerusalem Fund. They also lead by example with their determination and belief in the Qur'an and the teaching of the Prophet Muhammed, their sense of morality and fairness, and through their devotion to others.

All those traits are needed more than ever in the aftermath of the tragedies in Gaza City and Rafah. The incalculable weight of the rubble that once constituted a whole city now feels piled on top of two sets of shoulders already weary from the strain of war.

"When I go to bed I have my phone next to me. It sits there and I keep picking it up to read all the news and messages about Gaza that come in," Siham says. "Then, I turn it upside down and try to go to sleep. But the phone keeps dinging, so I pick it up again. I can't stop looking at the news and what's happened in Gaza that day. I try to close my eyes again, but I keep worrying about the fate of the people, particularly innocent children, and I worry that my generation has failed to restore Palestine and bring hope to Palestinians."

She found the death of six-year-old Hind Rajab especially painful. The young Gaza girl had been heard begging on her cell phone to be rescued after she was the only one left alive in her car that was reportedly hit by Israeli military fire. Several days later, her body was found, along with the bodies of five of her family members and two ambulance workers sent to rescue her. The Palestine Red Crescent Society accused Israel of deliberately blowing up the ambulance only a few yards away from where she was trapped.

Heartbreaking scenes are playing out in the whole Gaza Strip: children having their wounds stitched up with no numbing medication; children covered with blood crying for their family members; a baby just a few days old shot in the head while his mother nurses him. Those were a few of the eyewitness accounts described by five Dallas–Fort Worth medical professionals after returning from the crisis in Gaza.

"While we have addressed the physical damage, the emotional and psychological trauma endured by these families has not been discussed, and that is the one thing too [that's going] to last for a long time and their lifetime for sure," Dr. Syed Irfan Ali, a Dallas-based anesthesiologist, told the *Dallas Morning News*.

The other tragedy is that sixty-five years ago, Dr. Ramadan was thinking much the same thing, but nobody was listening. "I tell you, it's torture for us and for me," Tawfik says, referring to the more than 17,000 children who have been killed in Gaza. "You know that when we bought our home in Ada, we planted several small pine trees in the yard," Siham says. "One of them is now a hundred feet tall. I knew the deeper the roots went down, the harder it would be to extract them, so I knew those roots would keep us from fulfilling that dream of going home. Now, I cannot even think about being separated from my grandkids and not holding them close to me."

But Gaza has brought back a yearning she cannot dismiss: "I know for me in this period of time, my wish is that I will be able to visit Gaza before I die. I know there is hardly anything left, but I want to go there and stand in the middle of all the destruction because Palestine is not a building; it is the Earth and when I go there, I will not be looking up for a building that is no longer there. The attachment I have to the land will be pulling me down to the Earth. This is the feeling I have." Perhaps it is there that Siham will finally find peace. Too much has weighed too heavily on her heart for too long for her to know that precious feeling.

Tawfik is clear about what he misses and what he wants. He is like the man trying to row his boat on a choppy lake, gripping the oars with all his might to reach the shore. Al-Maliha is his safe harbor and always will be, even if the odds are against him.

When Za'al left, the house key was still in his pocket. Tawfik now carries it with him in his heart.

In 1999 Tawfik, Siham, and their six children joined other U.S. physicians and their families on a visit to Amman, Jordan, sponsored by NAAMA. It was arranged for some of the families to go to the West Bank, which is part of Palestine that has not been legally occupied. The eastern border of Palestine is west of the Jordan River, and Jordan's western border is east of the river. Both the East Bank and West Bank fell under the umbrella of the Hashemite Kingdom of Jordan after the 1948 Palestinian War.

"We went there and during that trip, we took another trip," Siham says. "We took a morning off as a family because our kids were with us, and we went to see Al-Maliha. As we got closer, the first thing we saw was a huge mall, known as the Al-Maliha Mall, where people from all over Israel went to shop."

From there, they drove past the remnants of the mosque where Tawfik prayed as a child and up a hill to where his house still stood. "Believe me, I tell you he suddenly took on the characteristics of an excited ten-year-old boy," is how Siham describes Tawfik. "He was saying things like,

'Oh, I used to sit on the steps here with my cousin, and this is the side of the house where I slept and tried to look through the metal parts of the windows there.' By the end, he was in tears."

As they walked up the hill to get a better view of Al-Maliha and the swath of open land that lay before them, Salam looked at her father and said, "Why can't we come back and buy this piece of land? Now we are Americans." Siham had to explain why that would never happen. She said they would not be allowed to buy property there because Al-Maliha was the place where their father, a Palestinian who supported the Arab nationalist movement and a Muslim, had his home taken away from him. To Israeli security forces, Tawfik Ramadan poses a threat. There is no way he would be able to own anything again in Palestine.

"Not in my lifetime, but I am hoping in any kind of way, hopefully in a peaceful way, that the Palestinians will get some rights to be able to get back to at least some of their own land and that our grandchildren will be able to experience it and say, 'Well, that is where my grandpa and my grandma were born,'" she says.

But the Green Wall Israel built to protect its citizens from the remaining Palestinian population won't keep Tawfik out of Al-Maliha. Neither will checkpoints and interrogations. His mind has other ideas. Tawfik still remembers coming home from school to play soccer with the other kids. He recalls how his father would return from Friday prayers with small gifts for his children in tow. Not long ago, he had a dream where he and his father walked up to the door of their home in Al-Maliha.

"I remember it all vividly, and it comes to me every day," he says. "I could not get over the first Nakba. And now I will not get over the second Nakba. It makes me doubt whether I will ever go home to Palestine. Probably not. But I have to have hope. We are Palestinians, and Palestine is in us and always with us."

THE END

PALESTINE HISTORY TIMELINE

1885 The term "Zionism" first coined by the Viennese writer, Nathan Birnbaum.

1896 Theodor Herzl, founder of the Zionist movement, calls for "restoration of the Jewish State".

1897 First Zionist congress takes place in Basel, Switzerland and the first Zionist organization is founded.

1907 Zionist leader Chaim Weizmann visits Palestine.

1908 First Palestinian anti-Zionist weekly newspaper is published by Arab Christian Najib Nassar.

1915 British cabinet member Herbert Samuel calls for the British annexation of Palestine in memorandum "The Future of Palestine".

1916 European Powers conclude secret Sykes-Picot agreement dividing future spheres of influence in Ottoman Empire territories.

1917 The Balfour Declaration promises a "national home for the Jewish people in Palestine".

1919 Emir Feisal presents a memorandum to the Paris Peace Conference, outlining the case for independence of Arab countries.

1922 The League of Nations grants mandate over former Ottoman territory Palestine to UK. Provisions include terms of the Balfour Declaration, including a "Jewish national home".

1933 Palestinians riot amid sudden rise in Jewish immigration from Nazi persecution in Germany.

1936–1939 Palestinian rebellion against the British Mandate and Jewish immigration.

1937 UK Peel Commission Report publicly recognizes conflict's irreconcilable terms and recommends partition of Palestine.

1939 UK issues White Paper limiting Jewish immigration.

1942 US Zionists meet in NY and adopt the "Biltmore Programme," calling for establishment of Palestine as a Jewish Commonwealth and for unlimited immigration.

1947 In February, UK proposes to relinquish its mandatory role and places the question of Palestine before the UN.

1947 (**cont.**) In September, the UN Special Committee on Palestine (UNSCOP) issues a report to the General Assembly with plans for partition or a federal state in Palestine.

In November, the UN General Assembly adopts resolution 181(II) which called to divide Palestine into an un-named "Jewish State" and an un-named "Arab State" with Jerusalem under UN trusteeship.

APRIL 1948 Deir Yassin massacre Zionist paramilitary groups kill hundreds of Palestinian Arabs in Deir Yassin, a village near Jerusalem.

MAY 1948 Great Britain terminates the Mandate over Palestine and Israel declares independence on 15 May. First large-scale displacement of Palestine refugees; 15 May becomes an official day to mark the Palestinian Nakba ("catastrophe").

The first Arab-Israeli War broke out when five Arab nations – Egypt, Transjordan (Jordan), Iraq, Syria, and Lebanon – invaded firstly the areas in southern and eastern Palestine not apportioned to the Jewish State by the UN partition of Palestine, and later, East Jerusalem.

Count Folke Bernadotte appointed UN Mediator in Palestine by the UN General Assembly. He is assassinated four months later by a Zionist militant group.

Security Council establishes a group of military observers to supervise truce, which later became UNTSO.

NOVEMBER 1948 UN establishes special fund to provide relief to over 500,000 Palestine refugees.

DECEMBER 1948 UN General Assembly passes resolution 194 calling for refugees to be allowed to return, Jerusalem to be under international regime, UN Conciliation Commission for Palestine (UNCCP) replaces UN mediator.

FEBRUARY-JULY 1949 Israel signs armistice agreements with Egypt, Jordan, Lebanon and Syria.

APRIL 1949 UN Conciliation Commission convenes Lausanne Conference to reconcile the parties.

MAY 1949 UNGA adopts Resolution 273 (III) admitting Israel as UN member.

DECEMBER 1949 UN establishes UNRWA to replace UNRPR (GA Resolution 302 (IV)).

1950 Israel moves its capital from Tel Aviv to the western part of Jerusalem, in defiance of UN resolutions, and the West Bank is brought formally under Jordanian control.

1964 Palestine Liberation Organization (PLO) is founded in Cairo.

1967 Six-day war Israel occupies West Bank, including East Jerusalem, Gaza, Golan Heights, and Sinai Peninsula.

In November, the UN Security Council unanimously adopts Resolution 242 (Land for peace).

1968 Establishment of UN Special Committee to Investigate Israeli Practices Affecting the Human Rights of the Palestinian People and Other Arabs of the Occupied Territories.

1973 Following the Middle East war of October, the UN Security Council passes resolution 338 calling for ceasefire, implementation of res. 242, negotiations between parties.

1974 The UN General Assembly and the Arab League recognize the PLO as the sole legitimate representative of the Palestinian people.

General Assembly reaffirms inalienable rights of Palestinian people to self-determination, independence and sovereignty, and refugee return (resolution 3236).

1975 In 1975 the Committee on the Exercise of the Inalienable Rights of the Palestinian People (CEIRPP) is founded by Resolution 3376 of the UNGA.

1976 The CEIRPP submits its programme to the Security Council and General Assembly to enable Palestinians to exercise their inalienable rights.

1977 Pursuant to UNGA Resolution 32/40 B, International Day of Solidarity with the Palestinian People is celebrated annually on 29 November.

1978 Following two weeks of secret negotiations at Camp David (USA), the Egyptian President and the Israeli Prime Minister agree on a Framework for Peace in the Middle East.

1979 The UNGA re-designates the Special Unit on Palestinian Rights as the Division for Palestinian Rights (Resolution 34/65 D).

1980 Israeli Knesset enacts the so-called 'Basic Law' on Jerusalem, proclaiming that "Jerusalem, whole and united" is the capital of Israel; the Security Council and GA resolution 35/169 E censure this law.

1981 UNESCO adds the Old City of Jerusalem to the UNESCO World Heritage Site list.

UN Security Council adopts resolution 497, calling on Israel to rescind action to annex the Golan Heights.

1982 Israel invades Lebanon with the intention of eliminating the PLO. After a ceasefire, PLO forces withdraw to neighboring countries. Despite guarantees of safety for Palestine refugees left behind, there are massacres at Sabra and Shatila camps.

1987 First "Intifada" begins in the Jabaliya Refugee Camp in the Gaza Strip.

1988 In July, Jordan renounces claims to the West Bank and recognizes PLO as "the sole legitimate representative of the Palestinian people."

In November, in Algiers, the Palestinian National Council adopts declaration of independence of the State of Palestine.

In December, PLO Chair Yasser Arafat addresses UN in Geneva; says Palestine National Council accepts UNSC Resolutions 242 and 338.

1991 Middle East peace conference in Madrid brings together all the parties to the Arab-Israeli conflict.

1993 Israel and the PLO sign the Declaration of Principles on Interim Self-Government Arrangements, also known the Oslo accords. Several "permanent status" issues are deferred for future negotiations.

1994 The Office of the UN Special Coordinator in the Occupied Territories (UNSCO) is established, and Mr. Terje Roed-Larsen of Norway is appointed as the first UN Special Coordinator.

1995 Israel and the PLO sign the Palestinian-Israeli Interim Agreement on the West Bank and the Gaza Strip ("Oslo II)".

1996 Palestinian general elections are held.

1997 Israel and the PLO sign the Hebron Protocol.

1998 Israel and the PLO sign the Wye River Memorandum, which consists of steps to facilitate implementation of previous agreements.

2000 In July, the US President Clinton convenes a Middle East Peace Summit at Camp David which concludes without agreement.

Ariel Sharon's al-Haram al-Sharif visit in September 2000 triggers the Second Palestinian Intifada.

2001 Outgoing US President Clinton proposes the Clinton Parameters for a permanent status agreement to resolve the Israeli–Palestinian conflict.

Shortly afterwards, the Taba Summit is held between Israel and the Palestinian Authority but fails to resolve the "permanent status" issues.

2002 The UN Security Council passes resolution 1397 affirming vision of a two-State solution to the conflict. The Quartet, consisting of the UN, the EU, the US, and Russia is established with a mandate to help mediate Israeli-Palestinian conflict and support Palestinian economic development and institution-building.

During a summit in Beirut, the League of Arab States adopts the Arab Peace Initiative.

2003 Roadmap for Peace is published by the Quartet and is endorsed by the Security Council in resolution 1515.

2004 The International Court of Justice (ICJ) issues Advisory Opinion on the legality of construction of a wall in the Occupied Palestinian Territory.

2006 In January, Hamas wins Palestinian Legislative Elections; forms Palestinian Authority government. The Quartet responds with Quartet Principles.

In July, Israel goes to war with Hezbollah in Lebanon.

2007 Israel imposes a blockade on the Gaza Strip after an armed takeover of Gaza by Hamas.

2007 (cont.) In November, the Annapolis Conference ends with parties issuing a joint statement committing to immediately implement their respective obligations under the Roadmap and working towards a peace treaty by the end of 2008.

2008 Israel broadens its sanctions and completely seals off the Gaza Strip.

Later in the year, Israel launches "Operation Cast Lead", a 22-day military assault on the Gaza Strip.

2009 Security Council passes resolution 1860 calling for a ceasefire in Gaza. HRC creates the UN Fact Finding Mission on the Gaza conflict to investigate violations of international humanitarian and human rights law. Their findings are issued in the "Goldstone Report".

2012 In November, Israel launches 'Pillar of Defense' an 8-day military operation against the Gaza Strip.

Later that month, the General Assembly adopts resolution 67/19 granting Palestine the status of non-member observer State in the UN.

2013 Direct negotiations between Israel and Palestine are held following an initiative by US Secretary of State John Kerry to restart the peace process.

2014 Israel launches a large scale military operation codenamed "Protective Edge" on the Gaza Strip.

2016 UN Security Council adopts resolution 2334, stating that Israel's settlement activity constitutes a "flagrant violation" of international law and has "no legal validity".

2017 US President Trump announces that the United States would recognize Jerusalem as the capital of Israel.

2018 US embassy in Israel moved from Tel Aviv to Jerusalem.

2020 US President Trump helps mediate Abraham Accords to normalize Israel's relations with some Arab States and proposes a Peace Plan.

2022 General Assembly adopts resolution A/RES/77/23 requesting the Committee to Commemorate the Nakba for the first time in the history of the UN.

2023 Israel launches "Operation Swords of Iron" against Gaza following Hamas attack. South Africa initiates a genocide case against Israel at the ICJ.

2024 International Court of Justice Advisory Opinion declares the Israeli occupation unlawful. General Assembly demands an end to occupation in 12 months.

2024 Following an investigation of war crimes and crimes against humanity, the International Criminal Court (ICC) issued arrest warrants for two senior Israeli officials, Benjamin Netanyahu, the Prime Minister of Israel, and Yoav Gallant, the former Minister of Defense of Israel. The request for a warrant against Hamas leader Haniyeh was withdrawn following his assassination and against Sinwar was withdrawn following his killing.

NOTE: *The list is from United Nation website as of the end of year 2024.*

BOOKS ON PALESTINE

BOOKS ON THE HISTORY OF PALESTINE

Palestine: A Four Thousand Year History by Nur Masalha – Traces the long history of Palestine, examining its cultural and political evolution over millennia.

Palestine: The Reality by J.M.N. Jeffries – provides a detailed analysis of the political and social situation in Palestine during the early 20th century. Jeffries critiques British colonial policies and the impact of Zionism on the Palestinian population, offering a critical perspective on the roots of the conflict.

Gaza: An Inquest into Its Martyrdom by Norman Finkelstein – Analyzes the humanitarian crises in Gaza and the political implications surrounding them.

Ten Myths About Israel by Ilan Pappé – challenges commonly held beliefs about Israel, exposing historical distortions and political narratives that support the Israeli occupation. Pappé deconstructs myths surrounding Israel's founding, its treatment of Palestinians, and its claims to legitimacy.

The Atlas of Palestine by Salman Abu Sitta – A detailed exploration of Palestinian geography, culture, and history, illustrated with maps and photographs.

Palestine 1936: The Great Revolt and the Roots of the Middle East Conflict by Oren Kessler – In Spring 1936, the Holy Land erupted in a rebellion that targeted both the local Jewish community and the British Mandate authorities that for two decades had midwifed the Zionist project. The Great Arab Revolt would last three years, cost thousands of lives—Jewish, British, and Arab—and cast the trajectory for the Middle East conflict ever since. Yet incredibly, no history of this seminal, formative first "Intifada" has ever been published for a general audience.

BOOKS ON THE POLITICS OF PALESTINE

The Question of Palestine by Edward Said – A foundational text that critiques Western perceptions of Palestine and examines the political implications of the Palestinian identity.

Palestine: Peace Not Apartheid by Jimmy Carter – critiques Israeli policies towards Palestinians, drawing comparisons to apartheid in South Africa. Carter advocates for a two-state solution and emphasizes the need for international pressure to achieve peace and justice.

Hundred Years' War on Palestine by Rashid Khalidi – explores the century-long conflict between Palestinians and Zionists, offering a historical perspective on the roots of the Israeli-Palestinian struggle. Khalidi highlights the impact of colonialism, Western policies, and the failure of peace efforts on the Palestinian plight.

The Ethnic Cleansing of Palestine by Ilan Pappe – argues that the displacement of Palestinians during the 1948 Arab-Israeli war was a deliberate campaign of ethnic cleansing. Pappe draws on historical documents to reveal how Zionist forces systematically expelled Palestinians to establish the state of Israel.

On Palestine by Noam Chomsky and Ilan Pappé – is a collection of dialogues between the two scholars, discussing the historical and political dimensions of the Israeli-Palestinian conflict. They critique Western policies, Israeli actions, and explore the prospects for peace and justice for Palestinians.

The Message by Ta-Nehisi Coates – Ta-Nehisi Coates originally set out to write a book about writing, in the tradition of Orwell's classic "Politics and the English Language, "but found himself grappling with deeper questions about how our stories—our reporting and imaginative narratives and mythmaking—expose and distort our realities.

BOOKS THAT HIGHLIGHT PALESTINIAN LITERATURE:

Mornings in Jenin by Susan Abulhawa – A powerful novel that follows the life of a Palestinian family over generations, capturing their struggles and resilience.

Gate of the Sun by Elias Khoury – is a novel that chronicles the lives of Palestinian refugees over several decades, blending personal stories with historical events. Through the experiences of its characters, the book explores themes of exile, memory, and the enduring trauma of the Nakba, offering a deep and poetic reflection on the Palestinian diaspora.

Men in the Sun and Other Palestinian Stories by Ghassan Kanafani – is a collection of short stories that portray the struggles of Palestinians, particularly refugees, in the aftermath of the Nakba. Kanafani's powerful narratives highlight themes of displacement, identity, and loss, offering a poignant exploration of the human condition in the context of the Palestinian experience.

Palestinian Literature and Culture edited by Salma Khadra Jayyusi – An anthology that showcases key works from Palestinian authors across various genres, providing a broad overview of the literary landscape.

In Search of Fatima: A Palestinian Story by Ghada Karmi – A memoir that reflects on the author's experiences as a Palestinian woman, her family's history, and the impact of displacement.

BOOKS OF PALESTINIAN POETRY

The Butterfly's Burden by Mahmoud Darwish – A celebrated collection from one of the most important Palestinian poets, exploring themes of loss, identity, and belonging.

So What: New and Selected Poems by Taha Muhammad Ali – is a collection of poems that reflect the personal and collective struggles of Palestinians, particularly those living in exile. Ali's work explores themes of loss, love, longing, and the resilience of the human spirit, offering a poignant and lyrical perspective on the Palestinian experience.

Enemy of the Sun: Poetry of Palestinian Resistance by Naseer Hasan Aruri – is a powerful anthology that showcases the work of Palestinian poets committed to resistance and liberation. The collection captures the emotional and political struggles of the Palestinian people, highlighting themes of exile, occupation, and the fight for freedom, with an emphasis on the role of poetry in inspiring and preserving the Palestinian cause.

Born Palestinian, Born Black by Suheir Hammad – is a powerful collection of poetry that explores the intersection of Palestinian identity and the African-American experience. Through her evocative verses, Hammad addresses themes of resistance, diaspora, and solidarity, reflecting on the struggles of both communities and the shared pursuit of justice.

If I Must Die: Poetry and Prose by Refaat Alareer and Yousef M. Aljamal – is a compelling anthology that captures the voices of Palestinian writers, offering poignant reflections on resistance, loss, and resilience. Through poetry and prose, the collection highlights the personal and collective struggles of Palestinians, addressing themes of identity, survival, and the longing for justice and freedom.

BOOKS THAT EXPLORE PALESTINIAN COOKING:

Palestine on a Plate by Joudie Kalla – A beautiful cookbook that blends personal stories with traditional Palestinian recipes, showcasing the richness of the cuisine.

The Gaza Kitchen: A Palestinian Culinary Journey by Laila El-Haddad and Maggie Schmitt – offers a rich exploration of Gaza's food culture, blending traditional recipes with personal stories. The book highlights the resilience of the Palestinian people through their culinary traditions, providing a glimpse into daily life under occupation while celebrating the flavors and history of the region.

Falastin: A Cookbook by Sami Tamimi – A soulful tour of Palestinian cooking today from the Ottolenghi restaurants' executive chef and partner—120 recipes shaped by his personal story as well as the history of Palestine.

Craving Palestine Cookbook: A Culinary Journey of Palestinian Flavors, Identity, and Generosity by Lama Bazzari – Craving Palestine is a not-for-profit cookbook showcasing over 100 beautifully curated recipes graciously donated by inspirational Palestinians from all walks of life, all of whom have come together in their love for food, poetry, and giving.

Dine in Palestine: An Authentic Taste of Palestine in 60 Recipes from My Family to Your Table by Heifa Odeh – Re-create traditional, flavorful Palestinian meals at home with this comprehensive collection of Middle Eastern recipes. From familiar favorites like Dawali (Stuffed Grape Leaves with Beef), Shawarma and Baklawa, to more complex meals like Musakhan, Palestine's national dish, Heifa Odeh has carefully adapted her family recipes with streamlined techniques, making it easier than ever to enjoy a taste of Palestine.